DIDGAH

ديدگاه

New perspectives on
UK-Iran cultural relations

BRITISH COUNCIL

British Council
10 Spring Gardens
London
SW1A 2BN
www.britishcouncil.org

ISBN 978 0 86355 753 8

Edited by Nick Wadham-Smith and Danny Whitehead
Designed by Navig8
Copyright © 2015 British Council

All rights reserved. No part of this publication may be reproduced or transmitted in any form or by any means, electronic or mechanical, including photocopy, recording or any information storage and retrieval system, without permission in writing from the copyright owners.

While every effort has been made to trace all present copyright holders of the material in this book, any unintentional omission is hearby apologised for in advance, and we should of course be pleased to correct any errors in acknowledgments in any future editions of this book.

The views expressed within this publication are the views of the individual contributors, and do not necessarily reflect the views of the British Council.

Contents

- 01 **Foreword**
- 03 **Preface**

- 09 **Overviews**
- 11 The Myth of 'Perfidious Albion': Anglo-Iranian Relations in Historical Perspective
- 30 Persian Studies in Britain: a brief review

- 47 **Working together in hard times**
- 49 Gassed: from the trenches of Khorramshahr to the Imperial War Museum
- 66 Bam: pictures of life, tragedy, hope and recovery
- 83 British imperialism and Persian diplomacy in the shadow of World War I (1914–1921)

- 127 **Working together in the arts**
- 129 The Contemporary Art Scene of Iran: cultural policy, infrastructure, dissemination and exchange
- 151 British Cinema in Iran: a brief history
- 170 Extending thresholds: Studio INTEGRATE on an architectural quest across continents
- 188 Irregular Channels

- 199 **Working together through language**
- 201 Bridge or Wall? English Language in Iran
- 224 Persian Language Teaching in the UK: challenges, potential and initiatives
- 239 Abalish: how English changed the language in Abadan
- 248 Owersettin the Rubaya'iat of Omar Khayyam

- 263 **Working together in education and science**
- 265 Higher Education in Iran, and UK-Iran cooperation
- 282 Iran and UK on the World Stage in Particle Physics

- 293 **Acknowledgments**

Foreword

The British Council is the UK's organisation for international cultural relations. Through cultural relations – the arts, education and society, and languages – we build trust through greater understanding, creating opportunities for the individuals and groups with whom we work across the world.

The British Council has been working in and with Iran since 1942. Although we currently do not have a physical office in the Islamic Republic of Iran, we continue to deliver a full cultural relations portfolio in partnership with UK and Iranian organisations, in order to build a better understanding between our two countries that may lead to greater trust.

Misunderstanding and misrepresentation in Iran and the UK are among the greatest challenges affecting bilateral relations. Cultural relations are among the most powerful tools that the UK and Iran have for addressing these twin challenges, and building trust for mutual benefit.

The British Council has responded to the positive developments in the bilateral relationship since the inauguration of President Rouhani in August 2013 by increasing the scope, scale, and impact of its cultural relations work with the Islamic Republic of Iran. Working with, and for the benefit of UK and Iranian partners, the British Council seeks to create opportunities for individuals and organisations in both countries.

This volume seeks to explore the past and present cultural relations ties between the UK and Iran, and make positive suggestions for future development. Despite the history of relations between the two countries being characterised by mistrust, cultural relations partnerships and respect for each country's arts, education sector, and linguistic heritage have remained extremely high. We hope that this volume demonstrates the strength and scope of some of those relations, and that it might provide inspiration for further and deeper cooperation and collaboration in these areas.

Preface

LORD LAMONT OF LERWICK

I am delighted that the British Council is finally seeking to return to Iran and that it is publishing *Didgah: New Perspectives on UK-Iran Cultural Relations*.

At the time I write this, it seems we may be at the start of a period when British-Iranian relations are on an upward trajectory. Some would say this is not before time.

When political and diplomatic relations are cool, one tends to hope that trade will be an avenue of contact. In recent years, that has been extremely difficult. But cultural ties have been and remain one of the ways in which citizens of the two countries can maintain some communication and understanding of each other. The arts can bring us closer when all else fails.

One of the great, indeed heroic, cultural events of recent years was the initiative of the British Museum in lending the Cylinder of Cyrus the Great to the Tehran Museum where it was viewed by hundreds of thousands of delighted Iranians. The Cylinder, from the 6th-century BC, is seen by some as an early declaration of human rights. Even President Ahmadinejad, not the greatest admirer of Britain, seemed pleased and keen to identify himself with this great event. Pessimists at the time forecast that Iran would not return the Cylinder but, of course, not only was it returned but it has continued to tour different parts of the globe to the joy of Iranians worldwide.

While there have been long periods of distrust and suspicion between Iran and Britain, there has also been a great deal of mutual respect – for each other's history, culture and traditions.

Ali Ansari writes in his article: 'The myth of Perfidious Albion remains especially potent because of the intimacy of an historical relationship which is profound, frequently affectionate and essentially respectful'. As he points out, for all the rhetoric about 'the Little Satan', Iranian politicians are often very keen to acquire British qualifications from British institutions. President Rouhani was not backward in the Iranian elections in mentioning his degrees from Glasgow University, although he had to clarify that it was from Glasgow Caledonia rather than the much older Glasgow University.

It is sometimes said that Iran is the last country in the world to believe that Britain is a great imperial power, manipulating everything behinds the scenes including even the United States government. Why has Britain has been demonised more than other countries such as the United States and Russia? Ali Ansari puts forward a number of highly ingenious theories. Some may seem far-fetched but I think they reflect the subtlety and complexity of the Iranian mind. I particularly was surprised and amused by his account of how George Bush's labelling Iran a part of the 'axis of evil' was attributed to British influence.

Iran, of course, was never a colony of Britain or, indeed, a colony of anyone. Iran suffered much self-interested interference by Britain without getting the benefits of British roads, training of civil servants or lawyers. I sometimes wonder if British-Iranian relations wouldn't be much better if Iran had in fact been a colony of Britain. Then they would have had a concrete British legacy instead of a bad collective memory of manipulation and interference.

For a long time, Britons viewed Iran through the lens of India. Mughal India was part of the Persianised world. The first Ambassadors from Britain to Iran were from the East India Company. British Civil Servants had to learn Persian to serve in

India, which, as is pointed out in the essays here, brought them not just into contact with the language but with wider Persian culture and values.

Even before the Empire, as Charles Melville points out, individual Britons developed a fascination with Persia – travellers, archaeologists, even mere romantics. This was followed by increasing academic interest: in 1888, Cambridge established its first lectureship in Persian and EG Browne was appointed. He also became involved with contemporary Persian politics including the Constitutional Revolution in 1905, which he strongly supported, though alas the British government did not. Quite rightly, he is commemorated today by a street named after him in Tehran.

Lord Curzon, Viceroy of India and Foreign Secretary, however, does not have a street named after him in Tehran, although he probably knew more about Persia and Persian culture than any British politician since and had a great academic interest in Persia. Unfortunately his policies only led to more criticism and opposition to Britain's role in Persia's internal affairs.

Many people when visiting Iran are startled by the lively arts scene. Iranian cinema is widely recognised throughout the world and continues to win many international prizes. But the visual arts scene also often surprises. This has had its ups and downs with the varying political climate. There was a great flowering of contemporary art under President Khatami but this was followed by a more restrictive regime under President Ahmadinejad. President Rouhani has indicated that he wants to move again towards much greater freedom for all the arts in Iran.

Adversity, tragedy and a sense of common humanity can bring people together in the most unexpected way. The Bam earthquake in 2003 in which 26,000 people died led to a sudden visit by His Royal Highness the Prince of Wales to Bam. Nevertheless there were, amazingly, political mutterings about 'interference'. Nevil Mountford writes movingly about what he found in Bam when he organised a photographic project in which ordinary people – the butcher, the policeman, the student – were invited to portray themselves in photographs as they wanted in the aftermath of the disaster. They sent the message that Bam was still alive and unbowed, full of dignity and humour.

In another moving chapter, doctor Shahriar Khateri compares his personal experience of mustard gas in the Iran-Iraq War with the accounts he heard at Ypres of chemical weapons in World War I. This led him to become a campaigner against chemical warfare and he recounts his efforts to establish the Peace Museum in Tehran.

One link between Iran and the UK is literature and above all, poetry. Iranians love poetry including Shakespeare. Today in Britain, poets like Rumi, Hafiz and Sa'adi are increasingly admired. Again, it was through India that knowledge of the classics of Persian literature reached England. However, Edward Fitzgerald's translation of The *Rubáiyát of Omar Khayyám* was different and it was only loosely based on the alleged Persian original. It was a bestseller in England and the United States but, as Charles Melville points out, created an image of Persia that had little to do with the reality.

There are many interesting chapters in this book. It covers an extraordinarily wide range of different cultural relations between institutions and individuals. These have developed despite the past, frosty, international background. I am very grateful to the British Council for having invested the resources, taken the initiative and shown the courage to bring to people's attention the richness, diversity, depth, colour and subtlety of Iranian culture and art. And, of course, it is the aim of the British Council to bring British culture even more to the attention of today's Iranians, particularly young Iranians eager for knowledge of the wider world.

As our political leaders attempt to bring about an improved diplomatic climate, this volume is a timely reminder of the great bridging power of culture and the arts. I hope that it will help lead to greater understanding, co-operation and trust between our two countries.

Norman Lamont
Lord Lamont of Lerwick
December 2014

Overviews

The Myth of 'Perfidious Albion': Anglo-Iranian Relations in Historical Perspective

ALI M. ANSARI

Dr Ali Ansari has published extensively on Iran. He is Professor of Iranian History and Director of the Institute for Iranian Studies at the University of St Andrews and President of the British Institute of Persian Studies

Whatever the future holds for diplomatic relations between the UK and Iran, it will be based on an understanding of a long historical relationship. That relationship may often be fraught but it has always been exceptionally deep and close.

In January 2002, President Bush of the United States declared in his State of the Union address to the nation that Iran, along with North Korea and Iraq, represented an 'Axis of Evil' which threatened the peace of the world. Ostensibly a speech intended for and directed to a domestic audience, this particular State of the Union Address, the first after the tragedy of 9/11, was always likely to include a more international dimension. Iranians across the political spectrum might differ on President Bush's assessment of the state of Iranian politics, but it would be fair to say that his decision to place Iran within an 'axis' that included its old foe Iraq was a matter of general consternation, frustration, and no little bewilderment. For the Reformist President, Mohammad Khatami, the speech proved a bitter blow to his policy of dialogue with the West. It was especially difficult to swallow in the light of his decision to provide assistance to the United States and its allies in the attack on Afghanistan that followed 9/11 and his critics lambasted the President for his 'naiveté' towards the West, and the United States in particular. One particularly distressed Reformist member of the Iranian parliament, in a desperate bid to absolve the Americans of such an egregious diplomatic error, discovered the true source of the mischief:

[The] European Union and a number of Asian and European countries have criticised Bush's position, describing it as inappropriate and wrong. Only England has supported Bush… England is behind those crises created in our country and the outside movements that support them. England is the one who motivates America to act brutishly. We must discover England's footprint in these events. In truth, England is the one who fuels events.[1]

After some years out of the limelight (having been supplanted by the United States as the Great Satan), and only some four years following the reestablishment of full diplomatic relations, 'Perfidious Albion' was back; and back with a vengeance that could scarcely have been appreciated in the warm glow of the Khatami presidency when the 'dialogue of civilisations' appeared to suggest a new era of sober inter-national engagements, gently deconstructing and laying to rest the paranoid fears of earlier generations.

Even discussions about the coup against Dr Mosaddeq seemed to have acquired a more scholarly tone as Reformists and progressives in the Iranian body politic turned their ire against domestic rather than foreign enemies, and berated them for their louche attitude towards the Mosaddeq premiership and their tendency to rewrite history in favour of Ayatollah Kashani.[2] Indeed, if the official British position was one of dignified, if frustrating silence, Iranians could at least point to an apology from the Americans[3] while their own conservatives in parliament had crassly decided to abolish the holiday commemorating the nationalisation of the Anglo-Iranian Oil Company in 1951, which they had somehow concluded was surplus to requirements.[4] The resultant public outrage, which saw the move quickly reversed, also, somewhat ominously, had led some to conjecture that the move had been made in response to a British announcement about their desire to pursue investment in the Iranian oil industry, confirming of course, what many already knew, that Britain stood behind the conservative 'authoritarian' establishment![5] It was perhaps a short step from this, to the outburst in the Majlis some two years later.

Of course, the fact that Britain had effectively been out of the limelight was grist to the mill of those who argued it had been manipulating events from behind the scenes all along. For Reformists struggling to contain the conservative backlash, the insult to apparent injury proved to be the surprise visit of Prince Charles to Iran, in his capacity as head of the British Red Cross, to visit the earthquake-ravaged town of Bam in January 2004. In the midst of what was due to become the first of a series of electoral clashes – in this case the parliamentary elections of 2004 – that would see reformists 'engineered' out of the electoral map, Reformists interpreted the first visit by a member of the British Royal family to Iran since 1979 in a somewhat different light.[6]

Anxiously awaiting a European riposte to what was widely described in the reformist press as an electoral 'coup', the surprise visit of Prince Charles was taken by many as a real slap in the face from Britain, and confirmation – if it were ever needed – that

Britain, up to its old tricks, had in fact backed the 'coup' all along.[7] It did not help that an anonymous diplomat, 'from a close European ally of the United States' and in the throes of nuclear negotiations, had unhelpfully commented to a journalists from AFP that, "These are issues that we have to deal with security people on – in other words the conservatives... The reformists have never been in the loop on these kinds of things. Having conservatives running everything may not be a reflection of the will of the Iranian public, but it will probably make our job as diplomats trying to deal with the people that matter much easier".[8]

But far from 'easing engagements', much worse was to follow. Indeed with the demise of the Reform government and the subsequent suppression of the reform movement, Anglophobia enjoyed a very public revival that arguably put the Great Satan in the shade. Indeed the new President, Mahmoud Ahmadinejad, not quite the conservative that Europeans had been hoping for, put Britain front and centre of his new foreign policy of confrontation. The British Embassy in Tehran came in for some particularly vitriolic criticism, including a bizarre allegation that a tunnel had been dug beneath the embassy to ferry prostitutes and spies in and out of the compound (the primary direction of travel was never ascertained), while moves were initiated to whip up public enthusiasm for the confiscation of the Embassy's summer compound in Qolhak.[9] Meanwhile petty harassment and the occasional demonstration finally coalesced in an apotheosis of engineered outrage resulting in (somewhat mature) students ransacking the British Embassy in 2011. By this stage, so restored and pervasive had the myth of Perfidious Albion become, that even sympathetic voices speculated that the assault on the embassy had in fact been engineered by the British themselves, in order to provide them with an excuse to remove their diplomats – the reason being, it was speculated, that an Israeli attack was imminent.

Ahmadinejad's vocal exploitation of anti-British sentiment tapped into a latent Anglophobia that enjoyed deep roots in Iranian political culture. It was by no means monochrome; as relations grew worse there was palpable frustration among Iranians at not being able to secure visas, even among those who actually believed in the omnipotence of British power. And those who could not quite agree with Ahmadinejad's posturing could certainly agree that the overthrow of Mosaddeq had been a 'bad thing'; a view that extended across the political spectrum to include those who had no particular affection for the Islamic Republic. For the Iranian-American diaspora it proved a particularly attractive way of combining their love of both America and Iran, as opposed to the Islamic Republic of Iran. Indeed as with the outburst from the Majlis deputy quoted above, by arguing that American errors had been forced on it by the 'cunning' British, the American state (and Americans in general) could be absolved of any serious guilt. For Ahmadinejad, appropriating Mosaddeq helped foster the narrative – which has not been without traction both in Iran and abroad – that the nuclear crisis was his 'oil crisis', and while many Iranians found his identification with the National Front Prime Minister a stretch, they were more willing to see parallels between relations with the West then and now. Indeed the narrative of the coup of 1953 ultimately segued nicely into the narrative of 'Velvet Coup' of 2009, with the British once again the villain of the piece.

The coup of 1953 is about as far back as popular memory will stretch. More educated Iranians will certainly be aware of British involvement in the 19th century through to the Constitutional Revolution, with some general if inaccurate appreciation of the Anglo-Persian Agreement and the imperialist machinations of Lord Curzon.[10] Curzon's contemporary, the Persianist Edward Browne, is also familiar as a friend of the Iranians, if for no other reason than a street continues to bear his name in Tehran, though most would be hard pressed to say what he actually did.[11]

But what is perhaps most curious in the popular imagination is the absence of Russia. Indeed, the other side to Ahmadinejad's official Anglophobia was an enthusiastic cultivation of relations with Russia, including a much-trumpeted state visit by then President Putin to Iran in 2007. Although some Iranians have cautioned about being too dependent on Russia, there seems scant attention paid to Russian behaviour towards Iran both before and after the revolution. Most people would certainly not be aware that Russia (as Lord Curzon would enthusiastically concur), throughout the last two centuries, posed a much greater threat to Iranian sovereignty than Britain ever did. It was the Treaty of Turkmenchai in 1828 that reduced Iran to the status of a second-rate power, confirming the loss of territories in the Caucasus; while the punitive nature of the reparations and the diplomatic privileges gained for Russia established the pattern for Iran's deteriorating relationship with Europe for the better part of the next 150 years. And, though seemingly hidden in the historical shade provided by the later Oil Nationalisation Crisis, it was Soviet Russia, in 1946, that sought to effectively annex Iranian Azerbaijan.

It is worth comparing the Treaty of Turkmenchai with the comparatively lenient Treaty of Paris of 1857, which ended the first and (to date) last Anglo-Persian War. Indeed so generous were the terms that it inaugurated a lengthy period of Anglophilia that was not to wane until the aftermath of the Constitutional revolution, when imperial priorities allowed Russia a free hand to suppress the Constitutionalists,[12] much to the anger and frustration of the revolutionaries who had sought British support for the establishment of a Constitution.[13] This sense of disappointment was to grow in subsequent decades and offers a significant clue to the reason why Britain occupies pride of place in the suspicions of Iranians. Like the Reformists of later years, the Constitutionalists had their expectations dashed on the altar of British Imperial, and later national, 'security' interests. But this sense of betrayal was predicated on something altogether deeper, and that was the nature of British power in Iran.

Indeed, the first point that must be borne in mind is that Britain, throughout much of this period, was on the strategic defensive in Iran. Its imperial priorities lay in its new imperial acquisitions in India, and the first systematic embassies sent to Iran at the turn of the 19th century were in fact dispatched by the East India Company, not the government in London. The embassy led by Sir John Malcolm was intended in the first instance to secure Iranian support against the Afghans, but, with the onset of the Napoleonic wars and French ambitions to secure Iranian support against both Russia and India, attentions turned to preventing other European powers from establishing a foothold in Iran. It should also be remembered that in this earlier period of engagement the spectre of Nader Shah loomed large in the European mind, and that Iran was not at this stage perceived as a weakened power subject to European aggrandisement. The prospect of an Iranian invasion of India was therefore not at this stage considered fanciful, especially if they could lay their hands on European military arms and training. It would take a protracted and somewhat one-sided war with Russia (1804–13) to lay those particular anxieties to rest. But just as these wars resulted in a Russian territorial move southwards, to be matched later in the century with further territorial gains in Central Asia, so too the balance of British anxieties moved from a concern of Iranian power to a broader fear of Russia ambitions. British intervention in Iran at this stage was therefore dictated to a greater or lesser extent at containing

Russia, and consequently if Russia gained advantage in Iran then British policy dictated that they too seek matching benefits. Iranian statesmen were likewise not averse to inviting Britain in when it suited them and in an effort to provide a counterweight to Russia.

This became most apparent in the aftermath of the Anglo-Persian war and the Treaty of Paris (1857) that followed, when a series of ministers sought British commercial investments that would help transform and modernise the Iranian economy. This high tide of British commercial ventures has largely been derided as the worst example of British economic imperialism and identified with the Reuters Concession of 1872 and the subsequent Tobacco Concession of 1890, both of which scandalised intellectuals both at home and abroad. But it is worth remembering that while such concessions were largely seen as the results of a feckless Shah earnestly seeking money at whatever cost to his country, the Reuters concession had in fact been undermined by the Foreign Office's lack of enthusiasm for such an extensive concession being awarded to a private individual, and the reaction it might provoke in Russia; and latterly condemned in no uncertain terms by Curzon.[14]

The Tobacco Concession, which was in many ways a more serious infraction, and a public relations disaster for Britain, was in many ways elevated to the status of 'national awakening' by none other than Edward Browne.[15] Although Iranian historiography (of which more later) has tended to see these concessions as the moment when the tide tipped against Britain in the Iranian mindset, the motivations and details show a more complex dynamic at work, in terms of not only motivations but also the British approach, which tended to be much less aggressive and much more sensitive to Russian reactions than is popularly recognised.

This complexity was exemplified by events in the first decade of the 20th century when Iran was in the grip of its first – Constitutional – revolution. As noted above, far from viewing the British with antipathy, Iran's constitutional revolutionaries actively sought British support for their political ambitions, and the British were not averse to providing it, even if diplomatic predictions of future political development proved as inaccurate as contemporary efforts.[16] What is perhaps most striking and of most disappointment to Iran's Constitutionalists is the ease with which Britain compromised its support in favour of broader imperial interests with Russia. Indeed one might even say British Indian rather than British interests, since in the subsequent Anglo-Russian convention of 1907, in which Russia and Britain agreed to divide Iran into 'concessionary' spheres of influence, Britain appeared to be content with retaining influence in Iranian Baluchestan. This only makes sense in terms of the defence of India, since Britain effectively forfeited any right of influence in the northern most populous areas (ceded to the Russian sphere) – a forfeiture which was to cost the Constitutionalists dear – and even more curiously, over south western Iran, where a British-Australian prospector by the name of William Knox D'Arcy was busy looking for oil. D'Arcy would of course discover oil in the following year, 1908, and this would in time transform Britain's relations with Iran, shifting the locus from India to Iran itself. But in 1907, Iranians would be forgiven for thinking that Iran was a very low priority for British policy-makers.

That they had expectations otherwise and found themselves repeatedly disappointed was in part a consequence of the cost of empire for Britain and the means by which she sought to compensate for this disadvantage, especially in the face of the Russian behemoth to the north. Although often misunderstood, British imperial government was probably more light-touch and financially prudent, if not austere, than is popularly recognised.[17]

Unlike the Russian empire, which enjoyed a surplus of relatively cheap manpower and could exercise this hard power at the whim of the Tsar, the British Empire operated within a wholly different environment which dictated that 'soft power' rather than hard power was the only efficient way to administer the empire and its interests. Commercial power lay at the heart of the imperial project and the exercise of military force was only used sparingly, and even then subject to the constraints of politics at home. In practical terms, though Britain was a financial superpower, it harvested these resources carefully and spent comparatively more effort on developing its diplomatic efforts. It may be interesting to note that the one occasion in which Britain did have to resort to force against Iran (1856) was also the occasion when its man on the ground, Charles Murray, was generally recognised to have been amongst the more inept of British diplomats in Iran.[18] Significantly, Murray had not previously served in India.

The importance of India in Britain's imperial priorities has already been noted and is widely recognised. But the importance of India as a gateway to the Persianate world is rarely noted if scarcely less important. Persian was the lingua franca of the Indian subcontinent until its replacement by English in the aftermath of the Indian mutiny. Officials in the East India Company were obliged to learn Persian in order to serve in India, and arguably the first modern dictionaries and grammars of the Persian language were produced in India for the benefit of this emerging civil service. British servicemen in India, however, did not just learn the language, they crucially acquired the cultural apparatus that framed it.

A good example is provided by Sir John Malcolm, the first diplomatic envoy sent by the government in India to Iran in 1800. Malcolm had left Britain for India at the tender age of 12 and saw extensive service there. He also, for a serving military officer, found time to learn several of the local languages, including Persian, to an exceptional standard. As he recounted in his memoirs, 'Sketches of Persia', Malcolm devoted a good deal of his time to reading and translating Persian works, ranging from historical works to 'fables and tales', "being satisfied that that this occupation, while it improved me in the knowledge of the language, gave me a better idea of the manners and mode of thinking of this people than I could derive from any other source".[19] In a particularly interesting letter written to his wife while on a sea voyage Malcolm wrote, "I have been amusing myself today with Persian poetry – from which... happy selections might be made in every flight of Muse. How nobly does Sadi (sic) commence advice to kings in the following two lines... 'Make mankind happy, and subdue without an army. Conquer the hearts of all – and be the conquering King of the World'".[20]

It would be interesting to speculate just how much of the acquired knowledge was subsequently put to good use by Malcolm and his contemporaries. Certainly Malcolm had an acute understanding of the importance of style over substance in many of the procedures that guided court and government etiquette in Iran. This cultural understanding won Malcolm many admirers though it would be too easy to see this cultural affectation as all one way. Although the early British orientalists – those who established the cultural frame of reference for future generations of British diplomats and travellers – were acutely aware of the limitations of Iranian government, they acquired a powerful affection for the Iranians themselves.[21] Even James Morier, whose highly popular 'Hajji Baba of Isfahan' was the cause of some consternation among his contemporaries, most notably Harford Jones Brydges, ensured that while his hero was a rogue, he was a lovable one for all that.[22] In short, the British diplomatic and political class cultivated friendships that were reciprocated by Iranians flattered with the attention and enthused with the prospect that they too could acquire the 'order' that had made Britain a great power. Indeed it could be argued that Britain spent the better part of the 19th century winning hearts and it was in many ways the repeated failure to fulfil the promise and match the expectation that ensured that the disappointment was especially acute when it inevitably came. British diplomats were themselves not oblivious to the contradictions that pervaded policy.

A poignant early example was provided in the memoirs of Edward Eastwick – perhaps not the most distinguished diplomat to serve in Iran but one for whom the incongruities of ideals and realities was only too apparent. As one royal governor of Khorasan protested, "I am at a loss to understand the behaviour of the English. England professes herself to be the ally of Persia, and yet she pertinaciously opposes measures which are absolutely requisite to secure the Persian frontier. England assumes to be the determined enemy of the slave trade, and has gone to enormous expense to liberate the African races, to whom she is no way bound save by the tie of a common humanity. It is surely, then, inexplicable that England should have never lifted a finger to save or rescue the hundreds of thousands of Persians who are carried off into slavery by the Turkomans. So far from that, England shackles and impedes every effort that the Persian government makes for the protection of its own subjects, and, by expelling Persia from Herat, and even discouraging a friendly alliance between the two countries, renders the tranquillity of Khurasan impossible". "I must confess", reflected Eastwick, "I thought there was a great deal of truth in the remarks of the Prince..."[23]

These contradictions were if anything to become more acute in the 20th century, with the discovery of oil. Iran was no longer viewed as a buffer state to protect British India; it became an important strategic asset in itself, and British policy no longer had to 'simply' contend with the divergent views of London and Delhi; there was now in addition a powerful corporate voice coming out of Abadan. Moreover, while British diplomats were often decidedly wary of some of the business ventures British subjects might get themselves involved in (and had occasion to defend these interests at arms length), Anglo-Persian Oil was a different venture altogether. Not only was it a strategic asset, but it was one in which the British government had a direct stake. This did not mean that criticisms of operational practice did not exist, but they tended to be more subdued and private for the simple reason that oil represented a strategic asset and interest which could not be compromised. This was not the same for example with the British Imperial Bank of Persia, whose gradual dismantling by the versatile Abol-Hasan Ebtehaj (a former employee) was viewed with sympathy by those British officials – especially in the Bank of England – who regarded the Bank's approach to Iran as anachronistic, and counterproductive to broader British interests.[24] The demise of the British Imperial Bank provided an interesting alternative narrative to that of Anglo-Iranian Oil (as it became known after 1934), and had the former been the signal event in Anglo-Iranian relations in the 20th century, the myth of the Perfidious Albion would have enjoyed considerably less force in the popular imagination.[25]

As it was, the confrontation over Anglo-Iranian Oil came to define British-Iranian relations for the modern era. Most of this is put down to the reality of the Anglo-American intervention that facilitated the overthrow of Dr Mosaddeq's government. But while this would have reinforced certain fears and prejudices it does not sufficiently explain the full force of this event in the public imagination and why it has been elevated over all others as the incident in Iran's modern encounter with the international community, trumping Russian interventions in the nineteenth century and wholly overshadowing their attempted annexation of Azerbaijan in 1946. Foreign intervention in Iran's domestic affairs had become a fact of life since 1828 and the prospect of a coup was never far from the popular rhetoric of the time. Indeed in many ways Mosaddeq's government expected a coup attempt to be made and understood that it was likely to involve the court and the young Shah, who was never quite the pawn in the affairs at this stage that historical convention would sometimes have us believe.

There is certainly some truth to the argument, as noted above, that expectations of the West were greater than of Russia, and that fears of a possible coup were quite different from the reality of the experience, which nonetheless shocked many educated Iranians. Even so, here, the shock was more directed towards the United States, and even more contemporary narratives promoted in the Islamic Republic tend to argue that Mosaddeq's mistake – his political naiveté – was to trust the Americans. Nevertheless, if the Americans are accused of an astonishing betrayal, there has been a tendency to accord them the same naiveté that has been thrust on Mosaddeq, inasmuch as they were clearly misled by the far more cunning British. (There is an irony here that should not be dismissed and that is that both British and Iranian perceptions of each other identified the other as cunning and duplicitous;[26] not always, it must be added, in an unflattering way).

In this sense the Americans have been absolved of any serious guilt and are instead accorded the lesser evil of having been, perhaps wilfully, manipulated by darker forces. This absolution of course allows for a certain room for manoeuvre where the prospect of future and/or current relations are concerned. It is certainly easier, for example, for Iranian-Americans to reconcile their affection for both countries by blaming American intervention in Iranian politics on a third party. Much the same process can be seen with respect to the Iranians themselves, who, rather than admit that they had lost faith in the nationalist prime minister, effectively 'Orientalise' themselves (in the Saidian sense), and argue that they too were hapless victims of foreign manipulation. The buck tends to stop with Britain in this hierarchy of manipulation (there are of course other layers, such as Zionists, Masons and Bahai's for example, but at least the last two have tended to be identified in some way or form with Britain) with the consequence that a whole range of otherwise guilty parties transfer their complicity to 'Britain' and reinforce this particular narrative.

This process of transferral has perhaps most curiously, if effectively, been seen in Marxist historiography, which has had a profound influence on the writing of history and politics in Iran in the 20th century. The dominance of Marxist historiography and political analysis among Iranian intellectuals helps explain why Russia and then the Soviet Union were gradually eased out of the narrative of colonial oppression and exploitation. The Russian Revolution had effectively rebooted this particular narrative with the Soviet Union occupying a far more sympathetic space among left-leaning Iranian intellectuals who identified the Shah with Western Capitalism, to which Russia, as the Soviet Union, no longer belonged. That these narratives should have become embedded at a time of growing education and mass communication only served to reinforce them within the body politic and made them harder to dislodge or amend and far easier to fix within society.

What is less easy to explain is the manner in which, even with this capitalist world view, the United States still takes second place to Britain. This, to be sure, has not always been the case, and certainly in the earlier days of the Revolution Marxist and Islamist revolutionaries vented their fury on a United States that was by all accounts the Great Satan. But it is also true that positions have periodically softened and as noted above, for the better part of the last decade, Britain has once again achieved pride of place. Some reasons for this have been outlined above and certainly a larger Iranian-American diaspora willing to discuss and dissect the coup of 1953 has helped this process, to say nothing of American intellectuals themselves. There is also the argument, applied similarly towards Russia, that the United States was not as easy to offend as the British. Indeed one of the arguments about the apparent Iranian preference for seizing British military personnel over American ones in the Persian Gulf was that no Iranian would risk antagonising the Americans.

But there is also an aspect that we have not touched upon, but which is in many ways both the most intriguing and interesting: and that would be the issue of a deeper respect. The myth of Perfidious Albion remains especially potent because of the intimacy of a historical relationship which is profound, frequently affectionate and essentially respectful. Even today for all the rhetorical bile that can be spilt, Iranian politicians often fall over themselves to acquire British qualifications from British Universities with the implicit assumption that the technical skills acquired are complemented by an unquantifiable degree of political (inner) knowledge.[27] Indeed even though Ahmadinejad's administration sought to diminish the status of British degrees, going so far as to argue that degrees in the humanities and social sciences would not be officially recognised, Iranians of all political leanings and positions have sought to acquire just these qualifications. The most notable recent example of course has been that of President-elect Rouhani, who was perhaps a little too enthusiastic in promoting the fact that he had an 'English' doctorate.[28] His achievement was prominently stated in his campaign material and, despite his having to qualify that he had gained his doctorate from Glasgow Caledonian rather than the University of Glasgow, this distinction will no doubt have been lost on the many Iranians who voted for him. That a presidential candidate should highlight this, despite the tremendous ideological suspicion of Britain, is testament to a much deeper and complex relationship in which a degree of mutual respect remains.

To fully appreciate the depth of this respect, one must return to the foundations of the relationship and the early British Orientalists, whose disdain for arbitrary Iranian politics (the root cause as they saw it of the widespread mendacity that existed in society) was in many ways surpassed by the affection and respect they had for Iranians themselves. Even Morier, widely considered to be among the most scathing of critics, was moved to comment positively on the Iranian aptitude for learning and adapting, such that "with their natural quickness [they] would have rivalled us in our own arts and sciences".[29] This affection and admiration was reciprocated, in part no doubt because it was easier to praise that which was distant (as opposed to say the Ottomans), but there is also little doubt that there was a profound respect for the British achievements, especially in the realms of politics and ideas. The Russians had force, the Americans had money, but the British understood politics.

For a people and a culture that had always considered themselves the masters of the art of politics, there was something to be admired, albeit reluctantly, in a people who, to reverse and paraphrase Morier's judgment, had rivalled the Iranians in their mastery and understanding of politics.

Notes

1. Hojjat-ol Islam Aliasghar Rahmani-Khalili, quoted in the ISNA website, 2 February 2002, BBC SWB Mon MEPol.
2. For a useful if dramatic summation of this narrative see the Iranian television drama Pedarkhandeh (Godfather), produced in 2005/6. For an account of narrative relating to Mosaddeq see Ansari, A, 'The Politics of Nationalism in Modern Iran', Cambridge, CUP, 2012, pp. 270–271.
3. http://transcripts.cnn.com/TRANSCRIPTS/0004/19/i_ins.00.html.
4. Arya, 28 Mordad 1378/19 August 1999, p. 3.
5. Sobh Emrooz, 1 Shahrivar 1378/23 August 1999, p. 5.
6. Yas-e No, 20 Bahman 1382/9 February 2004, p. 3.
7. Aftab-e Yazd, 23 Bahman 1382/12 February 2004, p. 7.
8. For a summary of Western views at this stage see Iran Conservatives to Ease Engagements, AFP, 18 February 2004. It is perhaps worth noting that the 'conservative' the Europeans had become so enamoured with was one Hassan Rouhani.
9. See in this regard Baztab.com, 30 Khordad 1386/20 June 2007. With regard to the tunneling, see Baztab.com, 22 Mordad 1386/13 August 2007.
10. A popular if wholly fanciful representation of this episode is provided in the prequel to Pedarkhandeh, Emirat-e farangi (The Foreign Emirate), which dealt with the rise and rule of Reza Shah.
11. There has been some suggestion that Edward Browne Street has been renamed but this does not appear to be true. Bobby Sands Street is of course nearby.
12. See in this regard Morgan Shuster's account of the Russian atrocities in Tabriz recounted in his *The Strangling of Persia*, Washington DC: Mage, 1987 (first published 1912), pp. 219–220.
13. See, for example, Hasan Taqizadeh, Persia's Appeal to England (1908), in Maqallat Taqizadeh, Vol. 7, Tehran: Shokufan, 1356/1977, p. 452.
14. Curzon, G N, *Persia and the Persian Question*, Vol. 1. London: Frank Cass, 1966 (first published 1892), p. 480.
15. Browne, E G, *The Persian Revolution 1905–1909*. Washington DC: Mage, 2005 (first published 1910), p. 57.
16. It is worth contrasting Hardinge's dispatch to Sir Edward Grey, received in London on 3 January 1906, with Cecil Spring Rice's General Report on Persia for the year 1906, also sent to Grey, the following year (received in London on 27 January 1907). Hardinge was decidedly sanguine about prospects for political change.
17. Niall Ferguson is particularly good on this point; see *Empire: How Britain Made the Modern World*. London: Penguin, 2004, p. 247.
18. Calmard, J, http://www.iranicaonline.org/articles/anglo-persian-war–1856–57; Wright calls him 'probably the clumsiest and most inept envoy ever appointed by the British government to the Persian Court'. Wright, D, *The English Among the Persians*. London: Heinneman, 1977, p. 23.
19. Malcolm, J, *Sketches of Persia*, Vol. I. London: John Murray, 1827, p. 128.
20. Quoted in Pasley, R *Send Malcolm! The Life of Major General Sir John Malcolm 1769–1833*. London: British Association of Cemeteries in South Asia, 1982, p. 31. Pasley notes that the verse from Saadi was reproduced in the letter in Persian. The translation noted above is Pasley's.

21. Pasley, op cit. p. 84.
22. Both Malcolm and Harford Jones Brydges make clear that their memoirs were written in part to refute the popular image that was taking hold as a consequence of the success of Hajji Baba.
23. Eastwick, E *Three Years Residence in Persia*, 1864.
24. See Bostock, F and Jones, G, *Planning and Power in Iran: Ebtehaj and Economic Development under the Shah*. London: Cass, 1989, p. 73; also Jones, G, *Banking and Empire in Iran: The History of the British Bank of the Middle East*. Cambridge: Cambridge University Press, 1986, p. 319.
25. Jones, G, op cit., notes that the Bank's closure 'seems to have passed almost unnoticed'; pp. 336–337.
26. See Jones, op cit., p. 318. British diplomatic dispatches characterized Mosaddeq as 'cunning and slippery'.
27. The most absurd case in recent memory was that of a minister in Ahmadinejad's government, Ali Kordan, who bought himself an honorary doctorate from the University of Oxford; see http://www.timesonline.co.uk/tol/news/world/middle_east/ article5079422.ece.
28. Since the term for Britain in Persian is inglis, the Scottish distinction is lost in translation, though it is a distinction that does come in useful if and when anglo-phobic tensions rise once again.
29. Morier, J J, *A Journey through Persia, Armenia and Asia Minor to Constantinople in the years 1808 and 1809*. Elibron Classic (2004), p. 366 (first published in 1812).

Persian Studies in Britain: a brief review

CHARLES AND FIRUZA MELVILLE

Dr Charles Melville is Professor of Persian History, and founder of Shahnama Project and Dr Firuza Abdullaeva Melville is Director of Research of the Shahnama Centre for Persian Studies, Pembroke College, University of Cambridge.

Britain's scholarly fascination with Persia intertwines with Empire, living in the spaces created by travel and diplomacy; its academic traditions in UK wax and wane, rise and fall like the dynasties they study.

In this short essay we aim to look back over some highlights of British engagement with Persian culture and the contributions that individual scholars and authors have made to the study of Iran and to fostering an understanding of the country. It is only relatively recently that this has taken place in the context of a formal academic environment. Before the establishment of University posts dedicated to Persian language and literature in the late 19th century, experience of Iran, interest in her culture and history, and the writing of books and other publications was the preserve of travellers to the country in a number of capacities – as diplomats, government agents, merchants and later businessmen, missionaries, artists, archaeologists, tourists and romantics.

Although to some extent, interest in Iran inevitably went in parallel with British imperial and colonial objectives, it would be quite wrong to suppose that such a motivation for knowledge of the country underlay every spirit of enquiry and every attachment formed. One would be hard pressed to find English accounts of their travels in Iran and the performance of their duties there that did not recognise the extent of Persia's ancient civilisation and cultural sophistication, however alien this might seem and however frustrating to deal with on an official level. It is also worth pointing out that, apart from a couple of brief and minor episodes in the mid-19th century, Iran has never been Britain's 'enemy' and whatever the relations between the two countries, Iran has never been a British colony, or a colony of any other country for that matter. The Oil Crisis of the early 1950s is perhaps the nearest Britain and Iran came to being foes before the current breakdown in relations at government and political levels. Otherwise, Britain's undeniable past of sometimes drastic and pernicious interference in Iran and her internal affairs was motivated by the desire to count on Iran as a reliable friend and ally, whose interests were hoped and intended to align with our own (first against France and then Germany and most of the time, Russia). Even if, as may be granted, this rosy and positive view of Britain's relations with Iran (surveyed in another chapter of this book) is unduly optimistic, we might conclude these introductory remarks by observing that, whether or not Iran is regarded by some as an opponent, it is better to 'know your enemy' than not to know him, and the British have led the way in their engagement with Persia's history and civilisation.

So, to concentrate on cultural relations against a colourful political background of mutual irritation and resentment, mingled with affection and respect, we may note that among the first British visitors to Persia who showed an interest in the study of the language was Sir Thomas Herbert (1606–82), who accompanied Sir Dodmore Cotton's ill-fated embassy to Shah Abbas in 1627.

Herbert included a short English-Persian glossary and phrase book in the second edition of his journal, *Some Yeares Travels into Africa and Asia the Great* (London, 1638), in which his sympathetic enjoyment of his journey shines through. Most other work on the Persian language and editing texts (e.g. of astronomical treatises) in the 17th century was carried out in Oxford and to a lesser extent Cambridge by scholars with no experience of the country. It was Britain's growing interest in India that proved to be the catalyst for progress in the study of Persian – the official language of the Mughal Empire – and indeed for a strategic interest in Iran. This interest remained marginal to and dependent on the concern for Britain's Indian possessions until the discovery of Iranian oil at the beginning of the 20th century: at this point, Iran became important in her own right. In fact, it would not be too much to state that while knowledge of Iran, her cities and physical geography was being generated by a series of increasingly frequent visitors and travellers – often taking the overland route to India – from the late 18th century onwards, it was in India that the study of Persian culture was advanced and through India, rather than Iran, that knowledge of the classics of Persian literature reached England.

The outstanding figure at the start of this period is Sir William Jones (1746–94), who, having learned Persian at Oxford, published his *Grammar of the Persian Language* (London, 1771) – before even arriving in Calcutta in a judicial capacity in 1783, where his most famous efforts as a linguist were made largely as a result of his study of Sanskrit. His *Grammar* was the first to put the study of Persian on a systematic basis and went through many editions, despite the criticisms it rightly attracted. Jones included a section on poetry at the end of his *Grammar* and published his *Poems consisting chiefly of translations from the Asiatick languages: To which are added two essays, I. On the poetry of the Eastern nations. II. On the arts, commonly called imitative*, the following year (Oxford, 1772). He also pinned down nicely the causes of the previous neglect of Persian and the reasons for studying it, while aiming to set out the means to do so:

Since the literature of Asia was so much neglected, and the causes of that neglect so various, we could not have expected that any slight power would rouse the nations of Europe from their inattention to it; and they would, perhaps, have persisted in despising it, if they had not been animated by the most powerful incentive that can influence the mind of man: interest was the magic wand which brought them all within one circle... and it was at last discovered, that they must apply themselves to the study of the Persian language, in which all the letters from the Indian princes were written (Jones, *Grammar*, 7th edition, 1809, pp. ix–x).

Jones recommended Sa'adi's *Gulistan* ('or Bed of Roses') and the *Anvar-e Suhaili* (a 15th-century version of the Fables of Bidpai) by Husain Kashifi as models of Persian literature and his influence was such that they remained set texts for the Indian Civil Service examinations a century later. Edward Eastwick (a former East India Company employee and later briefly, 1860–63, secretary to the British Legation in Tehran) translated the *Gulistan* in 1852 and the *Anvar-e Suhaili* in 1854. Turner Macan's first complete edition of Ferdowsi's *Shahnameh* (4 vols., Calcutta, 1829), dubbed by Jones as the 'Persian Homer', followed by James Atkinson's abridged translation (1832), and Matthew Arnold's *Sohrab and Rustum* (1853), brought Ferdowsi to a wider English audience. These and other poets, notably Hafiz, became household names in England; Jones had already identified Hafiz (the 'Persian Anacreon') as a major poet and offered elegant translations of his ghazals in his earliest publications.

Undoubtedly, however, the most influential and best known of all Persian literary works in England (as elsewhere) were the celebrated *Ruba'iyat* ('Quatrains') of Omar Khayyam, contemporary evidence for whose authorship is essentially lacking and who was more celebrated in his own time as a mathematician and freethinker. Edward FitzGerald's translation of the *Ruba'iyat of Omar Khayyam* (London, 1859) was, as is well known, only loosely based on a supposed Persian original and should be considered in its own right as a piece of Victorian English literature. Nevertheless, FitzGerald did base his verse on acquaintance with a manuscript in the Bodleian Library in Oxford, to which he was introduced by Edward Cowell (1826–1903), with whom he studied Persian and who later supplied FitzGerald with details of another manuscript of Khayyam that he had found in Calcutta. Cowell himself remained a significant translator of Persian poetry, particularly Hafiz. When he returned to England in 1867 to become the first Professor of Sanskrit at Cambridge, he translated two odes of the 12th-century poet Anvari together with E.H. Palmer (1840–82), professor of Arabic but also author of a *Concise Dictionary of the Persian Language* (London, 1876). It is worth underlining this point, that during the 19th century, as earlier, even Persian studies pursued in an academic context were promoted by scholars whose posts were not specifically in Persian.

The enormous popularity and success of Edward FitzGerald's *Ruba'iyat of Omar Khayyam* were something of a one-off phenomenon and the four subsequent editions to 1889 (the last published posthumously) had a great impact on English literature and following the first illustrated edition of 1884 – spawned an industry of sentimental or erotic images of Persia that had nothing to do with either the text or the realities of Persian society.

Meanwhile, the first accounts of England began to be written in Persian in the early 19th century, first by visitors from India and then later by students sent by Crown Prince 'Abbas Mirza; the most notable of these was the work of Mirza Salih Shirazi, who was in England from 1815 to 1819 and left a full description of his stay and of the British manners and institutions that he encountered. He introduced the printing press to Iran when he returned to Tabriz. Another student, Hajji Baba, studying anatomy and surgery among other things, on his return to Iran became the Shah's physician, and his name was used for the hero of James Morier's brilliant satire on Persian society, *The adventures of Hajji Baba of Ispahan* (London, 1824), which caused such outrage in Iran when it was discovered that it was written by an 'Englishman'. For the most part, however, visits to England and the knowledge of the country disseminated as a result remained few and far between throughout the 19th century, and probably had no impact on the understanding of British ways outside the political elites who dealt with the British in an official capacity within Iran.

James Morier was himself a diplomat and Minister Plenipotentiary in Iran (1814–15), and in addition, wrote two books on his various *Journeys in Persia, Armenia and Asia Minor* (London, 1812, 1818). These are valuable accounts of the country and, together with substantial works written by other contemporary officials with whom he was associated in this first flush of intensive diplomatic engagement with Persia, such as Sir John Malcolm and Sir Gore and Sir William Ouseley, contributed greatly to the increase in knowledge of the country and her long and rich history. Malcolm's *History of Persia* (2 vols., London, 1815) is the outstanding work of the period and it became a fundamental source for later authors, being also quoted by Persian writers. As A K S Lambton (1995: 107) remarks in her assessment of the *History*, 'Malcolm was not a professional historian, but he was deeply interested in the history of the people among whom he lived and worked... The popularity of his *History* in Persia showed that he both captured the Persian imagination and sympathised with them as they saw themselves.'

British travel literature throughout the 19th century is voluminous and rightly regarded as a valuable source of information about the state of the country under the Qajars. Perhaps the most important, in view of his significance for Anglo-Persian relations, is the celebrated work of George Nathaniel Curzon (1859–1925), *Persia and the Persian Question* (2 vols., London, 1892), written as a result of a three-month period in Iran in 1889–90, but also an intensive study of existing sources of information. Curzon went on to be Viceroy of India (1898–1905) and British Foreign Secretary in 1919, in which post he presided over the Anglo-Persian Agreement, through which he sought to rejuvenate Iran's fortunes under the exclusive tutelage of the British, believing fervently not only in Britain's role as an exceptional civilising power, but also in the absolute imperative of controlling Iran as a bulwark against the ever present threat of Russian encroachment on India. Despite his profound knowledge of the country, he was unable to see that his proposals were completely unacceptable to Iranian statesmen increasingly anxious to throw off foreign interference in their country, especially in the wake of the unwanted occupation of Iran in World War I. The Agreement was never ratified, but clearly contributed to the very negative perceptions in Iran of Britain's role in her internal affairs.

Curzon's Persia was a scholarly work and the turn of the 20th century saw several other important contributions from British authors writing outside the confines of academic institutions. Guy Le Strange (1854–1933), a man of independent wealth, visited Persia in 1877–80. After 1907, he settled in Cambridge and worked with Edward Granville Browne (see below), pioneering the study of the historical geography of Iran. H L Rabino (1877–1950) was a professional diplomat who spent many years in *Persia* in a variety of consular posts, particularly in the Caspian region, which he described in great detail in his book, *Mázandarán* and *Astarábád* (London, 1928). Both authors, and many other travellers to Iran, published articles in the *Journal* of the Royal Geographical Society, a vehicle for disseminating widely a knowledge of the country, its physical geography and geology.

In due course, the study of Persian became established in British universities. In London, a professor in Oriental languages was appointed at the newly founded University College, where in 1855, a Chair in Arabic and Persian was created to cater for the examinations for the civil service of the East India Company. The second incumbent, Charles Rieu, who made his fine reputation from his detailed catalogues of the Persian manuscripts being acquired by the British Museum, held the post from 1856 to 1895, before moving to take up the Chair in Arabic at Cambridge. Two courses in Semitic languages (1878) and Indian languages (1879) were established at Cambridge, where C E Wilson taught Persian for five years before becoming Professor of Persian at University College, London (1903–17). Wilson was among those who made available English translations of other important poets apart from Ferdowsi and Sa'adi, whose works had dominated the scene up till then, with renditions of Jalal al-Din Rumi and 'Abd al-Rahman Jami as well as Nizami's *Haft Paikar* (2 vols., London, 1924).

In 1888, the first lectureship in Persian was established at Cambridge and E G Browne was appointed to the post, which he held until 1902, when he became Sir Thomas Adams's Professor of Arabic until his death in 1926. Browne's influence on Persian studies was enormous and effectively marks the beginning of Persian as a sustained field of research in an academic context in Britain. Browne graduated in Natural sciences in 1882 and qualified as a medical student in 1887, becoming a Fellow of Pembroke College the same year. He then spent his 'year amongst the Persians', later published as a travelogue (London, 1893) documenting his one and only visit to the country. Thereafter he pursued a life dedicated to its most sympathetic study. Browne achieved work of fundamental and often pioneering importance in many areas of research, not least in the editing and translation of numerous texts for the E J W Gibb Memorial Trust, of which he was a founder member and the moving spirit, encouraging his colleagues, such as Guy Le Strange, to do likewise (Rabino's book mentioned above was also published in the GMS). Browne's masterpiece and most enduring work is his monumental *Literary History of Persia* (4 vols., London, 1902–24), in which an assessment of the major poets and prose writers, especially of the classical period – conceived as ending with Jami – is set within a detailed historical context. It is important to recall that his research was carried out almost entirely on the basis of manuscripts, as very few works then existed in printed editions. Browne's trenchant and often idiosyncratic views carried great authority and were in some cases, such as his negative appreciation of the *Shahnameh* or the literature of the Safavid period, such as to deter further investigations.

Browne's activities extended far beyond his academic studies; he was particularly engaged with contemporary events in Iran and especially the unfolding of the Persian Constitutional Revolution of 1905, on which he published extensively and, more significantly, the cause of which he championed actively within the British political establishment, attempting to influence public opinion through his lectures and letters to the press. In 1908 he founded the Persia Committee, together with H F B Lynch, attracting several MPs and journalists to the Persian cause and lobbying for Russia's withdrawal; he published photographs of Russian atrocities in Tabriz in 1911. His efforts were essentially unsuccessful, the British government taking a pro-establishment line against the constitutionalists; nevertheless, his outspoken and sincere support for the people won him enduring gratitude and respect in Iran, including an alleyway named after him in Tehran that has survived two changes of regime.

Among the Iranians with whom Browne worked, it is worth mentioning Mirza Muhammad Qazvini (1877–1949), who lived 35 years in Europe, mainly in Paris, before returning to Iran in 1939. Browne encouraged Qazvini to prepare several texts for the Gibb Memorial Series, and was among the few European scholars Qazvini praised for his efforts to establish high quality critical text editions. Among younger students, Browne's reputation and publications attracted 'Isa Sadiq (1895–1978), initially sent by the Persian government to study in France in 1912. In 1916 a brief visit to Browne in Cambridge led to a longer stay in the academic year 1916–17, during which he taught Persian and by his own account became far better acquainted with (and proud of) his own culture and history; Browne was clearly able to communicate his enthusiasm and love for Iran in such a way as to win the hearts of the Iranians themselves. 'Isa Sadiq went on to become head of the newly establish Teachers Training College in Tehran and ultimately Minister of Education.

Browne was one of a remarkable series of incumbents of the Sir Thomas Adams's professorship of Arabic who concentrated their interests on Iran. The previous holder (1895–1902) was Charles Rieu, the famous cataloguer (noted above). Browne was in turn succeeded by his former pupil, Reynold A. Nicholson (1868–1945), who is celebrated chiefly for his studies of mystical poetry and especially the magisterial edition, translation, and commentary on the *Masnavi* of Jalal-al-Din Rumi. Nicholson was followed in

1933 by C A Storey (1888–1967), whose *Persian Literature: A Bio-bibliographical Survey* (London, 1927), remains an indispensable research tool. His library and the bulk of his estate were left to the Royal Asiatic Society, London. The final link in this chain of 'Persian' professors of Arabic at Cambridge is A J Arberry (1905–69), who moved from London on Storey's resignation in 1947. Arberry's best and most useful work (apart from his translations from Arabic, including the Qur'an) was done in translations of Rumi, Hafiz, Sa'adi and 'Attar, bringing Persian literature and sufi texts to a wider audience. He also contributed to cataloguing the magnificent collection of Persian manuscripts formed by the American Chester Beatty and now housed in Dublin.

The Sir Thomas Adams's professorship of Arabic since Arberry has reverted to Arabists, but the strong tradition of Persian studies at Cambridge continued; the two leading figures were Reuben Levy (1891–1966) and later P W Avery (1923–2008). Levy had studied in Oxford and taught Persian there (1920–23) before moving to Cambridge in 1926. He was promoted Professor of Persian in 1950, the first to hold that title. Levy translated and edited several Persian texts including the *Qabusnameh* (Gibb Memorial Series, London, 1951; tr. as *A Mirror for Princes*, London, 1951) and made an abridged prose translation of the *Shahnameh* (London, 1967).

Peter Avery came to Cambridge in 1958 as Lecturer in Persian; while a student at SOAS he had already embarked on translating some of the *ghazals* of Hafiz together with the English poet, John Heath-Stubbs (London, 1952). This was the start of a long and fruitful collaboration, which led to their translation of the *Ruba'iyat* of Omar Khayyam (London, 1979). Avery also translated Farid al-Din 'Attar's *Mantiq al-tair* (Cambridge, 1998) and the *Divan* of Hafiz (Cambridge, 2007), both of which occupied many years. Perhaps equally close to his heart, not unlike Browne's, was an intense interest in contemporary events in Iran – many of which (unlike Browne), he witnessed at first hand. The rather personal tone of his *Modern Iran* (London, 1965) and later *The Spirit of Iran* (Costa Mesa, 2007), is typical of his empathy for the subject. In 2001 he was honoured with an OBE 'for the Promotion of Oriental Studies', and in 2008, he was presented with the Farabi Award by the Iranian government in recognition of his services to Persian culture.

Among these services was his role on the Board of Editors of the *Cambridge History of Iran* (7 vols., 1968–91), first as editorial secretary and then as an editor. His own volume, 'From Nadir Shah to the Islamic Republic' eventually brought to a conclusion this ambitious enterprise, started under the chairmanship of A J Arberry – who was succeeded by Sir Harold Bailey, professor of Sanskrit at Cambridge. Among the editors were several of those mentioned in this chapter, including Reuben Levy and 'Isa Sadiq. We should also note Ilya Gershevitch (1914–2001), Reader in Iranian Studies, the first and only holder of a post created in 1948 for the study of pre-Islamic Iran at Cambridge. Among the others also was Laurence Lockhart (1891–1975), a student of Browne's at Pembroke College, who returned to academic research after a career first at the Foreign Office in World War I, and then in the Anglo-Persian Oil Company, of which he became the first official historian. These were routes by which so many contributors to the study of Persia acquired their familiarity with the country and expertise in Iran's history. Lockhart wrote several valuable books, of which *Nadir Shah* (London, 1938) and *The Fall of the Ṣafavī Dynasty and the Afghan Occupation of Persia* (Cambridge, 1958) remain standard works. Activities in Cambridge were greatly boosted by the presence of the great Russian Persianist, Vladimir Minorsky, on retirement from SOAS in 1944 until his death in 1966.

So much emphasis is placed here on Cambridge because such a strong tradition of Persian developed there, and we will return to this at the end of this chapter; but first we should note some of the most important figures elsewhere.

It was not until World War I that the long-felt need for a centre dedicated to Oriental studies in the capital of the British Empire was translated into action. The School of Oriental Studies was established in London in June 1916, with Sir Denison Ross as its first director, who also became the first professor of Persian (1916–37). With E G Browne's encouragement, Ross was succeeded by Vladimir Minorsky, and then A J Arberry, both of whom ended up in Cambridge as mentioned above. After a short interval, the professorship of Persian passed in 1953 to Ann K S Lambton (1912–2008), the doyenne of British Persianists in the post-war era and also an editor of the *Cambridge History of Iran*. Lambton knew Iran well, having served as press attaché in the British legation in Tehran throughout World War II and playing an influential advisory role to the British government in the Oil Crisis of 1951. She wrote widely on mediaeval Persian history and theories of government, as well as producing a reference grammar that is still useful (Cambridge, 1953), and several studies on the Qajar period; but another important area of her interest and expertise was in land tenure (*Landlord and Peasant in Persia*, Oxford, 1953) and land reform (*Persian land reform 1962–66*, London, 1969), the latter based on extensive fieldwork and giving a favourable and essentially positive analysis of a process that attracted considerable criticism both inside and outside Iran. Despite her long and distinguished scholarly career, Lambton did not appear to demonstrate the same emotional devotion to her subject as E G Browne or, for instance, Peter Avery, and had no time for Persian poetry. After her retirement in 1979, the statutory chair in Persian at SOAS lapsed.

After World War II, there were several developments in Persian studies following official recognition of the importance of cultivating a knowledge of the languages and cultures of what was left of the British Empire, and new posts were created outside the existing triangle of Oxford, Cambridge and London. In Manchester, J A Boyle (1916–78), in the Foreign Office during the war, was appointed senior lecturer in Persian in 1950 and ad hominem professor in 1966. His main contributions were in the study of the Mongol period in Iran, including his annotated translation of 'Ata Malik Juvaini's *History of the World Conqueror* (2 vols., Manchester, 1958) and editing volume 5 of *The Cambridge History of Iran* (Cambridge, 1968), but he also translated 'Attar's spiritual *masnavi*, the *Ilahinameh* (Manchester, 1976).

At Edinburgh, Laurence Elwell-Sutton (1912–84) was appointed lecturer in Persian in 1952 and ultimately, like Boyle, gained a personal chair, in 1976. Elwell-Sutton had served in the Anglo-Iranian Oil Company, in the British Broadcasting Corporation (BBC), London, and as Press Attaché to the British embassy in Tehran, 1943–47. He was interested in many aspects of Persian culture, including folklore, prosody and modern politics, as reflected in his many published works including *Persian Oil: A Study in Power Politics* (London, 1955), and *The Persian Metres* (Cambridge, 1976). Like Lambton and Boyle, Elwell-Sutton also published a Persian grammar.

At Durham, the Department of Middle East Studies was a brand new creation in response to the Scarbrough report of 1947. F.R.C. Bagley (1915–97), formerly in the Foreign Office, became lecturer in Persian in 1958 until his retirement in 1981. He translated al-Ghazali's *Nasihat al-muluk* (London, 1964), and also published studies and translations of modern Persian literature, especially Sadeq Chubak (New York, 1982).

Sadly, cuts soon followed these developments and stifled the opportunities for growth in the field; the Persian lectureship in Durham (along with most of the Middle East department) was closed in 1989, although here W B Fisher (1916–84), editor of the first volume of *The Cambridge History of Iran* (Cambridge, 1968), gathered an active group in the Faculty of Geography in the 1960s and 1970s, with a strong interest in Persia, and Persian studies have since recovered. Elsewhere, too, most places managed to cling on to a Persian component in their courses. Manchester was fortunate to have in C E Bosworth a professor of Arabic Studies (1967–91) who devoted a considerable part of his research to medieval Persian history. Among his prodigious output are his standard works on the Ghaznavids (Edinburgh, 1963, 1977) and Sistan (Rome, 1968; Costa Mesa & New York, 1994), together with recent translations of the chronicle of Gardizi (London, 2011) and Baihaqi (3 vols., Cambridge MA, 2011).

A further important feature of the post World War II expansion of Persian was the establishment of the British Institute of Persian Studies as a foreign school of the British Academy in 1961. Much of the work supported by the Institute has been in the field of archaeology and particularly pre-Islamic archaeology, among the highlights of which should be mentioned the excavations at Pasargadae by David Stronach, the Institute's first Director. Like the university departments, the Institute has somehow managed to remain active through difficult times, largely due to the dedication, commitment and enthusiasm of the individuals concerned. Investigations of pre-Islamic Iran owed much to the decipherment of the trilingual inscription of Darius at Bisitun by Henry Rawlinson (1810–95); the study of Zoroastrianism has been served particularly by Mary Boyce (1920–2006) in London and R C Zaehner (1913–74) at Oxford.

Despite constraints of space, it would be wrong to omit from this brief survey the great contributions to the study of Persian art in this country. Among them should be mentioned Basil Gray (1904–89) author of *Persian Painting* (Geneva, 1961) and numerous articles on Persian art, and his collaboration with Laurence Binyon and J V S Wilkinson on the celebrated Exhibition of Persian art at Burlington House in 1931, which attracted a quarter of a million visitors and demonstrated the importance of such shows for widening public interest. The doyen of Persian art historians, Basil W Robinson (1912–2005), former Keeper of Metalwork at the Victoria and Albert Museum, was a prolific author of studies and catalogues of the main collections of Persian paintings in Oxford, London and Manchester; the collection of 54 of his *Studies in Persian Art* (2 vols., London, 1993) reveals a strong interest in manuscripts of Ferdowsi's *Shahnameh*.

We conclude on the optimistic note of the establishment of the Shahnama Centre at Pembroke College, Cambridge, where the great tradition of Persian Studies has been so strongly supported for over a century. Based on the work of the Shahnama Project since 1999, the Centre is now developing several other activities, including the series of exhibitions and cultural events under the title 'Shahnameh Forever', and a project to digitise and publish papers from E G Browne's archives, which are of such interest not only for the field of Persian studies and his correspondence with colleagues throughout Europe, but also his role in the dramatic events of the constitutional movement in Iran.

As this necessarily brief survey has shown, British interest in Persian culture has run in parallel with the diplomatic and political relations with Iran at least since the 17th century. This interest was partly practical but also fuelled by a genuine enthusiasm and an appreciation of the literature and ancient civilisation of the country that led to many discoveries and in some respects can even be said to have helped introduce Iranians to their own past. Recognition of British contributions to the study of Iran's rich history was able to offset and temper the otherwise largely negative image of Britain that was the inevitable product of her imperial presence in Iran: an unwanted presence that was all that most Persians experienced of the British until travel to Europe became more common. The legacy of this long and deep interaction is a mutual respect and admiration that persists in educated circles and is able to survive the secular changes in political affairs. Enduring cultural relationships have an important role to play in maintaining and improving diplomatic discourses.

Further reading

Afshar, Iraj *Rahnema-ye tahqiqat-e Irani* (Tehran 1349/1970).
Arberry, Arthur J. *British contributions to Persian Studies* (London, 1942).
Encyclopaedia Iranica, numerous articles accessible online, especially:
'Browne, Edward Granville' (G M Wickens, Juan Cole, Kamran Ekbal).
'Cowell, Edward B.' (Parvin Loloi).
'Curzon, George Nathaniel' (Denis Wright).
'Eastwick, Edward B.' (Parvin Loloi).
'FitzGerald, Edward' (Dick Davis).
'Great Britain ix. Iranian Studies in Britain, the pre-Islamic' (A D H Bivar).
'Great Britain x. Iranian Studies in Britain, the Islamic Period' (Charles Melville).
'Jones, William' (Michael J Franklin).
'Rawlinson, Henry ii. Contributions to Assyriology and Iranian Studies' (Peter T. Daniels).
Javadi, Hasan, *Persian literary influences on English literature* (Calcutta, 1983).
Lambton, A.K.S. 'Sir John Malcolm and *The History of Persia*', Iran 33 (21995), pp. 97–109.
Wright, Denis *The English amongst the Persians* (London, 1977).
Wright, Denis *The Persians amongst the English* (London, 1985).
Yohannan, John D. Persian poetry in England and America: a two hundred year history (New York, 1977).

Working together in hard times

Gassed: from the trenches of Khorramshahr to the Imperial War Museum

SHAHRIAR KHATERI

Dr Shahriar Khateri is a medical doctor and a veteran of the Iran-Iraq war. On the battlefield he was exposed to both mustard gas and the nerve agent Sarin. After the war, he studied medicine in Tehran and toxicology at Newcastle University, UK. In Tehran he co-founded SCWVS, an NGO supporting victims of chemical warfare as well as the Tehran Peace Museum. He publishes on war and public health, and the humanitarian consequences of chemical warfare, peace and disarmament.

The Iran-Iraq war (1980–1988) was the longest conventional war of the last century. Trench warfare was seen for the first time since World War I and nerve gas was used by Iraq in combat operations for the first time ever. As many as a million to 1.5m people died (on both sides) in the war, many more were wounded, and millions were made refugees. The resources spent on the war exceeded what the entire Third World spent on public health in a decade.

The Tehran Peace Museum begins to take shape
London, May 2005

My first ever visit to the United Kingdom was in 2005, to Edinburgh. I was there to attend the World Congress on Disaster and Emergency Medicine, where I gave a lecture about the aftermath of the mustard gas attack on the city of Sardasht in the northwest of Iran in 1987. I also spoke about the medical management of chemical casualties.

On my way back to Iran from Scotland, I could not leave without spending a few days in London. Of course, wishing to explore one of the most popular tourist destinations in the world, I had made a 'to do' list which I carried with me.

Most first time visitors to London head straight for the likes of Buckingham Palace, the Tower of London and Westminster Cathedral, but my list was a little different. My first stop was the Imperial War Museum.

Visiting the Imperial War Museum is more than just an insight into the major wars involving Great Britain and its people. It is an experience; an experience of war on all fronts, both home and on the front line. I was deeply moved by my visit.

GASSED by John Singer Sargent 1919. © IWM (Art.IWM ART 1460)

However, my visit did have another more singular purpose, and that was to see for myself the original painting by John Singer Sargent: Gassed. This famous painting, completed in 1919, was commissioned by the British War Memorials Committee to portray the horrors of the mustard gas attacks in the trenches of World War I. The painting depicts young men suffering from a gas attack. Unable to see, having difficulty breathing, they walk with the aid of two orderlies, one hand on the shoulder of their comrade in front, to the nearest dressing station.

This deeply moving artwork depicts the horrors of one of the most terrifying experiences in the history of modern warfare.

In a large and reverentially quiet room, I stopped in front of this expressive painting and looked at it for long time. Staring at the gassed soldiers with sightless eyes, I was suddenly awash with the bitter memories of my own war experiences during the Iran-Iraq War from 1980 to 1988. I was transported back in time to 18 years ago.

It was February 1987, at the front line near Khorramshahr, in the south of Iran along the Iraqi border. We had been engaged in heavy battles for over a week. Our troops had penetrated fortified Iraqi positions, and the Iraqis were making us pay. Artillery and mortar shells rained down on us with a vengeance, as did bombs from Iraqi planes.

It was hell. Dead bodies, both Iranian and Iraqi, were scattered across the field. The bodies were strewn like broken dolls over the war-ravaged landscape, resting on their sides, with limbs folded in awkward positions and heads blown off. The faces were frozen in expressions of fear, of pain – and, at times, of relief. The smell of blood and sweat was overwhelming. It's a smell that has never left me after all these years. It has permeated me through my pores.

I was scared, but still proud of myself for managing to join the army as a young volunteer to fight against the invaders. I was only 16 years old then but I felt brave and strong.

But in the midst of all that death, I thought of my mother, knowing how much she must be worrying. My older brother was badly injured with mustard gas in March 1985 and spent several weeks in hospitals, after recovering from his chemical burns, had returned to the war front, only to be killed a few months afterward in March 1986 when his body was left behind after Iraq's counter attack. My mother was never able to bury him and find comfort in mourning at his grave. His body was finally found, 15 years later.

My mother begged me not to go to the front. 'It's enough that I've lost one son,' she pleaded. But I didn't listen, wanting to follow in the footsteps of my hero brother. On that day in 1987, I was sure she was listening to news of the offensive and crying again, not knowing if her sole remaining son was alive or dead.

'Gas! Gas!' Soldiers began screaming in terror. I saw the ominous cloud drifting toward our trenches and my nostrils immediately prickled with the strange odour.

Our commanders shouted, 'Put on your gas masks. Be quick!' I donned my gas mask that very second and ran with the other soldiers in the opposite direction from the approaching poisonous vapour. It was difficult to breathe while running with the mask on. I felt that I might suffocate, but the other soldiers pushed me along. We were lucky. The wind changed direction and blew the gas cloud away from us. Looking back on it now, I know what a miracle that was. We would have lost many more comrades if the wind hadn't changed direction.

A few in our battalion were positioned exactly in the middle of the gas attack zone. I tried to return to the site to help them, but my commanders would not allow it. I removed my gas mask and felt my eyes burning for the first time. Around me, others were coughing violently and some had fainted. I overheard on an officer's radio that we had sustained heavy casualties. The gas killed many instantaneously. Others had critical injuries.

Well into the night, I received bad news. Some of my closest buddies had been killed in the attack. I started weeping but had to suppress the tears. My eyes were burning. I tried to scream, but it was too difficult to breathe.

My lungs were on fire from the gas.

The Iran-Iraq War

The Iran-Iraq War is known as the longest conventional war of the 20th century, lasting eight years from September 1980 to August 1988. It was also an extremely costly war to both countries and the region in terms of financial expense, deaths and injuries, as well as destruction to infrastructure and the environment. For the international community, one of the outcomes of the war was a realisation that stronger mechanisms were needed to prevent the use of chemical warfare agents.

Ypres, Belgium, November 2005

I received an invitation from the city of Ypres in Belgium to deliver a lecture at a conference called, 'Innocent Slaughtered', organised by the in Flanders Fields Museum to commemorate the 90th anniversary of the first gas attack of WWI in 1915.

Ypres is a picturesque, peaceful town in the Flemish part of Belgium. Walking around Ypres today it is difficult to imagine that it was once the theatre of some of the bloodiest battles of the Great War between 1914 and 1918.

Many historians and academics from around the world were among the participants of the conference including several British, French and German experts who talked mainly about the experience of their own armies in the WWI gas attacks.

One lecture, however, had a different theme and looked at the issue from another perspective. It was a lecture by Dr Peter van den

Dungen from UK's Bradford University entitled *'Civil resistance to chemical warfare during the First World War'*.

After Professor van den Dungen's lecture, I decided that once I had finished my own presentation, I would go and speak with him and share similar experiences from my own country. However, I had just finished my lecture on *'Mustard Gas Exposure and Long-Term Health Effects. Lessons Learned From Iraq-Iran War, the most recent large-scale use of chemical weapons'*, when he came over to talk to me.

Dr van den Dungen was clearly shocked to discover that many people in Iran, including thousands of civilian victims, were still suffering from adverse long-term health effects from exposure to chemical warfare agents. He was unaware that gas attacks had happened on such a large scale during the Iran-Iraq War.

After discussing the history and consequences of this war, Dr van den Dungen suggested that Iran should build its own peace museum. We agreed that there was a great need to educate people about these harrowing events and share new ideas on how to avoid such conflicts in the future.

At the time, the concept of peace studies and peace museums was very new to me. But, with Dr van den Dungen's persistence in sharing resources and his indispensible help, I soon fell in love with the idea of peace museums and the fascinating philosophy behind it.

That one short yet meaningful conversation was the first step on a long journey, which finally came to fruition with the establishment of the Tehran Peace Museum some six years later.

The History of chemical warfare

Throughout ancient and medieval times poisons were commonly used in warfare. From simple poisoned arrows to the chemical bombs we have witnessed in our lifetime, societies have tried throughout history to limit their use.

The first international agreement limiting the use of chemical weapons dates back to 1675, when a French-German agreement not to use poisoned bullets was concluded in Strasbourg. Over the next 200 years, large-scale development of chemical weapons became feasible due to industrialisation and the development of chemical technology.

In 1874, the Brussels Convention on the Law and Customs of War was adopted. It prohibited the employment of poison or poisoned weapons, and the use of arms, projectiles or material to cause unnecessary suffering. An international peace conference held in The Hague in 1899 led to the signing of an agreement that prohibited the use of projectiles filled with poison gas.

The first large-scale use of chemical weapons, in the modern era, occurred during World War I, on battlefields near Ypres in Belgium. In the course of that war, 100,000 tonnes of toxic chemicals, such as chlorine, mustard gas and phosgene were deployed, resulting in about 90,000 deaths and over a million casualties.

The horrors of chemical warfare experienced during World War I caused such outrage that many countries resolved to ban the use of toxic chemicals or chemical weapons in war for all time. This commitment resulted in the signing of the 1925 Geneva Protocol for the Prohibition of the Use of Asphyxiating, Poisonous or Other Gases, and Bacteriological Methods of Warfare. Iran acceded to the Protocol on 5 November 1929, while Iraq acceded on 8 September 1931.

The Geneva Protocol bans the use of chemical weapons in war, but does not prohibit the development, production or possession of such weapons. Many states signed the Geneva Protocol, but with reservations that they had the right to retaliate in kind with chemical weapons should they or any of their allies be attacked in such a way. Many parties to the Protocol also reserved the right to use chemical weapons against states that had not joined.

In the 1990s the international community succeeded in producing a treaty that would verify the destruction of chemical weapons worldwide as well as ensure the non-proliferation of these weapons and the toxic chemicals used in their manufacture. The Convention on the Prohibition of the Development, Production, Stockpiling and Use of Chemical Weapons and on their Destruction (otherwise known as the Chemical Weapons Convention, or CWC) was opened for signature on 13 January 1993 and entered into force in 1997.

Hiroshima, August 2006

A visit the following year to Hiroshima in Japan with members of the Society for Chemical Weapons Victims Support (SCWVS)[1] determined our resolve to create a peace museum.

It was in Hiroshima at the Peace Memorial Museum, where our delegation – mostly survivors of gas attacks – could see the devastating effects of the atomic bombs dropped on 6 August 1945 and effectively bringing World War II to an end. We saw parallels between our own suffering and that of our Japanese counterparts. And, in sharing the experiences in Hiroshima, we saw how survivors had become living history lessons for future generations. Not only did the Hiroshima survivors volunteer as guides in the Peace Museum, but served as eyewitnesses willing to share their painful experiences about the devastating effects of war and nuclear weapons.

Chemical warfare during the Iran-Iraq War

During the eight-year war between Iran and Iraq, Iraqi forces employed chemical weapons extensively against Iranian targets including both military personnel and civilians in border towns and villages. The agents used by the Iraqis fell into two major categories based on chemical composition and casualty-producing effects.

The most frequently used compounds included organophosphate neurotoxins, known as nerve agents such as Tabun, Sarin and VX. Mustard gas[2] was also used extensively.

Iraqi troops are reported to have used vomiting agents during their initial smaller attacks on the Helaleh and NeyKhazar zones in 1981. They then employed chemical weapons in August 1983 on the Piranshahr and Haj-Omaran battlefields and later in November 1983 on the Panjvien battlefield.

The first extensive chemical attack by Iraqi troops was carried out in March 1984, when they used tonnes of sulfur mustard and nerve agents against Iranian soldiers on the Majnoon Islands battlefields, along the southern border. Afterward, extensive employment of chemical weapons by Iraqi troops in March 1985 led to a large number of Iranian casualties, both soldiers and volunteer combatants. Following requests by the Iranian Government, UN specialist teams were sent to Iran in March 1984, April 1985, February/March 1986, April 1987, March, July and Aug 1988[3]. Based on the UN fact-finding team's investigations, the use of mustard gas as well as nerve agents by Iraq against Iranians was confirmed.

The reports were subsequently submitted to the Security Council and two statements were released on 13 March 1984 and 21 March 1986 condemning the use of chemical weapons. However, neither these two statements, nor Resolution 612 (May 1988) nor Resolution 620 (August 1988) secured the cessation of chemical weapons attacks by the Iraqi regime, which continued to violate international law with impunity.

The Iraqi regime not only used chemical weapons against military targets, but also frequently targeted civilian residential areas, especially border towns and villages. According to official reports, there were more than 30 chemical attacks against Iranian (and some Iraqi Kurds) non-military targets.

The main civilian attacks occurred in Sardasht (28 June 1987), villages around the city of Marivan (March 1988), Halabja, with the massacre of more than 5000 civilians (16 March 1988) and villages around the cities of Sarpole Zahab, Gilane gharb and Oshnavieh (May–June 1988). Even some medical centres and field hospitals were targeted by chemical munitions, which resulted in high casualties among medical personnel.

The most recent and accurate description of chemical weapons use by Iraqi forces during the conflict is the 2003 United Nations Monitoring Verification and Inspection Commission (UNMOVIC) report. This document estimates that 1,800 metric tonnes of mustard gas, 140 tonnes of Tabun and over 600 tonnes of Sarin were used against Iran using munitions that included approximately 19,500 aerial bombs, 54,000 artillery shells and 27,000 short-range rockets. In excess of 1 million Iranians sustained exposure to these agents during the war, resulting in thousands of deaths from their acute effects.

This tragedy was a horrifying epic in the annals of modern warfare, inflicting enormous suffering, which continues to the present day in the form of latent illness among tens of thousands of survivors.

Tehran and London, 2007

And so, the journey continued. In June 2007, the third year of our 'Peace Exchange' programme with citizens of Hiroshima[4], the SCWVS members and our Japanese guests from Hiroshima visited Tehran. A meeting with Tehran's then-Mayor, Mr Qualibaf, started a series of discussions about the importance of establishing a peace museum in the city. Mr Qualibaf, himself a veteran of the Iran-Iraq War, was enthusiastic about a peace museum in the capital. With the Mayor's support, the initial steps for creating a peace museum began.

Significantly, the starting ceremony of the Tehran Peace Museum Project on the 29th of June coincided with the memorial ceremony of the gas attacks on Sardasht. The municipality of Tehran kindly donated a building to the museum founders in the City's Town Park – *The Park e Shahr*. Located in the very heart of the capital, there is no better location than this beautiful and peaceful park. The Tehran Peace Museum was opened with temporary exhibitions and big plans for a permanent museum.

Before returning from Newcastle University where I was working on my PhD thesis[5], I got in touch with an Iranian-British friend who introduced me to two wonderful peacemakers from Wales. A meeting was set up for me to talk to them about our Peace Museum Project.

Over a delicious vegetarian meal in London, we shared our experiences and then they told me about the World Peace Flame[6] Project. 'Our aim,' they said, 'is to inspire people everywhere that the individual plays a crucial role in creating peace at every level. Our dream is as simple as it is ambitious: to light an eternally burning World Peace Flame in every major city or decision-making centre in the world.' It is a dream that they have cherished since 1999 and now there are Flames of Peace burning on five continents.

This conversation about inner peace inspired me deeply. I, too, was convinced that we in Iran should also collaborate with

Poster of the memorial ceremony for chemical warfare victims – April 2014

the World Peace Flame movement. I started thinking about the connections we could make with citizens from around the world in promoting a culture of peace.

In that meeting, I was given two candles to be taken to Tehran. Later that year, one of the candles was lit in a special ceremony in the temporary building of the Tehran Peace Museum.

The chemical warfare toll

During the Iran-Iraq War, an estimated one million Iranians, both military and civilian, were exposed to chemical warfare agents. More than 100,000 Iranians were documented to have received emergency medical care for chemical injuries. Half of those injuries were moderate to severe. During the war, at least 7,500 Iranians died immediately from chemical injuries[7]. Since the end of the war in 1988, several hundred have died of chronic complications due to mustard intoxication.

In 2014, more than 26 years after the end of war, approximately 75,000 Iranians are registered as receiving care for chronic effects from chemical weapons injuries (Table 1). Of these around 10,000 are civilians. An additional 25,000 civilians are estimated to be currently affected by chemical weapons injuries but not included in the national registry.

Unfortunately, Iraqi attacks also included citizens of their own county. In the Anfal campaign (1986–1989), the Iraqi military used nerve and mustard agents against Kurdish villages in the northern provinces of Iraq. About 5,000 civilians in the town of Halabja alone died instantly from nerve agent poisoning on 16 March 1988, and many other Iraqi towns and villages were also gassed in this campaign. It is estimated that at least 20,000 Iraqi civilians sustained moderate to severe chemical injuries. Ironically, many of them were evacuated to Iran for medical treatment.

June 2011, Tehran

Finally, the day we had all been working towards arrived and the following invitation letter was sent to several people in Tehran:

Dear Sir/Madam,

The day so many of us have waited for is here!

It is a special pleasure to invite you to the opening ceremony of the Tehran Peace Museum on Wednesday 29 June 2011 at 6pm. This date coincides with the anniversary of the gas attack on Sardasht and Iran's national day for Campaigning Against Chemical and Biological Weapons.

Your participation will be a great encouragement to the advocates who have worked long and hard to make the museum a reality.

Other international guests will include Japanese peace campaigners and the director of the Hiroshima Peace Museum as well as survivors of the infamous Halabja gas attack.

We look forward to welcoming you at 6pm next Wednesday at the meeting hall of the Park-e Shahr library on Behesht Avenue in central Tehran.

This was the birthday of the Tehran Peace Museum.
It was a long journey and on the way, many friends and peace activists from all over the world inspired me. I am grateful to those wonderful peace activists from Wales and those who founded the World Peace Flame Foundation. Distinguished academics in the Department of Peace Studies at the University of Bradford and the city's Peace Museum. My deeper understanding about the brutality of chemical weapons and the suffering of victims was made possible while completing my PhD at the University of Newcastle, I felt privileged to be guided by a team of accomplished academics at the medical toxicology centre.

And now, as a result of this support and guidance from so many British friends, the Tehran Peace Museum is a place for building bridges in developing a culture of peace throughout the world.

A view of the Tehran Peace Museum

2014, the Tehran Peace Museum

Today, the Tehran Peace Museum is a member of the International Network of Museums for Peace (INMP), offering the opportunity to connect with a global network of museums promoting a culture of peace throughout the world.

The concept of the museum is to facilitate peace education and develop peaceful environments drawn from the personal experiences of war survivors.

The museum encompasses exhibitions about the horrors of chemical and nuclear warfare. This is balanced with awareness programmes, bridge-building dialogues, connections with other peace museums and a comprehensive peace education programme catering for both younger and older members of society. It offers the space and opportunity for a community of learning within the museum and welcomes fresh ideas and initiatives from visitors and volunteers.

The Tehran Peace Museum is unique in its body of volunteers, men and women who have been directly affected by chemical weapons. They are involved in the Veterans Oral History Project and actively voice the need for creating peaceful societies in today's world.

July 2014, Tehran

As somebody who has witnessed the horrors of war and gas attacks, the suffocation of comrades and close friends and years later, being involved in the treatment of many patients who struggle to survive for being exposed to mustard gas, I feel a heavy responsibility on my shoulder to raise awareness against war and chemical weapons so that such a tragedy will never happen again, and that is why I am here at the Peace Museum.

Health Effects of Chemical Weapons (Nerve agents and Mustard gas)*

Nerve Agents

- Lethality
  Causes death within minutes via paralysis and asphyxiation (anti-cholinesterase effect).
- Acute effects
  Eye pain and blurred vision; runny nose, headache, vomiting. In severe cases, unconsciousness, seizure, foamy discharge from mouth and/or nose, coma.
- Chronic effects
  PTSD and other psychological effects.

Sulfur Mustard

- Lethality
  Death in only 1–3% of cases, usually from respiratory failure or sepsis leading to respiratory failure.
- Acute effects
  – Respiratory – swelling, blistering, lesions and fluid build-up throughout respiratory tract; possible interference with breathing.
  – Dermatological – swelling, blistering and discoloration on exposed skin and mucous membranes. Sulfur mustard is lipophilic, hence injuries are particularly severe in moist areas of the body – eyes, armpits, groin. Serious skin injuries require intensive treatment in burn centers and signal high level of exposure and systemic involvement.
  – Optical – Approximately 75–90% of persons exposed to mustard agent suffer eye injuries. The most common immediate sign of mustard gas exposure is swollen red eyelids; often temporary blindness. Acute eye injuries, involving lesions to the cornea and other parts of the eye, require intensive nursing care. After 6 weeks, many severe eye injuries resolve.
- Chronic effects
  – Respiratory – Chronic Bronchitis/Bronchiolitis, airways Injuries require repeated surgery, continuous medication, and a severely restricted lifestyle because of lung dysfunction and Dyspnea in many of the survivors.
  – Dermatological – Skin lesions eventually heal over but leave scarring, chronic itching and dryness of skin.

– Optical – corneal injuries sometimes go into remission and then return in a more severe form, corneal opacity and melting of cornea in many cases leads to corneal transplant.
– Mutagenicity – Mustard agents have DNA, RNA, and protein-alkylating effects; they are mutagenic, and extremely cytotoxic at low doses.
– Carcinogenicity – Sulfur mustard is rated by International Agency for Research on cancer-IARC.
– as a human carcinogen. Recent reports by Iranian scientists reveals that risk of cancer is significantly higher among Sm exposed population compared with normal population.
– Immune system – chronic immune system dysfunctions, which may affect the immune response of natural killer cells (NK) as well as T-cells. This may lead to higher susceptibility to infectious diseases and chronic inflammation due to the excess of inflammatory cytokines.

- **Psychological effects**
Post-traumatic stress disorder (prevalence 68% of men, 86% of women surveyed in Sardasht), depression (prevalence of 56% of those surveyed in Sardasht), anxiety; more severe among those who were children at time of attack.

Notes

1 The SCWVS is a Tehran-based non-governmental organization (NGO), founded in 2003 and operates on a national basis, many of its members are survivors of chemical attacks or their family members, it has also many volunteers with different backgrounds. Its main goal is to provide social and health support for victims of chemical warfare and to raise awareness against the use of chemical weapons and other weapons of mass destruction.
2 Sulfur Mustard.
3 The conclusions, based on field inspections, clinical examinations of casualties, and laboratory analysis of samples, were released as official UN Documents (S/16433, S/17127, S/17911, S/18852, S/19823, S/20060, S/20134).
4 The SCWVS from Tehran and MOCT association from Hiroshima began their exchange programme in 2004 as two NGOs from countries affected by WMD, to raise awareness against chemical and nuclear weapons and to build a cultural bridge between citizens of the two countries of Iran and Japan.
5 The PhD thesis was concerned with a joint project with an Iranian university examining the chronic health effects of exposure to mustard gas and searching for ways to help Iranian gas attack survivors. Since the exact mechanism of toxic effects of Sulfur Mustard is unknown, there is no effective cure for exposure related illnesses. This joint project focused on possible chronic impairment of DNA repair mechanisms in cells due to exposure to Sulfur Mustard.
6 The World Peace Flame is a foundation established by a group of citizens, it is dedicated to achieving peace through a process of education and the practical support of grassroots peace initiatives.
7 4,000 victims died from nerve or blood agents and 3,500 from mustard agent.

Bibliography

- Foroutan, Abbas, Medical Experiences of Iraq's Chemical warfare, ISBN:964-456-654-8, 2003.
- Unresolved Disarmament issues, Iraq's Proscribed Weapons Programs, 6 March 2003, UNMOVIC Working document.
- Hiltermann, Joost. A Poisonous Affair: America, Iraq, and the Gassing of Halabja. New York: Cambridge University Press, 2007.
- An Open Wound: consequences of the use of chemical weapons against Iran. Society for Chemical Weapons Victims Support SCWVS. Tehran Peace Museum, 2010.
- United Nations Security Council. Report of the Specialists Appointed by the Secretary-General to Investigate Allegations by the Islamic Republic of Iran concerning the Use of Chemical Weapons. S/16433, 26 March 1984 – UN Document S/18852, 8 May 1987 – United Nations Security Council. UN Document S/18866, 15 May 1987.

References

- Balali-Mood, M and M Hefazi (2006). 'Comparison of early and late toxic effects of sulfur mustard in Iranian veterans.' Basic Clin Pharmacol Toxicol 99(4): 273–282.
- Emadi, S N, J Aslani, et al. (2011). 'Comparison late cutaneous complications between exposure to sulfur mustard and nerve agents.' Cutan Ocul Toxicol.
- Ghanei, M and A A Harandi (2007). 'Long term consequences from exposure to sulfur mustard: a review.' Inhal Toxicol 19(5): 451–456.
- Khateri, S, Ghanei, M, et al., (2003). 'Incidence of lung, eye, and skin lesions as late complications in 34,000 Iranians with wartime exposure to mustard agent.' Journal of occupational and environmental medicine, 45(11): 1136–1143.
- ARC Monographs on the Evaluation of Carcinogenic Risks to Humans, Volume 100F (2012).
- Zafarghandi, Mohammad Reza, et al. 'Incidence of cancer in Iranian sulfur mustard exposed veterans: a long-term follow-up cohort study.' cancer 7 (2012): 24.

Bam: pictures of life, tragedy, hope and recovery

Nevil Mountford
Nevil Mountford is a photographer and a social anthropologist by training. In 2004 he founded Picture People, an organisation that provides creative opportunities to men, women and children affected by war, natural disaster or social disadvantage.

In the year 2003/1424 an earthquake measuring 6.6 on the Richter Scale struck Bam, an ancient desert town in southeast Iran, killing over 26,000. For those who survived, including 30,000 injured in the disaster, life was changed forever. It was also to change for the British photographer who joined them on the long road to rebuild a city and its lives.

They're quite hazy but my first memories date from late-1970s Iran. There's an achromatic photo that freezes time. I am playing in the sand by the Caspian Sea and there is an azure sky so enveloping that it makes you want to curl up in its embrace. It recalls bygone days when everything seemed idyllic and full of possibilities.

We left Iran in 1980, politely asked to leave by the new guys. I didn't know much about what was going on, and didn't for many years to follow.

After that. the closest I got to Iran was in 1997, in Doğubeyazıt, in the borderlands of eastern Turkey. Mount Ararat towered on one side, and the Kurdish singer, Şivan Perwer's music floated across the plains leading to Iran. Being on the doorstep of those early memories, watching travellers heading to the wonderlands of the east, urged me to follow in their footsteps one day.

Around 2002, I met Nick Danziger. His book, *Danziger's Travels*, had inspired me to explore life, and meeting him finally connected the dots. Around the same time I watched Michael Winterbottom's film *In This World*, which followed two Afghan refugees trying to reach a better life in Europe. What inspired me was that the actors were real refugees living in Pakistan and had no formal acting training. They created a reality that Hollywood could only dream of.

These epic tales of adventure and self-discovery prominently featured Iran, and brought those early memories into focus. They were my catalyst to grow and learn more, and they opened the doors to circumstance.

On Boxing Day 2003, a huge earthquake flattened Bam, an oasis town in the desert of southeast Iran.

Iran was calling me, and so I got a visa and retraced those earlier steps through Turkey. I arrived at the farthest edge of the country on a cold, rainy day. Ararat greeted me, as it had seven years previously, capped with snow, huge and domineering, full of myth and fable. Intoxicated by the highs and lows of travel, with that tingling butterfly feeling that urges you forward into the unknown, I crossed into Iran.

Iran, 13th May 2004
The road to Maku meandered around the mountains, Ararat towering behind all the way. In Tabriz I had my first experience of crossing death-defying Iranian roads and the first of many *chelo*

kebabs. I swerved Tehran, transiting to Esfahan instead. Here I explored the mosques and bazaars, and sipped tea on the Si-o-Seh Bridge. Once I got to Yazd, I decided to stay for a while.

There, I met Hans from Holland. He worked in Bam for Medair, a Swiss NGO involved in the relief operation. He invited me to come and take some pictures. Without hesitation, I took up his offer and arrived in Bam a few days later.

First impressions count. *Bam is levelled and looks like Kabul.* 26,000 died during that bitterly cold, early morning wake-up call. 75,000 were injured. The earthquake lifted the city meters out of the ground, plunged it back deeper into the earth, then finally settled.

Bam was an important point on the Silk Road, and had always been prosperous. Its fat, succulent dates were among the finest in the world, and legend recounts the story of the Prophet advising all to break their fast with a date from Bam. *The Arg-e-Bam*, a 3,000-year-old adobe citadel and a World Heritage Site, stood at one end the city, drawing tourists from far and wide to admire its hypnotic splendour. Bam had it all, and its inhabitants had few worries. After the Revolution, things changed, but the people adapted and life had gone on as normal in this oasis in the desert.

In the scene I saw before me, humanity was busy mimicking ants. Trucks were filled with rubble, motorbikes piled with cement sacks, and people were hurrying to and fro in a never-ending stream. All around were thousands of different faces. 'Outsiders' from the impoverished neighbouring Sistan and Baluchistan province had turned up – many to find work, but some to pretend they were survivors so they could claim a fridge and an air conditioner from the government. The pre-earthquake population of Bam was around 200,000. Now, with the disaster economy prevailing, it was almost back to the same figure, with many dubious business deals taking place.

That evening Hans and I went to a gathering at the Acción Contra el Hambre (ACH) house. Headscarves were thrown off, and Bam juice flowed. There were lots of people discussing cement, toilets, pre-fabs – all manner of disaster-related issues. I met Kevin from Merlin, who asked what was I doing. 'I'm a tourist', I told him. After some discussion, he gave me a job – to GPS map the health houses in Bam and its environs.

I did my job: *Latitude N:29°07'37.79" Longitude E:58°19'32.24" Altitude 1076 metres.*

That little job got me more. I took pictures of psychosocial centres for World Vision; Islamic Relief asked me to photograph their new pre-fabs in the camps. ACH asked me to photograph the goat distribution! I snapped away, feeling free. The people of Bam were all so welcoming, perhaps because many had jobs with NGOs and were mixing with the rest of the world. Being in a disaster zone is a paradox: out of intense sadness and loss comes a certain fulfilment. Iran had been pretty much closed off for a long time, but in Bam, it seemed the world was there. Sometimes it takes a catastrophe for people to wake up and realise that cooperation is the best way forward.

Bam was prime for a project. All my working life I had seen the finest photojournalism, but I had seen very little news about Bam. So I thought about giving the people of Bam an opportunity to tell their story through their own pictures, to cast them in the spotlight. Before I left, I told people that I would be back to give out cameras and make an exhibition.

London, Summer 2004

To make this idea a reality involved a lot of effort. I needed a sponsor, some cash, cameras, and to get into Iran again. First, a sponsor – Merlin; second, cameras – Kodak; and third, entry to Iran – visit the Iranian Embassy.

I submitted a visa application, but the months dragged on without reply. Kodak came up with 100 disposable cameras – that retro type once so ubiquitous in tourist shops. Merlin agreed to provide on-the-ground support and lend their name to the project, and I had the cash, but all this would be futile without an Iranian visa.

I read an article Lord Phillips of Sudbury had written on the need to engage with Iran. I thought he could be useful, so I wrote to him in June. By the time I heard back from him, in late September, I had almost given up hope. But it took a fraction of that waiting time for everything to change. He supported my application and I received a visa from the Iranian Embassy. On 1st October, I returned to Bam, and met the new faces I would be working with – the most memorable of whom was Patrick Parsons.

Patrick was a balding man in his fifties, clad in blue jeans and a photographer's jacket. He used to be a roadie for Queen, the rock band. He and his assistant, Leila, were a formidable team, who would bend the ears of anyone who tried to get in their way. Their job was to run the logistics of the Merlin program, and make sure any layers of Iranian red tape, bureaucracy or time wasting did not occur. For the most part they succeeded.

I found out pretty quickly that if you let Patrick tell his stories, he would be on your side. And you needed someone on your side in Bam. Patrick gave me a driver and a translator – Abdul Reza, and Sadegh. Abdul had a lazy eye, a result of the Iran-Iraq War, which he entered in its dying days. Before the earthquake, he was a taxi driver. His immediate family survived the upheaval, but the damage to his extended family was shocking – 14 died.

Sadegh had come from Shiraz 'to work for the people of Bam'. Hundreds of Iranians did the same, and those with language skills were in particular demand. They came from all over the country – Mashad, Tehran, Esfahan, Kerman. Their energy, youthfulness, and wish to connect with the foreigners in Bam was undeniable.

As we set off, Abdul said to me, via Sadegh's temperamental English:

'If we're going to do this project well, you're going to have to let me take control. I know everyone in Bam, and they will do this project well if I ask them. So we got to go to people I know. You need to give them time, the people of Bam are busy. Give them time.'

It was an honest and practical statement, so we made a list of what people did – musician, policeman, teacher, butcher, baker, shop keeper, tailor, cook and so on. Abdul said, 'I am the taxi driver.'

The first character we visited was Mohammed, a musician. Before the earthquake he played keyboards at weddings and other events. He got out an enormous, timeworn organ and plugged in. The deafening reverb shook the walls, and the caged parrot he kept desperately flapped its wings and added its own shrieks. Mohammed started to play some notes, and put a beat to it. He wanted to sing. And when he finished his piece, he accepted the little yellow Kodak camera and said, *'ghorbanet'*.

The next visit we made was to Akbar, who ran a guesthouse that was completely flattened. Akbar spoke brilliant English, and had the air of a university professor with his goatee and spectacles. He was rebuilding his guesthouse and garden. He wanted to get back to business as soon as possible. We all sat down to more tea. We were there for a few hours, talking about everything. I began to think, Abdul is right, this is going to take a long time.

That first day, we met perhaps ten people – men, women and kids. Their names would take up this entire narrative, but each and every one of them took photos for the project with genuine enthusiasm. Their names read like a toy-town list: *Mohammed, the Policeman; Abbas, the Butcher; Monaver, the Student* and many more. We were making a miniature ethnography of Bam, and there was no shortage of participants.

As the days went by, Abdul's promise of '*doing it his way*' eventually came to fruition and 65 people were taking pictures. We went everywhere in Bam, and the surrounding countryside – Baravat, Chelto, Biderano. I saw palm gardens that looked biblical, teeming with citrus trees. Here, you couldn't imagine the devastating earthquake, they were so peaceful and serene. Birdsong made you imagine fulfilment, and the trickle trickle sound of that most creative of Persian inventions – the *qanat* – kept these gardens lush and verdant. You could sit under one of Bam's three million date palms and watch the sunrays flicker down and feel a sort of euphoria. And against this backdrop, people all over Bam were taking pictures.

Two important people came into my life during those days. The first was Parisa Damandan, an enchanting soft-spoken lady from Esfahan. She said to me a few years later, '*Mainly I am a story teller, but now I am more of an archivist.*' Unbeknown to me at the time, Parisa and her project would form such a natural complement to mine it seemed our encounter was shaped by the immortals.

Parisa came to Bam, along with some volunteers, to dig through the rubble, not looking for people trapped underneath, but their photographs – some dating back to the turn of the century, some in colour, some in black and white, some with that kitschy painted effect so often found in this part of the world. A few years later she showed me what she had rescued. Thousands of pictures, capturing life before the earthquake struck. Her task was immense and so poignant and important.

The other person was Seifollah Samadian, a photographer, filmmaker and cameraman for Abbas Kiarostami, one of Iran's creative geniuses. He made a film called *Three Days and Ten Days* right after the earthquake. A long, silent sequence, so typical of Iranian cinema, defined the enormous scale of the disaster, as he passed row after row of Red Crescent tents that dominated the roadside. He gave me a copy of his film for the project.

I had been in Bam for more than three weeks and had met hundreds of people. I had shared their most sensitive stories. I had seen tears, laughter and smiles, but perhaps the most moving of all was when asking people, *'where is your favourite place in Bam?'* The response was often: *'it's the graveyard, because that is where all our memories are.'*

Bam graveyard was indeed a special place, and each Thursday afternoon, I went there to watch an incredible scene unfold in front of me. The noise from thousands of mourners was haunting, as prayers floated sprite-like over the headstones and into the distance. It seemed to me that the two places in Bam that transcended ordinary life were the graveyard and the Arg. The graveyard was a cacophony of sound, and the Arg, silently watched over the city and its people. Truly awe-inspiring.

In my notebook, on the day I was leaving Bam for Tehran, I wrote: *'Last day, few hours in Bam – going to be back in reality shortly. It's been the making of me over here…'*

London, November 2004

Back in London, I went through the photos. They were astonishing, and several had that wonderful tell-tale sign of an amateur making holiday snaps – the blurry pink hue of a thumb in the top right corner. There were few pictures of rubble and destruction – all the sights you see outside. Most depicted interior family life, posed amongst prize possessions – a fridge and a carpet. Others showed the graveyard and the Arg. The kids took pictures of themselves playing, riding donkeys and enjoying the simple pleasures of childhood. Some contained the poignancy of the tragedy, showing family portraits of the deceased. By this act of giving cameras, we were able to peer inside the family home and share the private times of others. Layers of cultural obstruction were removed, and it felt rewarding editing the pictures, putting together the story of Bam, one year after.

I wrote as an introduction for the show: '*The people of Bam chose to depict themselves as individuals with dignity and humour. And through these pictures the most evident thing is that Bam is alive, Bam is living and Bam will become better.*'

In the days leading to the show at The Spitz Gallery, many people got in touch. There were people from Iranian TV and radio, a lady called Diana Khalatbari, another luminous example of Iranian hospitality and kindness, asked to exhibit a model of a new school she was building in Bam. Lord Phillips agreed to make a speech at the show, and further support what I was doing. A package from Seifollah arrived containing a ten-by-two-metre encapsulated strip of photographs taken by Iranian photographers after the earthquake, showing Bam flattened and in trauma.

We had sent out invitations to everyone. We didn't know who would come, but a lot of people wanted to help make this a special show. Four hundred people turned up. Afterwards there was little time for anti-climax as I hurriedly returned to Bam with the stack of photographs to display in the Arg, for everyone to see.

Bam, December 2004

We went to the crumbling behemoth to see where we could put the pictures. Initially I wanted to place the picture boards in random spaces around the Arg, so people could wander, serendipitously stumbling across pictures in the rubble. This wasn't possible as the Arg was still fragile and dangerous, so we chose a spot in what was once a royal courtyard.

The pictures easily filled the space, and at night the Arg was illuminated. A benign eeriness filled the air, a sense the history of such a place. The pictures had found their home, and stood proud in memory of all those who died, and those that survived.

One day, the *Bad-e-Shaheed* or The Martyrs Wind, which blows in off the desert, collapsed and scattered all the boards. We went to pick them up, but found that others were doing the same. To cap it off, a rainbow hung over the Arg. It was a very special moment. Coincidentally the very same wind blew over the USAID tent, and in a richly comic moment not lost on the inhabitants, the *Stars and Stripes* that had flown on Iranian soil for the first time in a generation, fell again to the ground.

A few days later, after a lot of effort from countless people, the Bam Project wound down. It had been a wonderful success and achieved its aims many times over – the people of Bam were not forgotten. It seemed like a lifetime in the making, but its purpose was to facilitate the self-expressions of the people of Bam. They had never done this before on an international stage. And it went further than that – diverse people and entities co-operated in a meaningful way for the first time since the Revolution. The relief operation in Bam opened up Iran for a time, and whilst there were eyes and ears everywhere, the majority worked without

'It has been two years and four months since the earthquake. We haven't finished our house yet. We have only finished its metal structure. But we hope by God's will we will build it.'
Photo by Ali, the Truck Driver. October 2005

restraint. This signified a transformation that had not been seen in a generation. The Bam Project was a tiny part of this, but a part nonetheless. Leaving the city of three million date palms, with so many new friends and an enormous sense of pride and satisfaction – not just for me, but the 65 plus people who participated – left me emotional but resolute. The days ahead would be for reflection, and passing Ararat at 35,000 feet, with that azure hue all encompassing, the feeling that I was in the right place at the right time accompanied me all the way back home.

Bam, October 2005

I wanted to continue what I had begun in Bam. I thought if each year, we could produce a series of photographs, then not only could Bam be remembered, it would become an engaging visual study on how a city rebuilds itself after a disaster. I received a grant, and in October 2005, almost a year to the day since the first project began, I was back. Only this time, the undulating vivacity of a year earlier was missing, and despite some extraordinary times over the next few years, it would never truly be found again.

The anticipated departure of international NGOs and their inflated

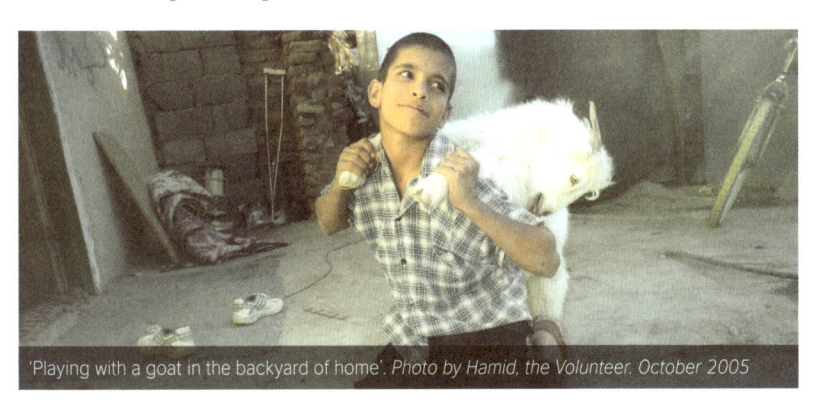

'Playing with a goat in the backyard of home'. *Photo by Hamid, the Volunteer. October 2005*

'My friend took this photo when I was playing with the donkey'.
Photo by Hamid, the Volunteer. October 2005

cash reservoirs caused a rude awakening for many who had grown used to the disaster money. A lot of people lived in a bubble for that first year after the earthquake, mistakenly believing their lives would improve. It was a naivety that would affect many, including myself.

Patrick and Leila were still there, but everyone else had gone. Abdul was my driver again, and Leila set him up with a crash course in what we were going to do, and the Second Bam Project began, with the theme of *Change* as a focus for taking pictures.

I was always writing about my experiences, and that year I summed it up with this: '*Bam remains a city where people have to try incredibly hard to survive and make their lives as they were before the earthquake. Coming back to Bam, many things had changed. Gone were the many NGOs, and with them the jobs of so many. There was a lonely feeling. Despite this, Bam was rebuilding itself.*

'*This is what happens in life. People arrive, and others leave. When you look at the photos from 2005, you see the beginnings of Bam coming back to life. You see colour in people's faces. You see new buildings, new couples coming together. You see the first baby born after the earthquake, and the first married couple. This was Bam, in 2005, and it will get better, a happier place.*'

'For the first days after the earthquake there was a lot of change in my life, and also in the city. Rebuilding of the schools, hospital and bazaar, makes life easy for the people. Preparing shelters for the people make a lot of difference in our lives. The most important things that have happened is rebuilding my house and the birth of my child.' *Photo by Hussein, the Watchman of the Arg. October 2005*

Bam, April 2006

I never spent much time in Tehran, except to visit Parisa and Seifollah. Returning from Bam, I would arrive in the morning, and head up to see Seifollah for a long lunch and conversation. His studio was a halfway house for photographers, filmmakers and artist types, hanging around with cameras dangling. It was a great place to depressurise from the travails of Bam.

Afterwards, I would ride out to Karaj, to see Parisa. Karaj is actually a suburb of Tehran, but it feels distant and pastoral. She lived in a forest, with a garden full of fruit trees. Her husband, Soheil, was a musician, and this coupling of artistic creativity made the evenings typically enthused with colloquy. Rifling through Parisa's boxes of negatives and prints would reveal wonders, many of them uncannily similar to those taken by the participants of The Bam Project. We spoke of exhibitions where one of *her* images would stand next to one of *my* images, reflecting two projects as equals, just as important as the other, except in one we would know who took what, while the other would be anonymous, dug out from the rubble, like a silent memory.

My times in Iran were so brief – just a nominal two-week press visa, with a ten-day extension. If I could I would have stayed months, because in Bam there was a blank canvas, and I wanted the people to paint it with their stories and their creativity.

Bam, February 2007

That year Michael Winterbottom gave us the rushes he had shot in Bam from *In This World*. They weren't used in his final film and were mainly scenes of the Arg, but we edited it together to make a short homage to the great monument. The dots were once again connected and I felt more and more that the project was as I intended – organic and meaningful, with contributions from many different people – photos, films and stories.

I spent a lot of time with Abdul's family, which gave me a beautiful insight into Iranian hospitality, where I was always the guest and looked after. When not driving around, visiting the participants and drinking endless tea, we would spend time in the countryside having picnics, with me gradually increasing my vocabulary of Farsi words and learning more about ordinary life in Iran – simple, compassionate and respectful.

'This kitten is the only one I tell everything to without fear or feeling shy'.
Photo by Jack Mandal. April 2006

The authorities allowed me the luxury of making this project without hindrance. I always looked forward to coming back and immersing myself in daily life, as one of very few foreigners in this part of Iran. The freedom to move around and talk to anyone was one of the defining successes of the project, and it exploded a few myths.

Bam, May 2008

My writings were always full of hope that Bam would return to normal. But the slow-burning political and social undercurrents began to create complications. That year I noticed queues at the petrol stations. Iran, with the fourth largest oil reserves in the world has to ration its own citizens. Food prices were rising too. It seemed like a struggle for just about everything.

'We decided to finish this year, as Bam has moved on from the disaster zone it was. It has a long way to go, and the people of Bam are tired, but they have not lost hope altogether.

'The photos you look at are as you see Bam now. We have tried hard to keep Bam where it should be, but other factors take over when we are not in control. As Abdul Reza said one rainy day in December 2004: "It's as if Bam was a dream that came to end… I want to see the bazaar full of people, I want to see the rush, the excitement of Bam… I want to see that day again."'

Those words were written on my seventh trip back, and the fifth project. Bam was tired! I was not to know it, but it was also the last time I saw Bam.

In March 2009 events in Iran prevented me from returning. After the disputed election and ensuing demonstrations, our friends in the Ershad had changed, and those who replaced them did not want us back.

The Bam Project, a visual narrative of a city on the edge of a desert, flattened by a massive earthquake, did not seem to interest anyone any more. I wanted to make a book, so the people of Bam could have something to remember, but no one would support it. I felt deflated as if I was letting everybody down, and Bam and Iran, would be relegated to the margins of my professional life. Several attempts over the course of the next few years led to sporadic moments of hope, but to no avail.

Then, out of the blue, I was asked to write this. It is at least an account of amazing times and people, of social conscience and genuine intention, and of enthusiastic naivety and mistakes.

And, its results – the 400-plus photographs taken over five years – display a unique sensitivity that is typical of Iran. Within that 3x2 frame, there were people's intentions to provide a narrative, not just to '*capture the moment*'. People would pose meaningfully with a symbolic reference to their situation – sometimes flowers, animals, palm trees or their cars – to illustrate what they had in their lives as they recovered and rebuilt. And what made this more exciting was that no one had any formal training in picture making. It was instinctive, and as it was made over time, you saw the ebb and flow of life and all its trials and tribulations.

One of the best photos shows *Hussein, The Watchman*, standing upright in the middle of the Arg where we had the show in 2004. It basks in the late afternoon yellow haze, with him, perfectly posed. The colours, composition and the message he attached, summed up the spirit of the project – *what does Bam mean to you?*

Another favourite was taken by *Jack Mandal*, (he had no moniker) holding up a kitten in his ramshackle construct he called home. He captioned it with the words: '*the kitten is the only one I tell everything to without feeling fear or being shy.*' And there is another by *Ali, The Truck Driver*, showing the skeletal foundation struts of a new building, with a tiny figure waving against a blue sky and palm trees, simply captioned: *'we're rebuilding Bam'*.

There are too many to write about, but all the pictures, when put together, tell the story of the Bam Project, and how the people took to it so enthusiastically, how they welcomed me with their kindness, smiles and friendship, and how they really did believe that life would get better.

'For those who have spent time here over the years, it is easy to feel romantic about an oasis in the middle of the desert, where people are living on the edge, but surviving by ingenuity and cunning. It is easy to feel content, when your mind has slipped into dreamy and never ending Bam sunsets, looking over the desert toward the mountains, when the sky turns red, yellow, orange and explodes over the horizon. It is easy to feel a long way from home driving at speed along the flat and straight roads in and out of Bam, looking at land trodden on over millennia. It is easy to feel peace and quiet drinking tea on a warm afternoon in a palm garden listening to birdsong and the sway of trees. And it is easy to feel that people will mend their problems when you are surrounded by kind and gentle folk. But when you take the beauty out of life in Bam, you are left with the harsh reality of a place that was ruined, and will, in the words of Abdul, 'take 50 years to become Bam again'.

For Abdul, for everyone I have met and become friends with, I hope that day comes to you soon. So you can see the real Bam, instead of the memory.'

British imperialism and Persian diplomacy in the shadow of World War I (1914–1921)

Dr Oliver Bast

Dr Oliver Bast, Maître-ès-Lettres, Dr.phil., is Senior Lecturer [Associate Professor] in Middle Eastern History at the University of Manchester where he co-directs (together with Dr Siavush Randjbar-Daemi) the Manchester Iranian History Academic Network (MIHAN). Bast currently serves as Honorary Secretary of the British Institute of Persian Studies (BIPS) and was recently elected Executive Director of the British Society for Middle Eastern Studies (BRISMES). His research focuses on Iranian history during the late Qajar and early Pahlavi periods. Recent publications by Bast include "Duping the British and outwitting the Russians? Iran's foreign policy, the 'Bolshevik threat', and the genesis of the Soviet-Iranian Treaty of 1921", in *Iranian-Russian Encounters: Empires and Revolutions since 1800*, ed. Stephanie Cronin (London & New York: Routledge, 2013) and 'Les *buts de guerre* de la Perse neutre pendant la Première Guerre mondiale', in *Relations Internationales*, no. 160 (2015).

Britain and Iran's complex political relationship in the years leading up to World War I and the complex negotiations that took place afterwards are key to understanding the modern history of Iran as well as the ensuing attitudes towards the British, some of which persist today. A hundred years after the Great War, a study of the two countries' diplomatic relationship helps inform the challenges facing them today.

1. Background: Britain and Iran since the early 19th century

British interactions with Iran predate World War I by several centuries but more formal diplomatic relations were only established in the context of the Napoleonic Wars. That Iran began to matter for Britain at the beginning of the 19th century was due to British concerns for imperial security in the face of Russian southeastwardly expansion. Thus, and one might say, naturally, most British envoys to Tehran were initially handled from India. Only in 1835 did the London Foreign Office manage to wrestle responsibility for Iran from India (except for the Persian Gulf, which remained under the oversight of the Bushire-based Political Residency that answered to India, not London). Nevertheless, Britain's main concern in Iran remained on keeping the Russians as far as possible from the borders of India. After having already tried once unsuccessfully in 1838, Iran made another attempt to exploit this very Anglo-Russian antagonism to its advantage in 1856. She tried grabbing Herat from the fledgling Afghan territorial state, a buffer zone between Russia and British India. Once more, however, the Iranians were rebutted by both the Afghans and their British allies resulting in defeat and the humiliating Anglo-Persian Treaty of Paris (1856). This unequal arrangement bestowed privileges on Britain vis-à-vis Iran – especially in terms of potential for British economic penetration – that were not dissimilar to those already enjoyed by the Russians as a result of the earlier Treaty of Turkomanchai, which Russia had imposed on a defeated Iran in

1828. Yet initially, the British government remained reluctant to cash in on those new-won privileges lest this would encourage the Russians to become more active themselves. Hence in 1872, British officialdom did little to support a British subject, Baron Julius de Reuter, who caused a Russian outcry when he managed to obtain a very substantial commercial concession from the Shah that was scheduled to be valid for a 70-year period. It covered, amongst other things, major transport infrastructure projects, including railway building and substantial mining rights and was utterly all-encompassing and far-reaching. Indeed Curzon later wrote that upon publication the concession had been 'found to contain the most complete and extraordinary surrender of the entire industrial resources of a kingdom into foreign hands that has probably ever been dreamed of, much less accomplished, in history.'

In the course of the 1880s, however, HMG's reticence would give way to a policy of encouragement of and support for British business engagement in Iran leading most notably to the establishment in 1889 of the Imperial Bank of Persia, a British–owned private company that succeeded in securing the monopoly for issuing Iran's banknotes. In fierce competition with Russia, Britain now engaged in a veritable scramble for concessions in Iran. One significant concession thus won by a British businessman in 1890, the so-called *Tobacco Régie*, a 50-year monopoly for the production, sale, and export of tobacco, would spark a major and above all unified backlash from the hitherto fragmented and thus rather impotent Iranian society. Although the Russians, ever keen to create problems for their British opponent in what had by now become the Great Game, also quietly fanned the flames from behind the scenes, the protracted protests against the *Régie*, which eventually forced Naser al-Din Shah Qajar to rescind the controversial concession in early 1892, mark the first instance of a co-ordinated country-wide challenge to the absolute power of the Shah. It was helped a great deal by the telegraph network that had been initiated back in 1857–8, and in the development of which, ironically, Britain had played an important part since the year 1863. The two most important social groups in the heterodox coalition of protesters of 1890–92, the Shi'ite 'clergy', or *ulema*, and the merchants and artisans of the bazaar would later rise again in a further struggle aimed at curbing both foreign encroachment as well as the Shahs' powers. This time, they eventually allied themselves to intellectuals who had begun framing the objectives of this fight in terms of effectively European notions such as constitutionalism, parliamentarism, and nationalism. The result was the victorious Iranian Constitutional Revolution of 1906. It made Iran a constitutional monarchy although the monarch in whom sovereignty remained invested constitutionally retained major prerogatives. Britain had lent a not insignificant support to the revolutionary struggle albeit more by default than by design, e.g. by allowing large numbers of Tehran's revolutionaries to take an extended refuge on the embassy's vast grounds, which were, naturally, off-limits for the regime's Russian officered security forces trying to crack down on the up-rising when it climaxed in the summer of 1906.

However, if the Iranian constitutionalists had hoped to thus have a long-term ally in Britain, a liberal democracy, especially against the encroachment of Russia, which was technically still an autocracy despite the changes wrought by the Russian Revolution of 1905, they would soon see those hopes squashed. When a Russian-supported counter-revolutionary interlude in 1908–1909, instigated through a coup d'état executed from the top by the then reigning Shah, Mohammad Ali Qajar, interrupted the bedding in of Iran's fledgling parliamentary democracy early and brutally, Britain would do next to nothing. Wider strategic considerations dictated Britain's reluctance to challenge the seeming reinstatement of absolute rule by the Shah with Russia's help. To be sure, the structural antagonism with Russia in the region had not gone away. Indeed, the Great Game in Asia was far from over. Yet, it was for this very reason that, in the face of Germany's rise on the continent, which presented distinct challenges to both Russia and Britain in Europe, the two powers decided to reduce their Asian rivalry's potential for the creation of tensions between them in an understanding that became known as the Anglo-Russian Entente of 1907 covering Iran, Afghanistan, and Tibet. The aim was to 'stay out of each other's hair' in Asia through the creation of buffer zones between one's respective empires. Russia's and Britain's coming to terms with one another over Iran was also helped by the fact that it was precisely in 1906, that Germany had finally decided to no longer turn a deaf ear to long-standing Iranian entreaties for greater involvement in the development of the country: a major German loan to Iran was being considered, and, encouraged by the German foreign ministry, the Deutsche Orientbank, a consortium led by Dresdner Bank was exploring erecting a branch in Tehran. While nothing came of this because the German bankers soon lost interest, the reality of the Anglo-Russian Entente of 1907 meant that Britain and Russia between them split Iran into three zones, namely a Russian influence zone in the North, a neutral buffer zone in the middle, and a zone of British influence in the Southeast, bordering British India.

It's an ironic twist of history that this British zone did not incorporate a region in Southwest Iran that by the eve of World War I would become a special focus of British attention because of its oil wealth. A British subject, the Australian businessman

William Knox d'Arcy, had obtained a concession for the extraction of oil in the South of Iran in 1901. Yet, the company that represented the concession by the time of the signing of the Anglo-Russian Entente had failed to find any oil thus far. By 1908 they were finally about to give up and leave when oil was at last struck, which led to the creation, in 1909, of what would become the Anglo-Persian Oil Company (APOC), the present BP. Still, this company continued to struggle. This was due to the poor marketability of its produce and the company would have probably been taken over by mightier rivals or indeed, gone under, had it not been for the narrow victory in 1913 of those far-sighted individuals in the British naval establishment that had been battling with their more conservative colleagues over the question of switching the Navy's fuel from coal to oil. Once the decision to switch had been endorsed, the British government proceeded to acquire a controlling stake in the oil company thus effectively saving the business. The British government intended this as an insurance policy lest the Navy would one day find itself being held to ransom by one of the major foreign oil companies. Yet despite now being effectively owned by the British state the company retained a large degree of commercial and operational autonomy; significant differences of opinion between the Foreign Office and the company's executives were not uncommon. Furthermore, the Navy's conversion to oil did not happen overnight. Thus, while important, the role of oil in British policy in Iran during the following years, i.e. during World War I, must not be overstated; other factors, still chiefly connected to the question of imperial security weighed far more heavily on the minds of most of those who had a stake in formulating Britain's policy toward Iran one the eve of, during, and immediately after World War I.

2. Britain and Iran during the war (1914–1018)

While the July Crisis of 1914 unfolded in Europe, Tehran was decked out in flags, banners, and other intricate ornamentations to mark a major celebration: the son of the above-mentioned illiberal Mohammad Ali Qajar Shah (who had been forced to abdicate in July 1909 after a second revolutionary upsurge had put an end to the aforementioned absolutist interlude) had come of age and was crowned as Soltan Ahmad Shah Qajar on 21 July 1914. When the war broke out at the beginning of August, it seemed a faraway affair that needed not unduly concern the Iranians.

This ceased, however, to be true when the Ottoman Empire entered the conflict siding with the Central Powers by attacking Russia in late October 1914. Now Iran, whose only military assets worth mentioning consisted of two units dedicated to domestic security rather than being armed forces able to take on an external attacker, namely a Brigade of Cossacks led by Russian officers and a Swedish-officered Gendarmerie, hastened to emphasise her neutrality. The Shah's official proclamation to that effect was announced on 1 November 1914. Yet it would not take long before the war would reach neutral Iran's territory. The presence of Russian contingents in the Northwest of Iran who had been stationed there since the Civil War that had followed Mohammad Ali Shah Qajar's counter-revolutionary coup in June 1908, jeopardised Iran's neutrality. As was to be expected, the Russians failed to heed repeated Iranian requests to withdraw their troops, which in turn provided the Ottomans with the perfect pretext to dismiss Iran's neutrality as a chimera. The first clashes between advancing irregular Ottoman units and Russian troops occurred around the turn of the year 1914. At this early stage of the war, British foreign policy makers concerned with the Middle East in London, in Cairo, as well as in India were merely watching developments in Iran with anxiety without getting involved yet. However, over the course of 1915 this stance would change dramatically.

There were two reasons for this. One the one hand, the (ultimately unsuccessful) Anglo-French naval assault on the Dardanelles that began in February 1915 had the alarm bells ringing in Petrograd. Thus the Russians hastened to stake their claim on the Straits vis-à-vis their allies, which gave rise to the so-called Constantinople Agreement of March/April 1915. The Anglo-Russian part of what was in actual fact not one integrated agreement but two initially rather un-coordinated bilateral arrangements between Russia and each of her Western allies, also stipulated the division of the whole of Iran into two zones of influence between Russia and Britain. Now, the neutral zone that the aforementioned Anglo-Russian Entente of 1907 had established in the centre of Iran was to be added to the British zone of influence, except for the city of Isfahan, which was to be allocated to the Russian zone. Both parties were to do as they saw fit in their respective zones, which provided additional ammunition to that influential yet hitherto unheeded minority in the Russian foreign policy establishment that had been advocating outright annexation of Northern Iran for some time already. There can be little doubt that if the stipulations of the Constantinople Agreement had come to pass, Iran would not only have seen her territorial integrity challenged but also suffered a major, potentially fatal, blow to her sovereignty as an independent state. At any rate, in the spring of 1915 this Agreement certainly meant that Iran moved up the agenda of British foreign policy making.

One the other hand, Britain's attention was also drawn to Iran by what may be called the 'German Moment' in Iran's World War I experience. This had been playing out since the beginning of

1915 when the German consul in Tabriz, Wilhelm Litten, liaised with advancing Ottoman irregular units and their local supporters to briefly take control of the city in a veritable *coup de théâtre* that shook the Russians, who had felt to have an unassailable grip on the region, and alerted the British. Throughout the spring and summer of 1915, German activity increased steadily with the Germans being able to capitalise on the hostility that many Iranians, especially the veterans of the Constitutionalist struggle of all political colours, harboured towards the Entente powers.

Britain and Iran's 'German Moment' in 1915

Ironically, the 'German Moment' came about merely as a 'by-product' of German initiatives targeting objectives elsewhere, with Berlin's initial interest in Iran having been rather limited. Latching on to an Ottoman initiative going back to the summer of 1914, German officials had drawn up plans to win over the Emir of Afghanistan, Habibollah Khan, for an attack on British India. These plans resulted in a German military mission led by Oskar Ritter von Niedermayer that was dispatched to Kabul in September 1914. It was followed, in the spring of 1915, by a small diplomatic mission under Werner Otto von Hentig. Initially, the two missions were merely to transit Persia quickly. Once there, however, some members of the Nierdermayer mission, who had been sent ahead as advance parties, became involved in astonishingly successful activities against the Entente in several Iranian cities. Isfahan, Kermanshah, Yazd, Hamadan, and Kerman were in the hands of pro-German groups by autumn 1915. Relying on this West-East axis of favourably inclined places, Niedermayer's and Hentig's missions succeeded in crossing Iran and made it to Kabul. The British responded to these developments by using their still intact consular presence in Eastern towns such as Mashhad, Qa'en, and Birjand in an attempt at sealing off Iran's Eastern border by setting up what became known the East Persian Cordon. In parts of the North this was achieved through an uneasy liaison with Russian forces while in other regions the British proceeded to the raising of local levies.

Another area where the 'German Moment' created headaches for Britain was Southwest Iran. There, a small unit of German agents headed by Captain Fritz Klein operating from bases within Mesopotamia attacked British oil installations in the area now known as Khuzestan while local khans, encouraged by the German agent Wilhelm Wassmuss, who had arrived in the region, which he knew well, in early 1915, threatened the British in both Shiraz, the capital of the province of Fars, and in Bushire, the port city on the Persian Gulf where Wassmuss had served as a consul before the war. As mentioned above, Bushire was the location of the British Political Residency for the Persian Gulf, i.e. the head-quarters of Britain's control of what contemporaries argued had become a 'British lake' by that time. In the face of Wassmuss' successful stirring up of anti-Entente activity in the region, in May 1915, the British found themselves forced to send in troops from India to occupy Bushire lest they would be driven from this strategic port by Wassmuss' local Tangestani allies led by their chief Ra'is Ali Delvari who has by now become a legendary figure in Iran. The British occupation of Bushire did, however, not prevent the city of Shiraz from falling into the hands of anti-Entente groups orchestrated by Wassmuss' colleague, the German consul Kurt Wustrow and supported militarily by pro-German local Gendarmerie units as well as, at least tacitly, by Qashqa'i tribal forces led by the tribe's chief, Esma'il Khan Sowlat od-Dowleh, who was known for his anti-British attitude. They succeeded in ousting the serving governor of Fars, Habibollah Khan Qavam ol-Molk, another tribal leader who had led his *Khamzeh* tribal confederation into a loose alliance with the British. It also resulted in the arrest of the British consul for Shiraz, William Frederick O'Connor, and his staff who were kept prisoners at the fort of Zayer Khezr Khan, another local chief based in the hinterland of Bushire that had been mobilised by the indefatigable Wassmus.

At the same time, the German foreign ministry initiated the establishment of an Iranian action committee in Berlin that was led by an exiled veteran of the Constitutional Revolution of 1906, the firebrand Seyyed Hasan Taqizadeh, whom the Germans had specifically brought over to Germany from his new home in New York. Generously financed by the Germans throughout the early years of its existence, this committee organised pro-German propaganda, anti-Entente activities, and would later publish the Persian-language newspaper *Kaveh* that took a hostile attitude to Britain and her Entente allies.

With all this taking place, Germany's key decision makers, which had been facing constant calls for action from lower ranking but very vocal civilian and military officials on the ground in Iran and at the centre in Berlin, finally endeavoured to seek a formal alliance with Iran in the autumn of 1915. However, the Iranian government headed by Mirza Hasan Khan Ashtiyani Mostowfi ol-Mamalek, even though the latter was considered to be germanophile, tried to play for time because he, like the rest of the leading politicians in Tehran where one short-lived cabinet had been replacing the other in close succession throughout 1915, did not wish to commit themselves to one side too soon, wherever their convictions might have lain.

Although Britain's Iran policy had long been woken up by now, a co-ordinated Entente response to the 'German Moment' had been hampered by the far from harmonious relationship between the British and the Russian 'men on the spot' whose animosity literally embodied the Anglo-Russian antagonism of the Great Game, the ministers Sir Walter Townley and Ivan Yakovlevich Korostovetz. It took for both of them to be re-called and replaced, which happened in the course of 1915, as well as for Raymond Lecomte's, the French minister in Tehran's energetic efforts at mediating between his allied colleagues, before the Entente finally moved seriously against the German threat that had been building up in Iran. Thus at last, in early November 1915, Russian troops advanced on Tehran with British (and French) connivance, leading to the pro-German element, including a sizeable number of deputies of the Iranian National Assembly, or *majles*, fleeing the capital southward, soon to be followed by the representatives of the Central Powers. They assumed that the Shah and his government would join them and transfer the capital to Isfahan. Soltan Ahmad Shah Qajar had indeed issued orders to that effect. The representatives of the Entente in Tehran that had rushed to the Imperial palace upon hearing these orders were nevertheless able to persuade the monarch to stay after lengthy discussions. Having secured the capital, where Mirza Abdolhoseyn Khan Farmanfarma now formed a cabinet that was considered to be pro-Entente, Britain and Russia proceeded to wiping out the German positions in the provinces. Russian troops cleared the Northwest and West of Iran defeating Germany's regional allies (mainly tribal units, in whom the German military attaché, Count Georg von Kanitz-Podangen, who had worked tirelessly to raise them, had held high hopes but who proved to be of very low fighting value in the face of regular troops) and driving over the border into Mesopotamia the Germans as well as the nationalist parliamentarians, intellectuals and clerics who had fled together with them from Tehran. This flight would become known in Iran as the *mohajerat* (the Secession). Conversely, the South of Iran was cleared of German influence by a new British-led

Iranian levy force, the South Persia Rifles (SPR) that had been raised by Brigadier Sir Percy Sykes after landing at the port of Bandar Abbas in the spring of 1916, accompanied by only a small contingent of Indian N.C.O.s but equipped with ample financial funds. After this, only a few German agents, notably Wassmuss, who would escape capture until after the war, were still holding out in the country.

Toward a 'true and lasting order' – British efforts to consolidate her position in Iran and the Russian factor (1916–1918)

Now with seemingly friendly governments being formed in Tehran and given that the British themselves had contributed significantly to putting an end to the 'German moment' alongside the Russians, London felt that the situation was ripe for a consolidation of Britain's position in Iran. In the negotiations that thus ensued, the Russians who were suspicious of British motives would not cease pointing to the Constantinople Agreement while the respective Iranian governments, though deemed friendly, were no pushovers. Yet, a compromise was finally reached by August 1916 in what would become known as the Sepahsalar Agreement (after the then Iranian Prime Minister, Mohammad-Vali Khan, Khal'atbari Tonekaboni Sepahsalar, Sepahdar-e Azam). The vehicle of a 'retroactive moratorium' on Iran's debt service obligations toward the Entente had provided a creative solution to the tricky issue of how to lend money to an Iranian government that was constitutionally obliged to seek parliamentary approval for any foreign borrowing but lacked a sitting parliament. A joint tripartite Russian-Iranian-British commission was to oversee the release of funds to the Iranian government under this scheme. While the Agreement stressed the notion of Iranian sovereignty in its preamble, the totality of its other clauses including the plans for the establishment of proper Iranian armed forces to be undertaken jointly by Britain and Russia were perceived as a complete sell-out to these two Entente powers in the eyes of the public. This led to a collective outcry when the Agreement was published in Tehran, which in turn caused the fall of Sepahsalar's cabinet. Britain's first attempt at a formal consolidation of her position in Iran since the outbreak of World War I had failed not least since the subsequent government headed by Mirza Hasan Khan Vosuq od-Dowleh dragged its heels over the formal implementation of the Agreement, which therefore remained in limbo. This did not, however, stop Vosuq and his successors at the helm of consecutive Iranian governments from gladly accepting the funds that had been released by the 'retroactive moratorium', which helped them to keep government going despite the otherwise near empty coffers of the Iranian treasury.

The summer of 1916 had also seen the Ottomans, who had defeated the British Mesopotamian expeditionary force at Kut in April 1916, occupying parts of Western Iran, which in turn allowed the politicians of the 1915 Secession to move back into Iran, namely to Kermanshah where they set up a Provisional (counter-)Government headed by Reza Qoli Khan Mafi Nezam os-Saltaneh, an aristocrat and former provincial governor. This Provisional Government was supported by German money and advisers but suffered from infighting as well as from frictions with both the Ottomans as well as the Germans who in turn were often enough seriously at odds with each other themselves. Before this development had the time to evolve into a significant problem for the British, the Iranian secessionists were, however, once more driven out of the country by February 1917 due to a new Russian offensive. Therefore, the events that unfolded in the remainder of

1917 would have a far greater impact on Britain's Iran policy than the short-lived Iranian Provisional Government of Kermanshah.

Already the first of the two Russian revolutions of this year, in March 1917, had reverberated ideologically throughout Iran thus e.g. giving heart to the Islamist-nationalist movement of the *Jangalis* (literally: those of the forest, in Persian: *jangal*) that had sprung up in the deep, impenetrable forests of the Caspian coastal province of Gilan under the charismatic leadership of Mirza Kuchek Khan, a local veteran of the Constitutional movement with a clerical background who combined loosely defined domestic social-revolutionary objectives with a strong anti-colonial, anti-imperialist agenda in the name of Islam and of Iranian patrotism. This period also witnessed the appearance in Tehran of a terrorist underground organisation that began targeting politicians that were suspected of holding pro-British sentiments, the so-called *Komiteh-e mojazat* (literally: Punishment Committee). The second Russian Revolution in November 1917, which led the Bolsheviks to denounce unequal treaties and unfair privileges in a passionate anti-imperialist appeal to the 'toiling masses of the East' in early 1918 on the one hand, whilst also explicitly recognising Iran's independence and territorial integrity in the Peace Treaty of Brest-Litovsk (March 1918) on the other hand, only deepened those trends and also led to the withdrawal of Russian troops from Iran. From the British point of view, this created a dangerous power-vacuum in Northern Iran and the Caucasus, which the Ottomans promptly exploited by launching a third offensive into Iranian territory in the summer of 1918. As long as the British who by that time found themselves embroiled in serious fighting with the Ottomans further to the West, namely in Syria and Palestine, had not yet defeated them there, their response to these new Ottoman threats to Britain's position in Northern Persia remained limited and somewhat *ad hoc*.

It gave rise to smaller military missions led by audacious officers such as Major-General Lionel Charles Dunsterville who fought and negotiated his way from Mesopotamia through Iran to Baku and back, or Commodore David Thomas Norris who was sent from Mesopotamia to the Caspian with a handful of men, two field guns and ample funds with the task of establishing a British flotilla in the Caspian, which was successfully accomplished. However, once the Ottoman leadership had effectively capitulated in late October 1918, and the war in the Middle East was officially over, regular British troops poured into Northern Iran to complement the control over the South that had been already achieved thanks to the aforementioned South Persia Rifles (SPR).

With the Ottomans defeated and the once mighty Russian rival embroiled in a Civil War, the path toward the desired consolidation of Britain's position in Iran now seemed to be not only wide open but the British could also hope to achieve much more far-reaching objectives than at the time when they concluded the ill-fated Sepahsalar Agreement two years earlier. The prospects for this seemed even brighter in light of the fact that British behind-the-scenes entreaties with the Shah in August 1918 had led the latter to once again assign the post of Prime Minister to Vosuq od-Dowleh. The British considered Vosuq to be 'their man' and agreed to pay the Shah a handsome special allowance for every month he would keep Vosuq in office.

At this point, a conventional description of Anglo-Persian relations during this period would therefore proceed by presenting a history of the inception and subsequent failure of the (in)famous so-called Anglo-Persian Agreement of 1919 from the perspective of the Earl Curzon of Kedleston, the then Acting and soon-to-be actual Foreign Secretary. I, however, having adopted a British point of view for most of what I have said so far, would like to propose inverting the interpretive gaze now and to look at the immediate post-WWI period that saw Britain playing a major role not only in Iran but in the whole of the Middle East, through the eyes of the Iranian foreign policy makers of the time, especially Vosuq and his close colleague in the cabinet, Firuz Mirza Firuz Nosrat od-Dowleh. As will be shown, these Iranian statesmen were farsighted enough to see in this period, which amounted to a veritable crisis of disintegration that practically annihilated the grip of Iran's central government on the country, not only grave danger but also plenty of opportunity.

3. Iran and Britian in the immediate aftermath of World War I (1918–1921)

The latter resided in the fact that even before they would gather in Paris in early 1919, the future peace-makers, most notably US-President Woodrow Wilson, conveyed the strong impression to the Iranians, and indeed to the whole world, that their negotiations would result in nothing less than the establishment of a completely new World Order built on a new approach to International Relations and peoples' right to self-determination. If Iran, which had officially stayed neutral throughout but had nevertheless become a badly damaged battlefield of the war, now succeeded in using this unique peace conference to secure, once and for all, her sovereignty and territorial integrity, which had been seriously called into question ever since at least 1907, if not since 1828, then Iran would have 'won the Peace' even though it had effectively 'lost' the war. Therefore, Iran's foreign policy makers during that period were chiefly concerned with formulating and then attempting to realise what I would like to call Iran's 'Peace Aims'.

Iran's 'Peace Aims' and Britain 1917–1918

In actual fact, the question of peace had been high on the agenda of Iran's foreign policy-makers right from the outbreak of the conflict. After the Russian revolution of March 1917 and the US's entry into the war in April of this year, even more attention began to be paid to the issue of peace. This is testified by the creation, in the summer of 1917, of an inter-departmental commission for the assessment of neutral Iran's substantive war damages (*komisiyun-e ta'yin-e khesarat*). Iran's foreign policy-makers clearly hoped that a register of damages having been established in a demonstrably systematic fashion would help the non-belligerent Iran gaining access to the deliberations of the major peace conference that was generally anticipated for the time after the hostilities would have stopped. Throughout the following months until the end of the fighting, the fundamental importance for the shape of the post-war world of this future peace conference and its potential for Iran increasingly pre-occupied Iran's foreign policy makers. In a report from late October 1918, an Iranian diplomatic report sent in from The Hague went as far as stating:

'The outcome of this conference will have far reaching consequences that will not cease to make an impact for long years to come. The deliberations of this conference will decide whether Iran will survive as an independent state or whether she will agonise and eventual die in political slavery. After this conference, there will be no judge left to which we could turn and plead for our just cause.'

Having been preparing systematically for peace ever since at least 1917, the Iranian government was able to react quickly to the new realities once the hostilities had indeed ended in November 1918. Only two weeks after the Armistice, on 24 November 1918, the Iranian cabinet presented the three major victorious powers with a demand for admission to the impending Peace Conference submitting an eight-point memorandum stipulating Iran's desiderata.

Once these claims had been submitted, the Iranian government did not waste much time waiting for reactions from the powers but hurried to put together their conference delegation with great speed, which embarrassed the British and annoyed the French.

Curzon who, not without some justification, considered himself an expert on Iranian affairs and who was undoubtedly the chief driver of Britain's Iran policy during those years, hoped to be able to strike a swift bilateral and largely exclusive deal with Iran. As mentioned above, this was supposed to formalise and bolster the already very strong position that Britain enjoyed in the country as a result of the war. Nothing could be more harmful to this objective than Iran's admission to the forthcoming Peace Conference. The Foreign Office therefore decided to obstruct Iran's attempts at gaining access as much as possible and it resolved to go as far as to pursue the aim of turning Iran into a mandate should the Iranians show themselves too bothersome.

Nevertheless, despite the very strong objections from the French and British governments, the Iranian government refused to cave in and on 17 December 1918 – hardly five weeks after the Armistice and the very day on which London (obviously unbeknown to the Iranians) had decided on their course of utmost obstruction – the Iranian delegation headed by Foreign Minister Ali Qoli Khan Moshaver ol-Mamalek set off on its journey to Paris where it arrived on 23 January 1919, five days after the official opening of the Peace Conference.

As far as this delegation's instructions and thus Iran's ultimate objectives are concerned it is important to note that the eight-point catalogue of demands that the Iranian government had presented to the major victorious powers in November 1918, was merely the skeleton of Iran's aspirations. In order to send the delegations on its way with a more fleshed out set of aims and objectives, the Iranian Prime Minister charged a commission of experts headed by Mohammad 'Ali Forughi Zoka' ol-Molk, an influential intellectual turned politician who would also become a member of the delegation, to work out Iran's peace aims in detail. In other words, the government of Vosuq od-Dowleh, that is conventionally viewed as being idle, irresponsible and hapless at best and as being the willing executive agent of the British at worst, embarked on the very same thing that Wilson's administration did with the Inquiry or indeed what the British government did with their Curzon and Milner commissions of 1917, namely setting up a body of experts with the aim of determining their nation's 'Peace Aims'; or to put it more generally, to prepare a major diplomatic initiative in a highly professional manner. The commission's final report, which Forughi had submitted on 8 December 1919, formed the basis for an interdepartmental meeting on 14 December 1918 where the Iranian Peace Conference delegation's instructions were drawn up.

   The thus determined Iranian demands would reappear in various guises and shapes throughout the following months (more of which later). According to whom they were talking to, Iran's foreign policy-makers would have to amend, modify, expand, and, more often, reduce them, as we will see. It is, however, possible to distil from all of this, five principal objectives that, to me, seem to have formed the core of Iran's 'Peace Aims':

1. The complete independence and sovereignty of Persia as a fully recognised member of the international community of sovereign states to be guaranteed by some sort of formalised, ideally multi-power, approval.
2. The international and, again, somehow formalised recognition of the territorial integrity of the Iranian realm and this favourably

with some territorial gains in the Caucasus, Transcaspia, and Kurdistan at the expense of the former Russian and Ottoman Empires.
3. Reparations for the damages sustained as a result of foreign interventions to be paid by Germany, the Ottoman Empire, and potentially also by Russia.
4. Economic independence for the Persian state at a formal level, i.e. with regard to the setting of custom tariffs, hiring of foreign advisers, contracting of loans and granting of concessions.
5. Attraction – ideally from several different powers – of financial, administrative and military aid – i.e. advisors, loans, investment, supply of equipment, technology and know-how – in order to undertake structural reforms that would benefit state-building and development.

Whilst the forthcoming Peace Conference looked potentially very promising for the attainment of those aspirations, it was also clear that Vosuq could not afford to ignore the very strong British position in the country. British troops occupied various parts of the country, the British government paid a monthly subsidiary of 350.000 Toman (ca. £100,000) to keep the basic functions of the Iranian state apparatus going, and it also helped to keep intact Iran's only remaining security force, the Cossack Brigade. But contrary to the established view, this situation did lead to Vosuq's turning into an obedient executive agent of the Foreign Office.

Negotiating on two fronts at once: Iranian Peace Aim diplomacy between Britain and the Peace Makers (January 1919–August 1919)

Hence, an offer to come to an understanding that the Prime Minister extended to the British shortly after the Iranian delegation had left for Paris, in early 1919, was by no means an attempt to stab Moshaver's mission in the back. In actual fact it was nothing else than the opening of a 'second front' in the struggle for the realisation of Iran's 'Peace Aims'.

Since, while engaging in preliminary talks with the British side, it was after all nobody else than the Iranian Prime Minister himself who, in early February 1919, instructed his mission in Paris to do whatever they could to secure Iran's admission to the Peace Conference. This instruction resulted in a rush of feverish diplomatic and propaganda activity on the part of the Iranian delegates in Paris and their helpers, who had in any case not exactly sat on their hands even before having been given the explicit green light from Tehran. On 14 February 1919, the delegation formally requested admission to the conference and on 23 March 1919, a substantial catalogue of concrete Iranian desiderata – *Revendications de la Perse devant la Conférence des Préliminaires de Paix à Paris* – was submitted. All the noise made by the Iranian delegates did not remain without repercussions in Paris, especially among the American delegation, which the Iranians had made their target of choice, although it was – curiously – the Italian delegation that had first raised the question of an Iranian admission to the conference at a meeting of the Council of Ten on 18 February 1919. Thereafter, US President Woodrow Wilson and his Secretary of State, Robert Lansing, also put Iran's desire for a hearing repeatedly onto the agenda of the deliberations, which proved to be a source of great concern for the British, given their aim to keep Iran out of the Conference at all costs.

In parallel to those activities in Paris, the Iranian government in Tehran had also given orders to its official and non-official representatives in the Caucasus, in Trancscaspia and in Kurdistan to make sure that the regional populations would 'spontaneously' flood the French Legation in Tehran with petitions asking for support for their wish to be allowed to 'come home into the Iranian motherland'. A number of other measures to propagandistically support the Iranian campaign for access to the Conference were also taken in Tehran at that time. Thus a preliminary report of the findings of the abovementioned inter-departmental commission for the assessment of Iran's war damages was sent to all foreign legations present in the Iranian capital and the Iranian foreign ministry published a collection of archival documents containing Iranian diplomatic correspondence from start of the war aimed at proving that Iran made strenuous efforts to defend its neutrality – the so-called Green Book of Iran's Neutrality.

These measures together with the loud diplomatic noises, especially vis-à-vis the US delegation, that the Iranian delegation made in Paris in the spring of 1919, and we say it again: made on the Prime Minister's own very special behest, proved to be an excellent tool in Vosuq's hands to put under pressure his British interlocutors in Tehran. By haunting the British with the spectre of an US-backed admission of the Iranian delegation to the Conference, Vosuq was able to force the British, who wanted to forestall any such admission by a speedy separate agreement with Tehran, to take a conciliatory attitude toward his own demands.

A closer look at these demands as can be found in a draft for an Anglo-Persian agreement that was transmitted to London from Tehran in early April 1919, reveals that what the Prime Minister put forward in Tehran to the British was in actual fact nothing else than a slightly modified version of what his envoy in Paris had submitted a few days earlier to the Peace Conference. Both the Prime Minister's draft agreement and the catalogue of Iran's desiderata submitted in Paris represented a series of demands the fulfilment of which, either way, would mean the realisation of Iran's already mentioned five principal peace aims!

The sophisticated diplomatic game that the Iranian Prime Minister had been playing is nowhere better illustrated than in a dramatic appeal for help that he submitted to the French government at the end of June 1919. Already since early 1919 and behind the back of his British interlocutors, Vosuq had been trying to establish a direct connection with his French counter-part, George Clemenceau. After several of Vosuq's attempts to reach the French government had been left without a response while the Iranian delegation in Paris had still not managed to gain formal admission to the conference, on 23 June 1919, the Iranian Premier contacted Charles Bonin, the French minister in Tehran and put his cards openly on the table.

Vosuq told Bonin that being pushed by the British, he would have no choice but to conclude a potentially exclusive bilateral agreement with them if the French government would not finally get its act together and immediately intervene on Iran's behalf at the Peace Conference. France should use her influence with her British ally to make sure that Iran's demands would be addressed by the peace makers in Paris. Vosuq's quite dramatic appeal to Bonin, which contained a curious denunciation of his own Finance Minister Mirza Akbar Masu'd Khan Sarem od-Dowleh (who is usually seen as an accomplice of the allegedly treacherous Vosuq) as a dangerous British spy, was seconded by a similarly passionate plea for French help submitted to Bonin by Vosuq's Justice Minister, Firuz Mirza Firuz Nosrat od-Dowleh.

Nevertheless, by the end of July 1919, Vosuq had to learn that the French government had chosen to ignore his desperate appeal for help. In the mean-time, with the signing of the Versailles Treaty and the departure of President Wilson, the Peace Conference had temporarily lost momentum, without it being clear when there would be new movement. And only then, with the Americans having been unable to deliver despite Wilson's and Lansing's (at least outwardly) sympathetic attitude, with the French refusing to intervene on Iran's behalf, and with the mentioned slow-down at the Peace Conference, i.e. in a situation where the chances to further the realisation of Iran's major peace aims in a multi-power framework seemed to have been reduced for an unforeseeable time, did Vosuq opt for what must have seemed to him as a second best solution. He hastened to conclude a bilateral treaty with the British, which largely resembled his very own draft proposal of April 1919, i.e. an agreement, that was based more or less on *his* terms, lest the British change their minds and use the weakening Iranian position in the negotiations to impose harsher terms.

The Anglo-Persian Agreement of August 1919: an end or a new beginning?

The treaty, which gained notoriety as the Anglo-Persian Agreement of 1919, was signed on 9 August and consisted of three different parts. However, only the content of the first two parts is well known:

There was, firstly, the agreement proper, made up of six paragraphs stipulating amongst other things the provision of British financial and military advisors and a railway building programme.

Secondly, the treaty contained a credit agreement providing for a £2 million British loan for Iran.

The whole treaty package was rounded off thirdly by a supplementary agreement consisting of a formal exchange of letters between the British representative in Tehran, Sir Percy Cox and the Iranian Prime Minister – some of them open, others secret. This supplementary arrangement has been largely neglected by the existing writing on the 1919 Anglo-Persian Agreement.

In the non-secret part of this supplementary agreement, the

British government declared its readiness to support 'reasonable' Iranian territorial claims and the Iranian request for reparations as well as to help Iran obtain a revision of all her international treaties. It has to be said that these assurances of support were termed in a quite vague and guarded way. However, they were still clear enough to justify the conviction on the part of the Iranians that they now had in the British a powerful ally who would champion their desiderata when the peace negotiations in Paris would finally resume in order to proceed toward the establishment of a New Order for the Middle East.

There can be no doubt that the Agreement, at least from the British point of view, seemed to provide for a very strong Iranian dependence on Britain for the execution of Iran's reform and modernisation agenda, even if the letter of the Agreement did not, strictly speaking, stipulate any British exclusivity at the expense of other potentially interested powers. Nevertheless, it is important to underline that the Agreement by way of the supplementary agreement also seemed to provide the Iranians with a strong and influential advocate for their territorial and compensational demands at the Peace Conference.

Furthermore, it should not be overlooked that the Agreement seemed to provide the Iranian government with some relief as with regard to the dangers that were to be expected from a revival of Russian imperialist designs on Iran, which at the time of the signing of the treaty loomed large over the Iranians given that the Moscow-bound offensive that General Anton Ivanovich Denikin's counter-revolutionary Volunteer Army had launched in July 1919 appeared to be unstoppable.

At any rate, a close comparison of the desiderata submitted by the Iranian delegation in Paris with the actual Agreement, the wording of which, as has been pointed out already, largely followed

Vosuq's very own draft proposal of April 1919, reveals that the Agreement despite all its obvious shortcomings still seemed to promise the realisation of at least five of the eight demands as submitted by Moshaver to the Peace Conference. In my opinion it is crystal clear that the negotiations pursued by Vosuq in Tehran and the efforts made by his own delegation in Paris were nothing else than the two sides of an identical coin.

Before this background, the infamous so-called 'bribe' received by Vosuq od-Dowle and two of his cabinet ministers after the signature of the Agreement must be considered as utterly irrelevant and this despite the relatively high sums that had been transferred. There can be no doubt whatsoever that under the specific circumstances of August 1919, Vosuq would have concluded the Agreement with the British anyway. Whatever he and his ministers might have told the British, his decision to sign the Agreement at that particular point in time and under the described-above particular circumstances had nothing at all to do whatsoever with the 200,000 Toman (ca. £60,000) that were paid to his private account as an advance on the planned British loan.

At this point it is worth noting that many a member of the Iranian elite of the time did see the signature of the Treaty as the optimistic beginning of a new era rather than as the tragic end point as which it is portrayed with the benefit of hindsight by the established orthodoxy, which tends to focus almost solely and exclusively on the domestic and international opposition to the agreement.

After all, with the signing of the Agreement and the replacement of Moshaver as Foreign Minister and head of delegation by Firuz, who left for Paris almost immediately, the Peace Conference was far from over for the Iranian government. Some of the staff of Moshaver's delegation stayed on in Paris and also the agenda of trying to obtain an international validation of Iran's claims through the Peace Conference remained the same, the only difference being that the Iranian decision makers now believed to be able to rely on Britain as a powerful advocate of Iran's desiderata vis-à-vis the other great powers present at the Conference.

As is well known, the Agreement encountered not only strong internal opposition from the Prime Minister's domestic political enemies but also met with massive French and then also American criticism. It appears that much of the internal opposition must actually be attributed to the outburst of hostility in the French media, the underlying causes of which have very little, if anything, to do with Iran but with the then culminating Anglo-British tensions over the mandatory custody of Syria. While Vosuq and Firuz might have been annoyed by the strong wave of international hostility toward the Agreement, they immediately set out to exploit it in order to squeeze out concessions from the British by arguing that the hostile international opinion could be placated easily by Britain publicly making a number of eye-catching clarifications, especially regarding Britain's readiness to support territorial claims and other Iranian demands at the Peace Conference. They argued that thus it would be made more obvious that the Agreement was actually in favour of Iran and not at all tantamount to the establishment of a British protectorate as was suggested by its French and other critics. In this context it also highly interesting to note that in September 1919, i.e. after literally all hell had broken loose against the Agreement in international public opinion, Vosuq encouraged the French minister in Tehran actively to make even more noise hinting that if only the international outcry would be loud enough there might be a chance to unravel the Agreement package and to reconsider everything with a view to a multi-power agreement under inclusion of certainly France and potentially other interested states, chiefly the US. This suggests that Vosuq might have fully anticipated the international outrage about the Agreement and might have conceived of it as some sort of a wakeup call for the French and the Americans whom he had not managed to bring on board by any other means despite his strenuous efforts to that effect throughout the course of 1919.

The false dawn of early Autumn 1919
Be that as it may, a well-publicised speech made by Curzon on 18 September 1919 at a reception in honour of Firuz who had travelled on from Paris to London, seemed to have provided at least some of the clarifications in favour of Iran that Vosuq and Firuz had been after. This is included an explicit denouncement of the Anglo-Russian Convention of 1907 (which greatly angered the representatives of the Russian *Ancien Régime* in London and Tehran). The international, especially the French, criticism did indeed recede somewhat although there are probably also other reasons for this including the fact in September 1919 the acrimonious Franco-British diplomatic row over the custody of Greater Syria had been solved in favour of the French.

For the Iranian government things seemed to brighten up at this point: Firuz' first meetings with Curzon and other Foreign Office staff had been very promising while Iran's relationship with France looked as if it was on the mend since Firuz seemed to have found in the person of the influential Philippe Berthelot a potentially sympathetic interlocutor at the Quai d'Orsay. Furthermore, Vosuq's attempts to stabilise the domestic political situation had also made some modest progress.

The feeling of being at the dawn of a new era was only to be reinforced by the rather promising looking negotiations that Foroughi, who continued serving with the Iranian Peace Conference delegation in Paris, had entered into with the Azerbaijani delegation and which resulted in a joint protocol for the establishment of a Confederation between the Republic of Azerbaijan and Iran. This seemed to open up totally unexpected perspectives for the realisation of the Persian territorial claims in the Caucasus.

As a result of this protocol the Azerbaijanis in Paris had asked Firuz to help them establishing a direct and high-ranking contact within the British Foreign Office. The Iranian Foreign Minister did not hesitate a second to use this mandate for an attempt to win British backing for an aggressive Iranian Caucasus policy. Pointing to the alleged convergence of British and Iranian interests in the region Firuz tried to sell to Curzon nothing less than the idea of an Anglo-Iranian condominium in the Caucasus!

Given that the extent of the mandate of the Azerbaijani delegation in Paris was somewhat doubtful, the Prime Minister in Tehran decided to gain clarity directly on the ground and began to prepare the sending of a special diplomatic mission to the government of Azerbaijan. Vosuq saw the initial task of this mission, which was also supposed to travel to Yerevan and Tiflis once having finished its business at Baku, as finding out about the true intentions of the Azerbaijani government with regard to the Confederation project. The mission could furthermore help solving a number of concrete issues that momentarily clouded the good neighbourly co-existence of the two states. For that reason Vosuq's initial instructions for his special envoy and close political associate, Aqa Seyyed Ziya' od-Din Tabataba'i, were of a rather technical nature. They did not yet contain a mandate for negotiations about the Confederation or indeed for any other potential means to further Iran's territorial aspirations in the area. After all, those would have to be pursued first at the Peace Conference where British backing would be available, or so believed the Iranian Prime Minister at this point in time.

One Agreement, Two interpretations – Disappointment in Britain and Iran's return to a feverish multi-power diplomacy (December 1919–May 1920)

At the turn from 1919 to 1920, the Iranian foreign policy makers would, however, become painfully aware that the seemingly so promising beginnings of October and November 1919 had in actual fact not been much more than a false dawn. As far as the Peace Conference was concerned, for the time being, not much, if anything, did happen in terms of Middle Eastern affairs. Furthermore, the negotiations with the Azerbaijani government that Vosuq's special envoy to the Caucasus had started soon after his arrival in Baku on 1 December 1919, ground to a complete halt because of a messy cabinet crisis in the Azerbaijani capital.

Nevertheless, the greatest disappointment for the Iranian side came when the British government refused to throw their support behind the modified list of Iran's territorial claims that Firuz had presented to Curzon in November 1919 believing that it represented those 'reasonable demands' for the support of which Britain seemed to have signalled her readiness in the supplementary section of the Agreement signed on 9 August.

In the course of the ensuing Anglo-Iranian conflict, the Iranian foreign policy-makers came to realise that their own interpretation of this Agreement did not match that of the British. The two sides had concluded the Agreement based on totally different premises and one thing was clear: Britain was not ready to support Iran seriously in her efforts to use the ongoing process of re-ordering the world at the conference tables in Europe for the conduct of a strong, independent and, at least by Iranian standards, ambitious peace aim policy.

Thus however, for the Iranian Prime Minister, the Agreement had become void of its deeper meaning. The Prime Minister's thorough disenchantment with the British is nowhere better expressed than in the comprehensive instruction that he sent to his Foreign Minister at the end of 1919: Vosuq ordered Firuz to make the British understand that failure to honour their promises of support for Iran's aspirations at the Peace Conference would jeopardise the Agreement as a whole.

It transpires from their correspondence that the disappointment of the Iranian foreign policy-makers with Britain knew no boundaries. However, given the balance of power at that moment in time, there was no other option left open to Vosuq than to try making the most of the economic and administrative support aspects of the Agreement while gradually manoeuvring Persia out again of the British shadow at a diplomatic level.

Indeed, at the beginning of the year 1920, this shift in the Iranian approach led to a number of diplomatic initiatives in all possible directions. At least four distinctive moves can be identified:

1. Vosuq od-Dowleh gives his special mission to the Caucasus a qualitatively different importance by amending the instructions for his special envoy. He raises the latter's mandate from the rather technical one he had been sent out with to a more political one. Seyyed Ziya' is now ordered to strive for a diplomatic deal with the Azerbaijanis that had to be pursued as long as the Azerbaijanis were still impressible by the allegedly privileged relationship that Iran enjoyed with Britain as a result of the Agreement.
2. At the Peace Conference, Firuz engages in frenzied activity that now again explicitly targets the French and the Italians. In April 1920, these efforts are actually crowned by something that can be regarded as a modest success. Despite a valiant diplomatic struggle, Firuz had not managed to gain access to the Conference of San Remo. Nevertheless when the powers that

were conferring in San Remo prepared the text of what was to become the Peace Treaty of Sèvres with the Ottoman Empire, Iran was explicitly mentioned as one power to be involved in the drawing up of the boundaries of the autonomous Kurdish entity north of Mosul that this Treaty provided for. We know fair well that nothing came of this because the Treaty of Sèvres was never enforced but I would argue that the real significance of the invitation to participate that was extended to Iran has nothing to do with the issue of the Kurdish borders as such (even if the Treaty had been ratified, the Iranian role would have been rather limited and it is doubtful if any territorial gains could have been made) but it rather lies in the fact that Iran was invited formally by the victorious powers to partake in the establishment of the post-war new world order and this as an active player and not as an object that others would have to make decisions about as it had been the case in 1907 and again in 1915!

3. There is an attempt to get the Americans involved in Iran after all and this quasi by the back door. On the Prime Minister's behest, Firuz begins negotiations regarding the granting to an American oil major of the so-called *Khoshtaria* concession pertaining to the Northern provinces of Iran that were not covered by the Knox d'Arcy concession of 1901 held by the Anglo-Persian Oil Company.

4. And finally in the spring of 1920, the Iranian Prime Minister begins to contemplate a normalisation of Iran's relations with Soviet Russia, the state which emerged as a totally new threat to the North after the Bolsheviks had unexpectedly managed to gain the upper hand in the Civil War.

With regard to this fourth point it is worth noting that the Iranian government had for a long time been rather more fearful of the Whites than of the Bolsheviks. During the first months of 1920 however, after the Red Army had embarked on a sheer unstoppable southward offensive against Denikin, Vosuq's security concerns grew daily. Nevertheless, Curzon could do nothing about Vosuq's increasingly desperate pleas for British troops, equipment or at least special financial aid to strengthen Iran's northern border. The Foreign Secretary might have liked to be more helpful but he failed to convince the military command to commit the troops necessary to defend the Caucasus or at least Iran from a potential Bolshevik attack.

Considering himself abandoned by the British in the face of what was perceived as a great danger, the Iranian Prime Minister was finally disabused of any remaining illusions with regard to the strategic utility of the Agreement that he might still have entertained. And hence there was no need any more to have any considerations whatsoever with regard to the approach to other powers. In his instructions for Firuz at the end of March 1920 Vosuq used drastic words to make this crystal clear and he did not fail to draw the only possible conclusion: On 26 March 1920, Vosuq instructed his Foreign Minister to prepare the ground for a special diplomatic mission to be sent to Moscow in order to reach an understanding with Soviet Russia.

This decision was accompanied by a cabinet re-shuffle, which saw the apparently genuinely pro-British Finance Minister Sarem od-Dowleh being removed from the government despite strong British objections. It is in those developments of late March 1920 that we must search for the roots of the Soviet-Iranian Treaty of 26 Februrary 1921, which is usually (and wrongly) credited to the regime that emerged from the coup d'état of 21 February 1921. The intellectual father and original initiator of this understanding with the Soviets was in reality nobody else than the 'anglophile traitor' Vosuq od-Dowleh!

In the meantime, the negotiations between Vosuq's special envoy to the Caucasus and the Azerbaijani government in Baku had resumed, and in one month a complex package of agreements was ready to be signed.

Although Seyyed Ziya' hailed it as a historic achievement, the Iranian-Azerbaijani Treaty of 20 March 1920 did not elicit much enthusiasm on the part of the Iranian Prime Minister. There were mainly three reasons for the rather lukewarm reception of the agreement in the Iranian capital. First, nothing, not even a token concession, had been achieved with regard to Iran's territorial claims against Azerbaijan. Second, the Republic could consider itself recognised by Iran without that Azerbaijan had to make any compensation for this. Third, there were a couple of glitches in some of the more technical arrangements that the experts in Tehran saw in need of mending.

But this alone did not mean that the Agreement as such had failed; the Prime Minister wanted Seyyed Ziya' to re-negotiate. However, the Bolshevik take-over in Baku on 27 April 1920 prevented this from happening. The coup rendered obsolete with one stroke all the undoubted achievements that the Iranian special envoy had obtained through his often cumbersome negotiations with the far from Iran-friendly nationalist government in Baku.

Before the background of the fall of Baku it is hardly surprising that we see the Iranian Prime Minister intensifying his efforts to woe the Bolsheviks, and this against the explicitly expressed wishes of the British. When Firuz had muted the idea of an Iranian-Soviet agreement in a meeting with Curzon in early April 1920, the latter had nearly lost his temper and quasi *forbade* the Iranians to pursue any such plans. Confronted about this by Cox in Tehran, Vosuq hastened to play down his intentions: it was only a question of making friendly noises to placate the Bolshevik government but of course nobody had the plan to conclude an agreement with them. However it was exactly this, the sending of an Iranian mission to Moscow for the negotiation and conclusion of an agreement that Vosuq proposed to the Soviet government in a radio-telegram on 14 May 1920!

By May 1920, the Iranian Prime Minister was clearly busy trying to increase his diplomatic room for manoeuvre. It seems fair to say that with his proposal to negotiate an agreement with Soviet Russia, Vosuq had himself put the first nail in the coffin of the Anglo-Persian Agreement, at least as far as its strategic dimension in the sense of a special relationship with Britain was concerned. This did not mean that the Iranian government was not inclined to try benefiting from the economic and administrative support component of the Agreement, and this ideally without having to give anything back to the British. After all Vosuq was experienced in the art of taking from the British without giving. During his first premiership in 1916/1917, Vosuq had demonstrated this when he, as we saw above, shrewdly obstructed the ratification of the Sepahsalar Agreement but had no problem whatsoever with starting to reap the financial benefits for the Iranian treasury provided for by this Agreement.

However, on 18 May 1920, the Red Army landed at the Iranian port of Anzali and occupied parts of the Caspian province of Gilan. A few weeks later followed the declaration of the Socialist Soviet Republic of Iran by an unlikely coalition of Iranian communists parachuted in by the Russians and the local *Jangali* movement, which as mentioned above, had been already revolting against the central government since around 1915. Iran's rapprochement with Soviet Russia that had seemed well under way was all of a sudden severely called into question.

Defying Lord Curzon: Iran's successful appeal to the League of Nations (June 1920)

Once again the Iranian Prime Minister responded with a two-fold strategy to the new situation. On the one hand he continued to talk to the Soviets via Firuz, his Foreign Minister who, form his base in Paris, exchanged telegrams with his Soviet counter-part, Georgij Chicherin.

On the other hand, Vosuq loudly denounced the invasion and instructed Firuz to appeal to the League of Nations. Against the very staunch resistance of the French and British governments that both strongly opposed an Iranian hearing by the League, albeit for different reasons, Firuz managed to bring Iran's complaint onto the agenda of a League council meeting to be held in London on 14 June 1920. This then resulted in a follow up meeting two days later.

At a first glance the results of this demarche seemed meagre: the fact that Soviet Russia was not a member state and not recognised by most nations anyhow made it impossible for the League to act as an intermediary in the conflict. The resolution that was nevertheless passed on 16 June 1920 did also not look much: it amounted to a declaration of moral support for Iran and the seemingly superfluous counsel given to Iran to try and negotiate directly with Soviet Russia.

Those historians who have had consequently nothing but scorn and ridicule for the Iranian League appeal fail, however, to understand that the true significance of this demarche did not lie in its result with regard to the Soviet Russian intervention but in the very fact that the two council meetings took place at all, and that they led to a resolution, the passing of which had been dependent on the vote of the Iranian representative! This was highly significant for the status of Iran as a fully-fledged, sovereign member of the international community; a member whose territorial integrity was internationally recognised even if the international community could momentarily do nothing to help Iran defending it. The two League council meetings and the unanimous [!] resolution passed on 16 June 1920 had been the litmus test for Iran's membership in the club of sovereign nations.

And it was exactly for this reason that in the face of the extremely stiff Anglo-French opposition Vosuq had been so adamant, or as one British diplomat had it, 'obdurate' that Iran's complaint be heard by the League. The sources show that neither the Iranian Prime Minister nor Firuz had any illusions about the League's power to restrain the Soviets. No, for Iran's foreign policy-makers, the Soviet invasion provided the ideal pretext to establish Iran's membership of the League beyond any doubt. This was an important achievement given that until this point Iran's membership had been questioned time and again, especially by the French who had kept claiming that the Anglo-Persian Agreement of 9 August 1919 simply nullified Iran's right to be a member of that organisation.

In comparison with the beginning of Vosuq's premiership in August 1918, Iran's international standing had been enhanced. There can be no doubt that this consolidation of Iran's international position was the result of Vosuq's intelligent diplomacy even if the Anglo-Persian Agreement had turned out to be a failure. Under the specific circumstances of its conclusion it had appeared as the second best solution for the realisation of Irans's collectively defined 'Peace Aims' and when those circumstances changed, and the Agreement did not turn out to be what the Iranian side had hoped it would, Vosuq had not hesitated for one moment to draw the appropriate conclusions by attempting to manoeuvre Iran gradually out again of the British shadow.

The Prime Minister's problem, however, was that in June 1920, next to nobody was prepared to recognise this. In a way, this is not even very surprising because Vosuq's diplomatic achievements were not that easy to appreciate for his compatriots. They consisted to a large degree in indirect confirmations, in having prepared the ground, and in having started processes that would come to fruition after he had been forced to step down from office in late June 1920. With the privilege of hindsight and after the assessment of the documentary evidence, however, one can easily see that Vosuq was no foreign power's willing executioner. On the contrary, since his appointment in 1918, Vosuq had steered Iran quite successfully through an extremely volatile international situation that could easily have ended with Iran being transformed into a mandate of the League of Nations. His foreign policy had been based on what had been collectively established as Iran's Peace Aims in late 1918.

However, Vosuq had been unable to rally his contemporaries behind his foreign policy. His Achilles heel was public opinion. Despite his indubitable awareness of the increased importance of this factor in international politics, Vosuq had not been able to shake off the label of British lackey that his domestic political enemies had successfully attached to him. His tendency to operate in a political style that would have been more suited to the pre-constitutional period than to the post-war era, where public approval was paramount for any politician unable or unwilling to establish a dictatorship made him an easy target for his political adversaries. His Cabinet fell in late June 1920 once he had lost the backing of the Shah.

It was left to others to see through the programme of foreign policy for which Vosuq had laid the foundations. Under his successors the negotiations with American firms regarding their potential taking up of the disputed *Khoshtaria* oil concession and about American loans for Iran continued as much as there were new feelers being put out toward France. On the other hand, attempts to make the nation-building aspects of the Anglo-Persian Agreement work did also continue. Most importantly however, in the late summer of 1920, we see the Iranian mission to Moscow that Vosuq had envisaged finally making its way to the Russian capital.

26 February 1921: the end of World War I in Iran

Leading the Persian delegation to Moscow, Moshaver ol-Mamalek, Iran's special envoy started the negotiations with Soviet Russia at the beginning of November 1920.

The ensuing Iranian-Soviet Treaty of 26 February 1921 sealed the arrival of Iran in the post-war era. For all its major shortcomings, it put Russia and Iran on a degree of equality that looks gigantic by comparison with everything that had been in place since 1813. At the same moment in time there can be no longer any question of a British protectorate over Iran. The 26 February 1921 marks the definitive end of World War I for Iran. It is thus perhaps an even more important date in Iranian history than Reza Khan's coup d'état that occurred just a couple of days before with the connivance and support of the British military authorities in Iran but apparently unbeknown to Britain's diplomats. With the Iranian-Soviet Treaty of 26 February 1921 on the one hand, and the formal cancellation of the Anglo-Iranian Agreement on the other hand, the way was clear for a gradual retreat of the remaining British and Soviet forces from Iranian territory. Iran, a member state of the League of Nation whose incontestable membership had been, as it were, 'consummated' by her appeal in June 1920, was about to regain her complete sovereignty.

The two most prominent of the five major Iranian 'Peace Aims' had been achieved; namely, internationally recognised sovereignty and territorial integrity even if Persia had not managed to make any territorial gains and the Capitulations were still in existence. Reparations (Peace Aim number three) could not be secured but economic independence (Peace Aim number four) had been obtained, at least in a formal way. New customs agreements, a resumption of economic ties with Germany, and the arrival of the American financial adviser Arthur Millspaugh would soon become illustrations of a newly found room for more independent economic policies even if British economic influence remained very strong especially via the Anglo-Persian Oil Company.

The long term projects for the country's modernisation and development as contained in Peace Aim number five could now be tackled under the increasingly authoritarian, if not eventually dictatorial, leadership of the 1921 coup's strongman, because the external frame of the Iranian realm had been secured beforehand. The future Reza Shah would have nothing but scorn for the Qajar governments that preceded his coup d'état. Perhaps he should have been more grateful because, it was from them, and especially from Vosuq and his skilful Peace Aim diplomacy between 1918 and 1920, that he inherited external borders that had been strengthened securely against the seemingly eternal doubt, under which they had languished ever since the early 19th century.

4. Conclusion

Iran's interaction with Britain in the shadow of World War I or rather the way it was and continues to be remembered collectively by the Iranians has significantly shaped subsequent Anglo-Iranian relations. Thus the fact that Britain's role in Iran during the 'long' World War had been experienced and began immediately to be remembered mainly under the rubric of the 'Hidden Hand of the British' (*Dast-e penhan-e Engelis*) which had nothing but a nefarious influence in Iran was utterly formative for the views of an aristocratic member of the Qajar state's elite who gained his first experiences of high office during those exact years holding the title of Mosaddeq os-Saltaneh. Some thirty years later, this skilful Qajar administrator, renowned constitutional lawyer and fearlessly outspoken parliamentarian would become the champion of Iran's 1951 oil nationalisation and serve as Prime Minister during the ensuing acrimonious Anglo-Iranian dispute until his turbulent downfall in August 1953, to which Britain actively contributed from behind the scenes. Although a whole raft of other factors impacted upon what would become famous as the 'Coup d'état of 19 August 1953', the perception of Britain's role therein, continues having a negative influence on Anglo-Iranian relations to this day, both at government level and in terms of Iranian public opinion.

Thus even though it might sound utterly farfetched, in theory at least, the question begs to be asked whether a thoroughly constitutional and Modern Qajar dynasty would not be still in place today in a slightly territorially larger Iran if, in the interest of capitalising on shared interests and for the gain of mutual benefit, in 1919, Britain had stood by its lightly given promise of support for Iran's demands at the Paris Peace Conference; since this in turn might have indeed allowed for the undoubtedly positive, i.e. modernising and nation-building, elements of the Anglo-Persian Agreement to be carried through under Vosuq od-Dowleh in a reasonably consensual fashion adhering to if not the letter than at least to the spirit of the 1906 Constitution and thus in return perhaps having spared Iran the very painful experience of being modernised by the authoritarian, if not, by the mid-1930s, dictatorial Reza Shah.

Leaving such counter-factual flights of fancy to one side, it remains to note that Anglo-Iranian exchanges since the 'long' World War I are actually also very rich in examples of fruitful co-operation, not least in the commercial, but even more so, in the cultural and educational arenas. Building on the multiple instances of mutual gain on those levels while trying to draw lessons from an analysis of Britain's and Iran's more conflictual interactions at the political level during the last one hundred years, might actually allow the decision-makers in both countries to find a greater degree of common ground today. This would help them to better rise to the major regional security challenge that has arisen for both Britain and Iran during the course of the centenary year 2014 as an unexpected, yet perfectly explicable legacy of World War I.

Working together in the arts

The Contemporary Art Scene of Iran: cultural policy, infrastructure, dissemination and exchange

HAMID KESHMIRSHEKAN
Dr Hamid Keshmirhsekan is Research Associate, London Middle East Institute, SOAS, University of London and Professor of Art History, critic, editor and writer working in Iran and UK.

The current world of Iranian visual arts is increasingly influential and open to influence. The global market for art plays a sometimes controversial role and international exchange could offer crucial support to curators in their work.

This essay will introduce a broad overview of the post-Revolution Iranian art and cultural policy and its association with official cultural strategy. It will look at art infrastructures – such as institutions and exhibitions – publications, education, dissemination and exchange mechanisms, and the politics of the market and its impact on art practice. In order to clarify the past and possible future engagements of Iran with other cultures, and of their engagement with Iran, it is necessary to address the mentioned issues within the structure of Iranian art scene. Here this is important to understand how the UK, alongside other countries, has contributed to an evolving relationship throughout this time.

The 1979 Revolution produced profound yet contradictory changes across the social and cultural spheres of Iranian life. Iran's art scene was affected considerably, with modernism now giving way to an art based on revolutionary aspiration and ideological Islamic thoughts. The official cultural and artistic policies of the Pahlavi were brought to an abrupt halt. Hence the Pahlavi's identical doctrines of nationalism and modernism were frozen together too. Modernism in art was realised mainly with various trends and forms which were influenced and inspired by the atmosphere of European and American post-war artistic movements and what had no connection to the mass public and ideological preferences of the revolutionaries. Revolutionary art created narratives around revolutionary slogans and articulated an ideological or political message, as well as expressing social commitment. This, combined with their simple, understandable form and execution, increased their popularity and acceptance among the masses. This so-called 'committed' or revolutionary art[1] was encouraged and supported, especially in the first decade after the Revolution, by the cultural section of the revolutionary government, which fully controlled all artistic activity.

Much of this revolutionary art was produced by a group of young ideologically minded artists who shared common socio-political, revolutionary and certain religious interests.[2] In 1981 a group of poets, film-makers, writers and musicians came together to establish the Artistic Centre of Islamic Propaganda Organisation (Howzeh Hunari-i Sazman-i Tablighat-i Islami).

During this period, art centres were established in various ministries and militia units, including the Farabi Foundation in cinema, the Martyr and Veterans Affair Foundation (Bunyad-i Shahid va Janbazan) and the War Propaganda Army-Staff (Sitad-i Tablighat-i Jang) – all of which supported the revolutionary arts.

The major official body of cultural and artistic affairs in post-Revolution Iran, however, was the Ministry of Culture and Islamic Guidance (Vizarat-i Farhang va Irshad-i Islami), which had been established through the merger of the two pre-Revolution Ministries of Culture and Art and Information and Tourism.[3] All these institutions were to support the revolutionary 'committed' art that then became rather an ideological art based on the official interests.

Fig. 1

During this time revolutionary artists filled exhibition halls, civic institutions and public spaces such as the Tehran Museum of Contemporary Art (the most important venue for art), which is affiliated with the Ministry of Culture and Islamic Guidance, with large propaganda paintings, posters and murals commemorating the Islamic Revolution and revolutionary struggles. This situation established TMoCA's potential as a platform for ideological propaganda.[4] Furthermore, with the Cultural Revolution in 1980 which caused the temporary closing down of all universities (they were reopened in 1983), art institutions came under the complete control of the ideological revolutionary thoughts and teachers were more often from the members of Artistic Centre of the Islamic Propaganda Organisation whose head was appointed directly by the Supreme Leader.

In the years immediately after the Revolution, exhibitions were often held to mark particular anniversaries (especially of the Revolution itself) in public spaces such as the TMoCA (figs 1, 2).

Heavily influenced by the politicised atmosphere of those years, these shows included various kinds of paintings and graphic and calligraphic works (now conveying a clear religious or political message) by revolutionary committed artists, as well as a range of traditional arts such as coffee-house (*Qahveh-khaneh*) paintings and miniature paintings. None of these exhibitions, however, were curated based on a certain curatorial strategy.[5] This continued almost throughout the whole decade of the 1980s (mainly paralleled with the Iran-Iraq war – 1980–88).

The end of the war in 1988 opened a chapter of political 'reconstruction' and brought about a period of artistic renewal in Iran. By the end of the 1980s various commercial galleries that had been closed were reopening, while other new ones were gradually springing up. They began to exhibit non-political and non-ideological art. This period also saw the gradual organisation of national exhibitions in which various kinds of modernistic approaches were presented, although very cautiously. TMoCA, under the Centre of the Visual Arts (Markaz-i Hunar-hay-i Tajassumi-i Kishvar), a subdivision in the Ministry of Culture and Islamic Guidance, began to recognise various branches in visual arts. The centre had been established in 1983, and was classically directed by the head of the TMoCA. In 1990 it began organising regular national biennials (and in a few cases triennials), including painting, photography, sculpture, ceramics, illustration and cartoon. Alongside these exhibitions, the museum held lectures and conferences, which, in the early 1990s at least, considered issues of cultural and artistic

Fig. 2

identity and how it could be preserved against the 'mighty storm of Western culture'. At the same time, there was a growing ambition to participate in the international art scene. A look at exhibition catalogues and conference proceedings of the time shows a gradual growing interest in contemporary international art movements, without explicitly defending that kind of art. The formal stance of Iran's officials still clearly promoted resistance against 'other cultural norms' of 'cultural globalisation' or so-called 'Westernism'. The aim, however, seemed to be to find a balance between positioning the country in relation to the global culture while at the same time confronting 'Western aggression'.[6]

The third phase of post-Revolution art in Iran began with the election of the reformist president Mohammad Khatami in 1997. It was a defining moment in Iranian cultural policy and artistic movements, meaning there was a relaxation of control on visual arts activities, including those in major public and commercial galleries. Exhibitions and art activities grew rapidly in big cities, especially in the capital Tehran. The visual arts assumed a new significance not seen since the Islamic Revolution. In particular, TMoCA began to hold non-political and non-ideological exhibitions. Therefore the museum, and in particular the Centre of Visual Arts, played a key role in promoting various forms of contemporary Iranian art. For example the centre began to support commercial galleries in Tehran and other cities through funding and collaborations.[7] Galleries during this period were also freed of the requirement that they gain the centre's approval for each show they wanted to mount.[8] This marked a decisive reduction in government control of artistic affairs. The museum and the centre also supported the visual arts through the establishment of organised programmes, including giving their biennials more comprehensive aims while also directly involving the newly established artists' societies and holding thematic exhibitions of contemporary Iranian, European and Asian art. Worthy of mention are exhibitions at the TMoCA, such as Joan Miró in 2000, Arman in 2003, Heinz Mack in 2004 and Gerhard Richter in 2004, as well as contemporary Japanese art in 2005. Perhaps the most significant exhibition held at the museum was the *Turning Points: 20th-century British Sculpture* in 2003 (figs 3, 4), when artists Bill

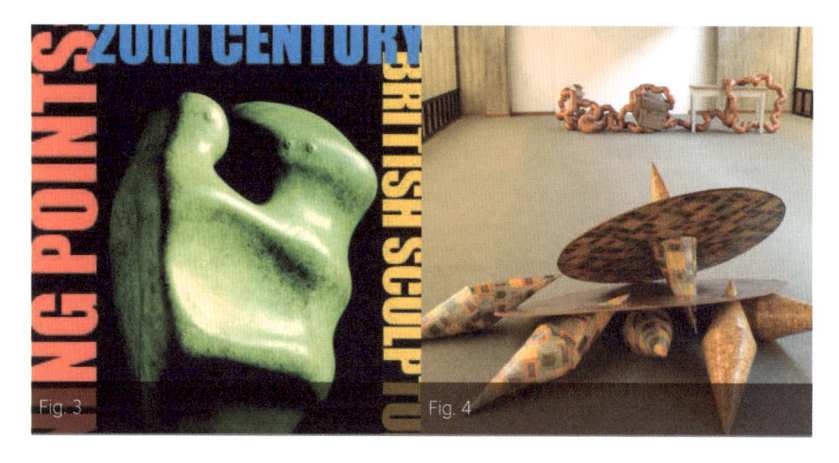

Woodrow and Richard Deacon, among other artistic and cultural figures, were invited to be present in the show.[9] This indeed signalled an important shift in the artistic relations between Iran and Britain. At the same time, a number of unprecedented exhibitions of contemporary Iranian art were held in the UK, among others were the *Iranian Contemporary Art* at the Barbican Centre in 2001 and an exhibition of the same name held at Christi's London in 2003. All these, plus other similar initiatives, indeed fostered Iran-UK cultural and artistic exchange in that period and the effect of these initiatives later materialised in the works of the contemporary Iranian art scene. A great hope was arising that this would be a beginning for further mutual cultural relationships. National and international gatherings and discussions on different aspects of contemporary art and culture were also organised within the museum. The number of art publications and public places exhibiting visual arts grew considerably. Moreover, the museum increased its international activities by establishing links with other international art institutions and museums by lending works from the Western collection of the Museum (many of which had been unseen for years) and through a number of exhibitions of Iranian artists in Europe, America and Asia.[10] One example was the presence of Francis Bacon's unique triptych, Two Figures Lying on a Bed with Attendants (1968) from the TMoCA's collection in his retrospective exhibition at Tate Britain in 2004 for the first time since the work was purchased in the 1970s. This period was also important in attracting a wider range of practising artists and in establishing new perspectives for artistic practice, partly affected by those mutual exchanges, and the consolidation of an artistic community.

The presence of Iranian artists in international artistic exhibitions such as the Venice Biennale in this period of the early 2000s[11] was the direct result of the opening of cultural boundaries. Exhibitions of European and Asian art in Iran during those years resulted in the creation of an atmosphere in which Iranian artists became determined to stand alongside their counterparts around the world and fully participate in the contemporary international art scene. Those years also brought success to certain Iranian artists through exhibitions outside the country, and received recognition and awards in international exhibitions such as the Asian Art Biennial in Bangladesh, the Beijing International Art Biennial in China and the Sharjah Art Biennial.

The year 2001 saw the establishment of the Iranian Academy of the Arts, which was affiliated to the presidency. According to the Academy's charter, its activities should focus mainly on 'Islamic' and Iranian and Eastern art – both traditional and contemporary.[12] 'International' – perhaps meaning Western – contemporary art was considered less important.[13] Established as a centre for artistic policy-making, the Academy did not have a mandate to get involved in artistic activities, though it nevertheless organised various exhibitions from the Islamic world including calligraphy, posters and painting, mainly in the Academy's newly established gallery, the Saba Cultural and Artistic Centre. With its biennales of contemporary art from the Islamic world, the Academy also held various conferences on broad subjects including the philosophy of art, traditional art, and art and globalisation (fig 5).

Fig. 5

Its activities declined, however, after the dismissal of the founder and director Mir Hossein Mousavi as one of the consequences of the controversial election in 2009.

If Khatami's presidency enabled a cultural and intellectual explosion, giving voice to new ideas in art as well as in social and political issues, the election in 2005 of Mahmoud Ahmadinejad as president of the Islamic Republic marked another huge shift. After 2005, the official attitude towards art echoed the first phase after the Islamic Revolution. This can be seen in exhibitions, such as that held at the TMoCA in 2006, that looked at 'resistance', in reference to Palestine-Israel conflict. This continued throughout the second round of Ahmadinajad's presidency, after the 2009 controversial election, with more restrictions imposed from the official bodies on art and culture activities. In this period, officials promoted traditional, Islamic and revolutionary values, while at the same time encouraging extreme xenophobia towards the West. The response from the artistic community was apathetic about this ideology, and the majority of the community, including the artists' societies, overreacted culturally against this situation by refusing to participate in public shows.[14] Since there was a limited chance for showing their work in official venues such as the TMoCA, they had to focus their attention outside the country through the private sector. Various exhibitions of Iranian art and artists were held in Europe, the UK included, and America during recent years. At an international level, only two major exhibitions were organised in TMoCA by the cultural attaché of the German embassy in Tehran, namely *Käthe Kollwitz & Ernst Barlach* in 2008 and *Gunther Uecker* in 2012 which displayed works of the German contemporary artist. These exhibitions, however, could never re-establish the heydays of the museum, both in terms of quality and the number of the visitors.[15]

During recent years, there has been little intention to promote Iranian art internationally through the public sector. Apart from national biennials (not perhaps held very regularly), the annual Fadjr International Festival of Visual Arts (on the annual celebration of the Islamic Revolution)[16] (figs 6, 7); and also art expos are the only major events; all within the state's politics of culture. These exhibitions are conventionally held in the public

Fig. 6   Fig. 7

art centres and museums, under the Ministry of Culture and Islamic Guidance, in particular the TMoCA and the Niyavaral Cultural Centre and also the Saba Cultural and Artistic Centre, under the Iranian Academy of the Arts. The administration's ideological cultural view is obviously not in favour of any kind of critical or so-called alternative art practices; usually denoted by new media, site specific works, or performances, which are rather being practiced in private sector or through the artists' individual networks. At its best, the aforementioned official events limited themselves to a small portion of the cultural aims and ideologies of the country. Since the election of Hassan Rouhani last year, the moderate president who won the election with his promise of moderation, 'hope' and 'contrivance' against the former extremism, it is hoped that these circumstances will change. Although there has not yet been a fundamental change within official artistic policy, the election brought to an end the pessimism felt by the artistic community and private sector towards any effective official policy for art. The former excessive lack of inclusivity had turned against the status quo and created powerful commercial or even alternative sectors. It was when by the late 2000s the art scene in Iran was growing in parallel with cultural funding centres operating within the private art sector. At the same time the increasing level of production was seen by individuals and private institutions in this area.

Let us now briefly consider the non-official events. There are indeed private art competitions and prizes, (including MOP CAP[17] and Persbook[18]) (fig 8) which have attracted a greater number of

Fig. 8

emerging artists who would not accept restrictions imposed on them by official regulations. There are also a few websites or art centres which aim to build platforms for young artists and facilitate the introduction of contemporary Iranian art in the international art spectrum, and on some occasions hold exhibitions of foreign

Fig. 9

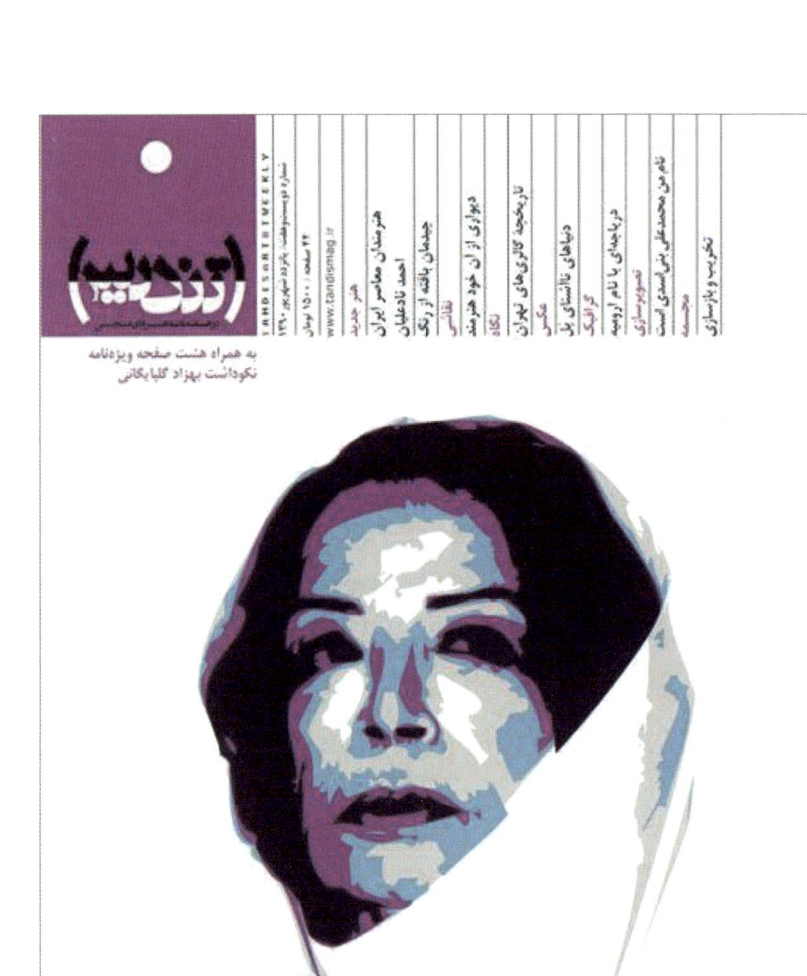

artists in Iran.[19] By the late 2000s, Tehran's commercial galleries and art centres established a series of international projects temporarily invested in an art scene that promises an alternative to institutional norms. There have also been small curatorial projects structured within the private sector. The inclusion of emerging artists, together with panel discussions and events, little presented in the Iranian art scene before, are organised in a few private galleries which introduces a recent development in art practice in Iran. There is, however, an excessive lack of reflection on the theoretical side involved in curating contemporary art and the issue of curatorial strategies. The range of issues relating to curating contemporary art exhibitions is expanding but it is mainly discussed in practical terms with insufficient attention being paid to the underlying theoretical discourses involved.

It is within this context that the role of publications, in particular periodicals, is essential in terms of knowledge production and theorising. Aside from some online magazines, mainly in Persian, dealing with various aspects of contemporary Iranian art, there are only a few periodicals focused on the visual arts. These include those published by formal institutions, such as the Iranian Academy of the Arts and Howzeh Honari which typically emphasises the Islamic and revolutionary aspects of art.[20] The key and much more widespread contemporary art periodicals are, however, not related to any official institutions. The bi-weekly publication *Tandis*, in print since 2002 (fig 9), the quarterly *Herfeh hunarmand* (Profession: Artist) (fig 10), established in 2004, and the quarterly *Art Tomorrow*, established in 2010, are the most important ones. The latter a bilingual (English–Persian) journal that includes contributions on contemporary art issues from international scholars. It covers regional and international art discourses, as well as focusing on Iran and the Middle East.[21]

Fig. 10

The past decade has also seen a flow of interest in the Iranian art market regionally, across the Middle East, and internationally. World politics and the state of the economy are at the least partly responsible for this recognition. This recent development of the regional art market, in particular Christie's biannual auctions in Dubai, has been further exemplified in art fairs, auction house sales and exhibitions which have not been without benefit to modern and contemporary Iranian art. In line with this development, the local market has also largely been affected. More commercial galleries and large art centres have been created during very recent years. The Tehran annual Auction, established in 2011 (fig 11), which basically follows the patterns of international auctions but on a national scale, is a recent private development in this field. This market, however, is in favour of a certain kind of artworks and media and so is not inclusive[22] (figs 12, 13). And it is this very tendency which has dominated the interest of many commercial galleries too. Nevertheless, the number of newcomers is increasing and several young collectors are likewise joining the club. Given the current economic instability of the country and the high amount of liquidity in the hands of a small cluster of rich people, to them art would be indeed less risky as a commodity investment. There are other reasons for growing interest in collecting contemporary (here rather in this case, modern) art locally mainly by a new generation of rich new buyers. One reason is to gain prestige – perhaps the same important demand as for the rich elsewhere – that one could attain by collecting art. This has created a problem *i.e.* the market is

Fig. 11

Fig. 12

Fig. 13

becoming very rarefied. The issue of exclusivity here again is the case. The art market has provided to some extent a local, regional and international channel of possibility for particular genres of art to be developed. However one should not expect to see the presence of all genres of contemporary art represented by works in this sector. This might be threatening for the position of a large group of practicing artists, in particular amongst the emerging younger generations who are not willing to comply with this system. Therefore, it is not surprising that a growing number of young artists are attempting to be successful in this market and produce works whose sale would be guaranteed. Examples are calligraphic works and fashionable social subjects (fig 14).

As for art education, during the past two decades the university system – both government and Azad universities – has developed with a growing number of institutions both in the capital and other provinces, all following a centralised system of curriculums under the Ministry of Science, Research and Technology (Vizarat-i Ulum, Tahqiqat va Fann-avari). Art faculties which offer various fields of fine art and applied arts, ranging from bachelor to PhD levels, accommodate a great number of visual arts students. However, what can clearly be identified is a great lack of attention to the changes in the education system and any international exchange with other foreign institutions. This has resulted in a failure to keep up-to-date with curriculums and fields of study. The most common example of this, which occurs in practical fields, is an obvious ignorance of theoretical foundations. The subjects of contemporary art theory

Fig. 14

and art history, in particular, have suffered within this system. This has affected the students and graduates who have made a great number of practising artists. An existing lack in current art education – in particular the contents and quality of theory based courses – in Iran and an imperative need for appreciation of critical theory and art theoretical foundation in contemporary art practice would make it essential to think about this deficiency. Furthermore, there have not been other educational platforms, such as conferences (national or international), large curatorial projects and accompanied theoretical discussions by the public institutions and museums during recent years. Despite these deficiencies, the huge number of young art students and artists maintain their hunger for knowledge and the demand for subjects of contemporary art remains very high. Only a few private institutions which have started their initiatives during past decade are trying to respond to this need. These institutions have attracted a great number of students who have failed to receive necessary educational training within the university system. There is, however, still an urgent need for observation of theoretical and practical aspects involved both in theory and practice in contemporary Iranian art which makes the issue of education extremely crucial.

On the whole, although art production and its market is flourishing in Iran, there is still a great need for more attention to be paid towards the issues of education, and establishing strong theoretical foundations that will support the study and understanding of this art. These factors are essential if contemporary Iranian art is to be sustainable and able to participate in the highly competitive and shifting contemporary international art scene. One of the solutions could be resuming international cultural relations through art institutions and the organisation of mutual events and educational programmes, where there will be opportunities to exchange ideas, knowledge and develop new cultural connections. The establishment of private initiatives within the private sector and collaboration and funding support of international institutions could indeed play a crucial role. A solid joint relationship that could foster the bilateral a cultural initiative such as that which on different occasions was realised between Iran and the UK, will certainly be instrumental. Given that during recent years UK has played a role as the most important platform for the introduction and dissemination of aspects of contemporary Iranian art through events, including the first comprehensive international conference on 'Contemporary Iranian Art: Modernity and the Iranian Artist' held at Oxford University in 2004; the aforementioned exhibitions, and more recently the *Recalling the Future: post revolutionary Iranian art* exhibition held at SOAS; University of London in 2014; the MOP CAP competition based in London; the London Middle East Institute, SOAS, conference on 'Contemporary Art from the Middle East' in 2013; all these demonstrate that UK is receptive to looking at Iranian art. There is therefore a great potential to build up bilateral educational programmes based on mutual interests with the aim of filling the gaps and meeting urgent needs in Iranian art education, in particular helping to build capacity in art theory and curatorial practice.

Notes

1 For the concept of committed art, see Hamid Keshmirshekan, 'Discourses on Post-Revolutionary Iranian Art: Neo-traditionalism during the 1990s', *Muqarnas XXIII* (2006), pp. 132–35ft.
2 These artists had had their first major show in the Ershad Assembly (Husseyniyya-i Irshad) in Tehran in 1979, just after the Revolution. This marked the beginning of the Centre of Islamic Thought and Art (Howzeh Andisha va Hunar-i Islami) later under Islamic Propaganda Organisation (Sazman-i Tablighat-i Islami).
3 This new body was first called the Ministry of Islamic Guidance (Vizarat-i Irshad-i Islami) in 1980, and then in 1987 was named the Ministry of Culture and Islamic Guidance.
4 Some exhibitions during the first two years after the Revolution included *Activist Painters* (1979 and 1980), *Revolutionary Graffiti* (1979), *The Palestinian Resistance Movement* (1979), *Drawings by University Students in Tehran* (1979), *Mexican Revolutionary Murals* (1980). (Helia Darabi, 'Tehran Museum of Contemporary Art as a Microcosm of State's Cultural Agenda', in *Contemporary from the Middle East: Regional Interactions with Global Art Discourses*, ed. Hamid Keshmirshekan, IB Tauris, London, New York, 2014, forthcoming).
5 Apart from the Tehran Museum of Contemporary art, the major centres were the Niyavaran Cultural Centre and the Azadi Cultural Centre.
6 See Hamid Keshmirshekan, Modern and Contemporary Iranian Art: Developments and Challenges', in *Different Sames, New Perspectives in Contemporary Iranian Art*, ed. Hossein Amirsadeghi, Tames and Hudson, London, 2009, p.29.
7 Apart from the Barg Gallery and other major official galleries linked to the Tehran Municipality, more than sixty galleries were active in Tehran during this period and many more in other Iranian provinces.
8 After this period, under Mahmoud Ahmadinajad's cultural administration, the requirement for approval before each exhibition was once again implemented.
9 See Helia Darabi, 'Tehran Museum of Contemporary Art as a Microcosm of State's Cultural Agenda', p. 249–50.
10 There were a few international activities already organised by the Ministry of Culture and Islamic Guidance before this period. Among others the first major international festival of Iranian art and culture since the Islamic Revolution was inaugurated in the German city of Düsseldorf in September 1991. For an entire month, the principal art galleries of Düsseldorf were devoted to this major endeavour. See Hamid Keshmirshekan, 'Discourses on Postrevolutionary Iranian Art', p. 156.
11 The first presence of contemporary Iranian art in the post-revolutionary period was in the 50th Venice Biennale in 2002.
12 R Jalali, 'guft-u-gu ba ductur Namvar Motlagh dabir-i farhangistan-i hunar: tafakkuri khas nisbat beh jahan-i islam', *Sharq* [daily newspaper], no. ccclxxxii, 1383/2005, p. 14.
13 Ibid.
14 After the election in 2009 a major number of artists and art activists, including artists' societies, signed declarations advocating a boycott of collaboration with government institutions which lasted until the 2013 election of President Hassan Rouhani.
15 See Helia Darabi, 'Tehran Museum of Contemporary Art as a Microcosm of State's Cultural Agenda', p. 254.

16 It includes two sections: National (painting, sculpture, calligraphy, pottery & ceramics, Persian Painting – the standard official categorisation of visual arts) and International (poster design, photography and cartoons.

17 MOP CAP stands for the Magic of Persia Contemporary Art Prize which is a biennial art prize organised by the Magic of Persia, a UK based charity. The introduction to the MOP CAP reads, 'MOP CAP is a worldwide search for the next generation of contemporary Iranian visual artists who have the potential to make a significant impact in their field. The goal of the prize is to provide an opportunity for emerging artists to gain international exposure, and to engage in artistic experimentation and cultural exchange...' http://www.mopcap.com/about/.

18 Established in 2010, Persbook is an annual online contemporary art competition 'Culture can be transmitted and expanded through General Media without any geographical borders'. persbookart.com.

19 One can name Sazmanab contemporary art centre. Established in 2009, it 'is an independent non-profit art center in Tehran. It 'supports artistic work in a wide range of media through exhibitions and events, residencies for artists and curators, educational initiatives, workshops, talks, and publications. By establishing local and international relationships, as well as diversifying both the practitioners and audiences of contemporary art, Sazmanab aims to support and expand the knowledge, appreciation and practice of contemporary arts in Iran...' http://www.sazmanab.org.

20 For further study of art publications in post-revolution Iran, see Hamid Severi, 'Mapping Iranian Contemporary Art Publications and Knowledge-Production', in *Contemporary Art from the Middle East: Regional Interactions with Global Art Discourses*, ed. Hamid Keshmirshekan, IB Tauris, London, New York, 2014, forthcoming.

21 See ibid.

22 This market is particularly in favour of certain modern Iranian masters, mainly those belonging to the 1960s and 1970s, and as usual more marketable media such as painting, sculpture and on much smaller scale photography.

British Cinema in Iran: a brief history

EHSAN KHOSHBAKHT
Ehsan Khoshbakht is an Iranian author, film critic, jazz scholar and architect.

It is a history which spans the promotional films of the British Council, in the 1940s to TV series such as *The Sweeney*, *Miss Marple*, *Sherlock Holmes*, and *Edge of Darkness* in 1990s. Sporadically, but often enthusiastically, British cinema and television productions have been highly appreciated in Iran and the UK's identity has been on display in many and various ways.

Introduction
The late 1980s: one Friday evening in a small city in northeastern Iran. A family has gathered around the television set, an old Philips model housed in a gigantic black wooden cabinet. They are sat in two semi-circles – the elders on the couch, and the youngsters casually settled on the floor. Everyone is mesmerised by the black and white images of a long-distance runner. The picture is rough, grey and muddy. For the man onscreen, running is freedom itself; a temporary detachment from the banality of his life. For the Iranians watching, the

freedom of this long-distance runner is a temporary detachment from the banality of their lives.

Suddenly, only a few yards from the finish line, the weary runner stops. He just stands there and watches his own defeat with a grin on the face. The whole family are shouting at the TV pleading for him to carry on, as if he was in the room, or they were in Nottingham. The runner doesn't move an inch. The race is lost with a smile. Though the family are disappointed, the screening is, for one of them at least, an introduction to something new; nothing short of a revelation.

In post-revolutionary Iran, when the distribution of foreign films in cinemas was close to nil and home video was banned, Iranian national television, reluctant to acquire new content, filled its weekly Friday evening programme with whatever was available from their archive. It was in this context that British cinema of the 1940s to the early 1960s was revived on Iranian TV. The grim, realist, socially conscious and unglamorous look of these films perfectly suited the agenda of filling the programme schedule without provocation.

Only a short time prior to these weekly TV screenings, however, these films had been shown in their complete forms, and most of the time in their original language, at the tail-end of a golden age of film culture in Iran, which had started three decades before the revolution. The British films shown in Iran in the 1980s and early 1990s were, in fact, part of a dormant period after two vibrant eras, occurring from the late 1920s to 1951 and from the late 1950s up to the late 1970s respectively. During both periods British film was highly present in Iran. British documentaries and British commercial genre films flowed into country, the import of each motivated by different aims.

Here I will give a brief history of the presence of British

cinema in Iran since its earliest days. In the process, I will highlight some of the problems involved in perceiving and assessing these films in Iran, as well as how the politics of the time were invariably inseparable from the films shown. It is a story of inconsistent efforts made by both the British and the Iranians to promote British cinema. Two breaking points that inevitably influence this history are the 1953 CIA-MI6 supported coup against the Prime Minister Mohammad Mosaddegh and the 1979 Revolution which led to certain restrictions, misinterpretations among Iranians' perception of British culture in general, and British cinema in particular.

Compared to the more easily traceable influences of American, Hindi and Italian cinemas in Iran, the British film might be somewhat less visible, but a historical study will show that the British cinema had been widely distributed and promoted in Iran, as well as praised and occasionally studied by Iranians.

First golden period: the documentary movement

British distributors had a place in Iran's popular chain cinemas beginning in the early years of the 20th century. What distinguishes the period from the 1920s to World War II is the overlap of commercial screenings, overseen by private companies, with what can be seen as ideological screenings, organised by government or semi-official institutions to promote a particular culture – in this case the British way of life. Such screenings consisted of educational, instructional, propaganda and short films, usually shown in a package with an animated film or a comedy just to add a touch of entertainment.

For these purposes, British mobile film units were sent to Iran and could travel around the country setting up 16mm or 35mm projections in small provincial cities and villages to show predominantly educational and newsreel films. Just as important as the capital city of Tehran for the British was the Abadan province – the centre of oil refineries in Iran. Following the establishment of the company in 1908, the mobile film units of the Anglo-Persian Oil Company were actively screening newsreel and short films for the public and the oil workers.

The British documentaries were short, compact, informative and fast-paced. An important part of these exhibition schemes was the inclusion of documentary content about, or issues related to, Iran. These films reinforced stereotypes about 'Persia' and the Middle East. For example, British Instructional Films (active between 1919 and 1932) produced several short travelogues as part of its *The Heart of Asia* series, which Hamid Naficy argues "demonstrate that British interest in Iran partly derived from its colonial interests in India and that Western films projected an Orientalist representation of Iran as a wild desert and pre-modern, exotic land, one traversed by intrepid westerners."[1]

In the lead-up to World War II the British films shown in Iran became increasingly charged with propagandistic messages, to compete with equally influential German films. After the Tehran

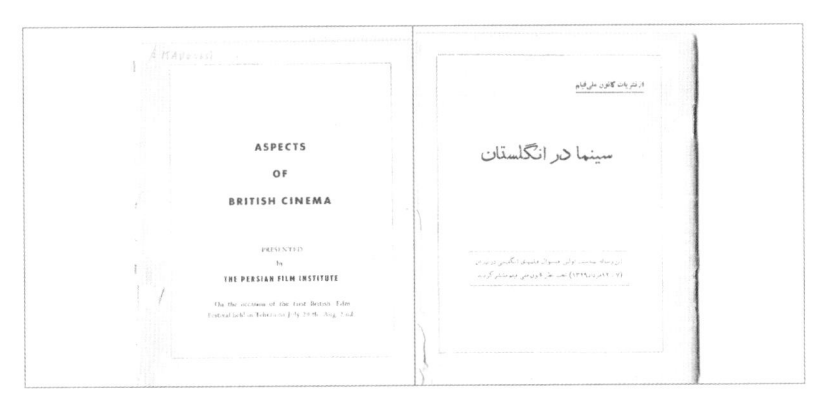

Conference of 1943, held between the 'Big Three' and when all German influences were purged from Iran, this rivalry shifted towards a tight competition with Russians and Americans.

Responding to the necessities of the time, the British started the first newsreel cinema in Tehran in 1943. Many British newsreels shown in Iran were about international affairs, but some were focusing specifically on the relations between Iran and Britain. Among various companies active in Iran, the British Movietone News catalogue lists nearly one hundred films about Iran, made between 1939 and 1958 – some of them with Persian titles[2] (there are apparently some with Persian voiceovers too, which I have not been able to see), which indicates British interest in making the material accessible for the Farsi speaking audience.

During the war, the mobile film units become increasingly active to support their strategic interests in a neutral country such as Iran. Another major factor which drastically increased the number of British films in Iran was the complete halt on domestic production in Iranian cinema's longest period of hibernation, between 1936 and 1948. In 1946–47 alone the British Council, then the key organiser of such screenings, held 47 screening events – on average one event per week – which usually featured two or three films and newsreels. Among the innovative methods used by the British was the screening of films to a specialised audience, such as showing football films to footballers, or police films to the policemen of Tehran; or organising children's film events, when selected schoolchildren could watch an "elementary biological film, sport film, 'life in Britain' film, scientific film and a Mickey Mouse film."[3] Later, Nilla Cook, a United States attaché in Iran from 1941 to 1947 and a rival to the British, went as far as to claim that people watched British documentaries for the last part of the event, which featured a Mickey Mouse film.[4]

This is only one example of the many clashes between the British and the Americans in their film programmes for Iran. A prime example of the rivalry and exchange between the two powers in their attempts to conquer the exhibition market in Iran was the classic documentary *Grass* (1925), a film shot in Iran, produced by a Hollywood studio (Paramount Pictures) and directed by Merian C Cooper and Ernest B Schoedsack (who would put their talents together again later to make *King Kong* among other productions). Fearing the Iranians' reaction to the depiction of the primitive life and poverty among the nomadic tribes of central Iran, the Americans never screened the film in the country in which it was made.

Grass was not shown in Iran until after the Allied powers had forced Reza Shah into exile. It was only then that the British came into the picture; they bought the rights to the film, edited a shorter version, and ingeniously substituted the patronising intertitles with a patriotic voiceover, spoken by one of the luminaries of Persian literature, the scholar Mojtaba Minavi. Even more interesting is the role of the British Council is distributing this shorter version of *Grass*, not only in cinemas but also (in a 16mm version) in industrial, cultural and educational institutions.[5]

Providing an overview of various film activities in Iran during the 1930s and 1940s, Naficy argues that in comparison with other foreign film units, the British were the most successful because their endeavours had been 'more serious in tone, more educationally oriented and more diverse, and its nationwide reach was wider than the American or Soviet efforts.' He also adds that the British notably exhibited "creativity in film presentation and audience preparation."[6]

The first golden age of British (documentary) cinema in Iran was interrupted when the movement towards nationalising the oil industry began and the legitimacy of British interests was questioned. Led by Mossadegh, the movement succeeded and a law was passed declaring the oil resources nationalised in 1953. Anti-British sentiments were manifested in the widespread rejection of British films. In their place, anti-British propaganda films were shown, including certain films produced in Nazi Germany such as *Ohm Krüger* (Hans Steinhoff, Karl Anton, Herbert Maisch, 1941)[7], about a "statesman who fought a heroic war against Germany's arch-enemy, Britain."[8] The reissue of the film, which was originally intended to prepare Germans for the invasion of Britain, showed the extent to which cinema was reflecting strong political currents and the fragility of British efforts in Iran.

Almost three decades later, shortly after the 1979 Revolution, the subject of British imperialism was revived in debates, statements, as well as the selection of films for cinemas. It was then that *Ohm Krüger* returned to Iranian cinemas 40 years after its initial release, in retribution for the British support of the Shah.[9]

Second golden period: British art house cinema vs. Norman Wisdom

The second golden period of film culture in Iran, as well as British cinema's presence in the country, began in the early 1950s and continued until the Revolution in 1979. In December 1949 the first film club opened in Tehran: The Persian Film Institute was opened by Henri Langlois's former Iranian assistant, Farrokh Ghaffari. Thanks to Ghaffari and some of his contemporaries the notion of cinema as art began to fascinate educated Iranians. Although this slowly growing cinephile culture was essentially Francophile in tone, the Persian Film Institute's first curated programme was a five-night festival of British cinema which ran from 29 July to 2 August 1950, supported by the British Council. For this event Ghaffari wrote the bilingual programme notes and a short introduction by John Grierson was included.[10]

This historically significant event was in all likelihood the first introduction to British cinema, initiated by Iranians and supported by the British, which didn't claim to present either an up-to-date picture of the British Film Industry or an historical survey of its development; it was, rather, as Ghaffari wrote, 'more in the nature of an experiment.'

In the brochure, before focusing on titles such as *A Matter of Life and Death* and *Odd Man Out*, Ghaffari gives a brief history of British cinema and explores the concept of the then still undefined documentary film. He declares that this very first film festival is intended to combine entertainment and art, showing both "box office type cinema", as well as "films which may be classified as great cinema and it is this kind of film which raises the cinema above a cheap and vulgar amusement to the higher level of an artistic medium." Ghaffari concludes that "if this British Film Festival can pave the way for an International Film Festival in Teheran [sic], we should consider our efforts worthwhile."[11]

This important and rather influential experiment indeed led to other, similar events for introducing foreign films to the Iranian elite. However, it was not until 1971 that the first Tehran International Film Festival materialised – and British cinema was a strong presence. Over the previous year, at a time when the boundaries between the art house and commercial cinemas were not as distinct as they are today, many classics of British cinema found their way onto Iranian screens. The most popular British cinematic goods imported into Iran were, in order of distribution, comedies (Ealing, Norman Wisdom and beyond), Hammer horrors and James Bond films.

The Iranian reaction to British comedies, especially those starring Norman Wisdom – whose popularity in Iran was unmatched by any other British star – is a phenomenon which invites its own specialist research. Needless to say, the imaginative Persian dubbing, with added jokes in local accents, and the underlying themes of class tension – a favorite theme of many Iranian films – were crucial to the success of British comedies in Iran. In the case of Norman Wisdom, being subversive within a very small, tightly controlled society was particularly attractive to Iranian moviegoers.

Around the same time, the members of the intelligentsia, preoccupied with the French idea of the 'filmmaker as auteur', rediscovered Alfred Hitchcock as the ultimate auteur figure. He became the only English filmmaker whose respectability remained fully intact in subsequent years – and was to be rediscovered, once more, after the revolution.

In spite of the ready access to a wealth of British cinema, as well as an increase in the number of film journals and the introduction of film reviews in various publications, the perceptions surrounding British cinema didn't change drastically on the whole. The discussion of British films during this period of Iranian film criticism is curiously devoid from any allusions to their country of origin. The subjects of national identity and politics are mostly absent in the case of British films, while more awareness is shown in the appreciation of American, Italian and French cinema.[12]

The 1960s and 1970s saw an increased spread of British cinema, following the massive success of numerous titles, and the reappearance of many British films on Iranian national TV. After the initiation of a second channel in Iran, with the aim of broadcasting cultural programmes and selected films (and which might have been modeled on BBC2), British films were not only seen in every household but also discussed in critical studies and reviews published in the journal of radio and television, *Tamasha*. Later on in the Seventies, a nearly complete season of Ealing comedies on Iranian TV became possibly the most significant export of British culture to Iran.[13]

At the end of the 1970s, however, the Revolution made all of these efforts futile. In the ensuing years the revolutionary climate undid much of the international cultural work of the previous years, especially with regards to the reception of Western cinema. But contrary to a widely held belief, film culture was not as violently interrupted as it might have appeared from outside. British cinema continued to exist and remained popular in Iran, even under the severe Islamic rules imposed on the distribution and exhibition of films.

After the revolution: Norman (again), Nazis and beyond

Film production in Iran ceased in the turbulent days leading up to the popular 1979 revolution, unintentionally paving the way for another period of regular international cinema screenings. Yet, due to a revolutionary climate, the expectations of cinema had drastically changed since the 1970s. What was previously programmed for a clandestine university screening was now the norm for the mainstream cinemas. Iranian screens were flooded with revolutionary, leftist, or anti-imperialist films from European and South American cinemas. A staggering 310 films were screened in only 27 cinemas in Tehran (200 of them enjoying a second run) and many of the other titles belonged to a large group of films banned by the Pahlavi regime.[14]

Leftist or Islamist, what most revolutionaries had in common was their rejection of the US and Great Britain for their interfering and imperialist presence in Iran. That attitude hindered American and British films from competing in the market, leaving the field open to films from the Soviet Union and the leftist cinema of Italy, France, Chile and Eastern Europe; eventually, all were banned so as to 'purge' the Islamic Republic.

From October 1982, the content production unit of Iranian TV resumed its film acquisition activities (this time, purchasing rights from Eastern countries from the Soviet Union to Japan) and the Friday evening film broadcast was reintroduced into the weekly schedule. The criterion for selection was simply that the films be 'safe', without overt or subversive political, religious or sexual insinuation; preferably films in which female bodies are fully covered; films without flamboyant heroes or heroines. This meant that British cinema had a fair chance of returning to an Iranian viewership.

During the years 1983 and 1984, British films (along with films from Japan) were allocated most of the rather small film slots on Iranian TV and many classics of British cinema were revived, such as *A Night to Remember*, *Ill Met by Moonlight*, *Lawrence of Arabia* (also in cinemas) *Cromwell*, *A Man for All Seasons*, *The One That Got Away*, *The Ipcress File* and *The Wrong Box*.[15]

This period was also marked by the invasion of Iran by Iraq, which gave rise to the eight-year Iran-Iraq War. It is probable that no country has shown as many anti-fascist films over a ten-year period as Iran did then; many of them were British war films, whose depictions of Hitler and the Nazis were now seen as metaphors for Saddam Hussein and the Ba'athis. In that context, Britain of the

1940s was the perfect emblem of wartime Iran, whose capital was being bombed by Saddam. The war was understood by Iran as a means of defence against an evil force, and its post-war landscape was demonstrably affected by the casualties, ruins and the economic and moral crisis of a long, exhausting conflict. British films were perfectly responding to both sides of the coin. In Which We Serve, The Dam Busters and The Cruel Sea were wartime favorites on Iranian TV and The Third Man, Brighton Rock and Mandy perfectly reflected the reconstruction years. Even the successful re-release of four old Norman Wisdom films in Iranian cinemas might have had something to do with their escapist nature during this tumultuous period in Iran's history.[16]

By 1985, Iranian Channel One's list of broadcast films featured more titles from Britain than anywhere else. These included films by Robert Hamer, Charles Frend and David Lean, all made before the 1960s.[17] Most were subject to some form of censorship, from cutting scenes to modifying the story through dubbing. A curious case of such alteration was *Sleuth* (1972), starring Laurence Olivier and Michael Caine. The wife of the character played by Olivier – and the subject of Caine's 'immoral' quest – was dubbed so as to become his daughter, thereby 'purifying' the plot of adulterous lust and transforming the story's cat and mouse game into a surrealist courtship comedy.

The arbitrary revival of British cinema on Iranian TV coincided with a more thoughtful re-evaluation of film history via the translation of film texts, undertaken by post-revolutionary film journals, most prominently *Film Monthly*. However, the place of British cinema among these new critical assessments was minimal, and the history of British cinema still largely unknown. Even a hastily assembled reference guide to British cinema published in 1992[18] couldn't fill the historical gaps and misunderstandings about British films.

Around the same time that the British embassy in Tehran was reopened for the first time since the revolution, the most successful series on Iranian TV was the 10-year-old *Secret Army*, then showing for the first time in Iran, which immediately became a cult series. Its success, coinciding as it did with improving diplomatic relations, led to a flock of British TV series on Islamic Republic TV. Predictably, all of these TV productions became hugely popular in Iran and have been shown many times since, including *The Sweeney* (1975–78), *Miss Marple* (1984–92), *Sherlock Holmes* (1984–1994), *Edge of Darkness* (1985), and *Agatha Christie's Poirot* (1989–2013).

Contemporaneous with this Anglophile cultural trend was an attempt to widen the scope of the Fajr Film Festival (previously known as Tehran Film Festival). Its 14th edition, held in 1996, introduced a strand about British cinema and literature with more than 18 films, including David Lean's *Brief Encounter*, *Hobson's Choice* and his Dickens films, as well as Shakespeare adaptations by Laurence Olivier and Kenneth Branagh. These films appeared at the Fajr Festival on an almost annual basis, programmed as part of different strands. For instance, the Hitchcock films in the 'British film and literature' season – *The Farmer's Wife*, *The Man Who Knew Too Much*, *Sabotage* and *The Thirty-nine Steps* – were programmed again 10 years later under the title 'Hitchcock: The British Years'.

Perhaps the most interesting film selected for the 'British cinema and literature' season was Michael Radford's version of *1984*, during the screening of which a paramilitary Basij group, unhappy about the selection of the film, attacked people waiting in the queue and shaved the heads of randomly selected men in the middle of the street.[19]

Such incidents demonstrated the general confusion in post-revolutionary film culture, as well as exposing the conflict between the radicals and reformists in their cultural politics. Another example of the paradoxes within the official conception of cinema was the re-emergence of Hitchcock as an 'auteur' filmmaker and the publication of *Hitchcock, Always a Maestro*, a voluminous book on the British master issued by, of all places, the Art Centre of the Islamic Propaganda Organisation. Aside from translated essays by British, American and French writers, the book contained contributions from different generations of Iranian film critics.

The following years, up until the present, were marked with the re-authorisation of home video, an almost systematic growth in the underground market for foreign films, and the spread of digital television via satellite receivers, which meant a freer access to a wider range of content. The effects of this shift in the cultural climate and the movement of cinematic activities from public screening houses to private homes were evident when a retrospective of Mike Leigh in 2009 met with a less than enthusiastic audience. The reason was not too difficult to comprehend: the festival was showing censored versions in poor quality copies, while thanks to the digital revolution people could see the films, uncut, in the freedom of their homes.[20]

The television broadcast of recent British Oscar winners *Slumdog Millionaire*, *The King's Speech*, and *12 Years a Slave* have been equally unsuccessful; not because of any lack of potential for attracting millions of viewers in themselves, but because long before their broadcast they have been available in much better quality versions, uncut and with Persian subtitles on the bootleg DVD market, for less than 50p.

Thus, the beginning of a new era was also the end of a particular phase in the history of Iran. No longer were millions of people, due to a severe lack of choice, watching the same images and somehow sharing the same emotional wavelength, stirred by classics of Alfred Hitchcock or Norman Wisdom.

Conclusion

Due to the many interruptions in the history of British film exhibition in Iran, as well as the changing currents of social history and the burgeoning cinephile culture, it becomes a difficult task to assess its impact on Iranian film culture over a period of many decades. In terms of influence, the timely distribution of British documentaries in the early years was no doubt crucial, even if the lack of proper documentation makes it difficult to realise to what extent they fostered the subsequent growing interest in British cinema per se. The traces of a more cultivated interest becomes apparent in the 1950s, when Iran became arguably the most receptive country in the Middle East to British films, ingesting anything from Ealing comedies to kitchen sink dramas.

The dual role of British films early on – educating and commercially exploiting viewers – was later reduced to a straightforwardly commercial one, and in absence of British film distributors in post-revolutionary Iran to a non-commercial form of 'safe' entertainment. However, I have briefly explained how these very same conditions led to the rediscovery of British classical cinema by a new generation of Iranians; a more thoughtful appreciation of British films came into existence, which has also been reflected in Persian film literature in recent years. Those British films seen in post-revolutionary Iran, regardless of the number of screenings or how mangled the films have been, have at least played an instrumental role in preventing the total cultural disconnection between Iran and Britain. Occasionally, as in my own experience with *The Loneliness of the Long Distance Runner*, they have provided small cultural shocks with intriguing and lasting effects.

Despite the lack of proper contextualisation – and the lack of regional differentiation through dubbing – British films have remained accessible to mass audiences. If some of the elements of these films – alluding to the 'Britishness' of products, places, names, costumes and manners – have been largely unnoticed by the public, their realist approach, their class-conscious stories, their documentary look, and the spirit of solidarity of the war films have nevertheless resonated well with Iranian society at various times.

Owing to many restrictions in the pre-digital Iran of the 1980s and 1990s, Iranians continually tend to approach cultural products from the West with a real thirst, comparable to the way in which the Western arts were secretly treasured in Eastern bloc. A film such as *The Lavender Hill Mob* was more than a comedy for many Iranians; it was a view of British life, a glimpse of an alien culture, or "a window open for a bit of fresh air," as Behzad Rahimian says.[21] In spite of the TV programmers' hard work to avoid controversial content, they were in fact showing a range of British films which were subversive in many ways. The subtle, understated commentary of British films on issues such as gender, class and repression were secretly transmitted to Iranian households via popular genres such as the comedy, thriller and melodrama.

At times when the likelihood of establishing dialogue between Iran and Britain has seemed dim, British films have acted as agents of cultural affinity among the viewing public, regardless of their intended purposes and specifically where titles have been spontaneously rediscovered from within Iran.

Notes

1 Naficy, Hamid, *A Social History of Iranian Cinema, Volume 1*, Duke University Press, 2011, pp 157–58.
2 For instance, see *Iran Delegation Visits Scotland* (1955).
3 Naficy, Hamid, *A Social History of Iranian Cinema, Volume 2*, Duke University Press, 2011, p. 24.
4 Ibid.
5 Naficy, 2011, pp. 106–7.
6 Naficy, 2011, p. 16.
7 Rahimian, Behzad, This author's interview with him in July 2014.
8 Welch, David, *Propaganda and the German Cinema 1933–1945*, I.B.Tauris, 2001, p. 229.
9 Rahimian, Behzad, 2014.
10 *Aspects of British Cinema*, The Persian Film Institute, 1950.
11 Ibid.
12 The first annual poll conducted by one of Iran's leading film journals *Mahnameye Setareye Cinema* [Film Star Monthly], published on March 21, 1967, picked Michelangelo Antonioni's *La Notte* as the best film of the year, yet it was Laurence Olivier who was selected as the best actor, for *Bunny Lake Is Missing*. Other British winners of 1967 were Douglas Slocomb, for his cinematography on *The Servant* and Richard Macdonald for his set design on *Modesty Blaise*.
13 Rahimian, 2014.
14 *The Pale Face of Cinema in 1980*, Keyhan Newspaper, March 18, 1980.
15 Film Monthly, No. 11, p. 35.
16 Ibid, p. 32.
17 Film Monthly, No. 35, p. 23.
18 The book in question is *British Cinema: From Beginning to 1992*, edited by Bizhan Ashtari.
19 The incident remembered in a short video by filmmaker Niyaz S Sellers entitled *Memories of a 70s Film Buff*, 2014.
20 This author personally witnessed the failed Leigh retrospective in Tehran, which marked his last festival-going experience in Iran too.
21 Rahimian, 2014.

Extending thresholds: Studio INTEGRATE on an architectural quest across continents

MEHRAN GHARLEGHI OF STUDIO **INTEGRATE**
Studio INTEGRATE is an architecture, design and research studio based in London and Sydney. It was founded by Iranian architects Mehran Gharleghi and Amin Sadeghy in 2011.

Architecture in Iran enjoys a long tradition, with a continuous history stretching back millennia. It has always harnessed the latest technologies of the times to erect splendid and comfortable living spaces in challenging environments. Modern Iranian architecture grapples with the different demands and challenges of the contemporary environment; a tireless search to push the boundaries of existing forms took a pair of Iranian architects from their successful practices in Tehran to the lecture halls and studios of London.

It was eight in the morning. We were excited. The promised lecture from a group of architects and researchers from the Architectural Association School of Architecture (AA) in London was taking place in Tehran. We couldn't take the chance of missing the event, so we arrived there early. Apart from the lecturers, there were only a few people in the room. We picked a seat in the second row behind the speakers, who were, unbeknown to us, about to play a significant role in our lives. Michael Hensel started his talk in a rather unusual fashion. He started walking up and down the stage while describing the space he was creating around him. He left the stage and walked towards the audience and expressed how quickly the space transformed as he was getting closer to the audience. My heart started beating faster. It was shocking and we were all paying close attention. The lecture became increasingly elaborate as it continued. He went on to explain the impact of campfires on their surrounding environment and concluded his talk by showing some of the projects completed by the AA, describing how materials, environment and form can be synthesised in sophisticated forms and architectural artefacts. We were fascinated by the architectural outcome and the arguments. We had to find out more. Our journey had begun.

Our conversation with Michael continued over the next two days. We became friends and decided to go on a trip to see a few cities in Iran including Yazd, Isfahan, Abyaneh and Kashan. During the trip we talked about architecture, the environment, society and the role of architects. Another level of understanding of the buildings that we had lived with our whole lives started to unfold throughout our journey. At one point we sat under the wind tower of Dolat Abad Garden in Yazd. It was a hot and sunny day, but inside it was shaded and made comfortable by a cool breeze which filled the space through a large wind tower over the main hall. We were sitting around a shallow pool under the wind tower while Michael was talking about how architecture can improve the quality of our lives regardless of any political situation. This trip had

Figure 1: Dolat Abad Garden

Figure 2: CARPET image

a profound effect on us. We were looking at our own architecture through a new lens. We realised that it was possible to join a global movement with our background in Iranian architecture.

We decided to learn more and join the Emergent Technologies and Design masters course at the AA, the most advanced school of architecture in the world. Emtech was co-founded by Michael Hensel and Michael Weinstock in 2002 and holds a leading position in advance design in the academic world.

Leaving everything behind to join the AA was a difficult decision. We had already established our practice in Iran, after working with well-known architects for a number of years. We had won a number of competitions and had two projects under construction. We had one year to apply to the AA and join the course. This period was one of the most dynamic for us. We started to improve our English and researched the topics we had touched upon with Michael further. We applied this knowledge to competitions such as the International World Carpet Trade Centre, of which we were announced as one of the winners. This was the first time we used an existing morphology – the motif of the Persian carpets – and transformed it into a new skin which had the capacity of environmental and light modulation. A building which was utterly contemporary but at the same time culturally rooted. It had established a relationship with its environment, context, culture and programme. There was still a long way to go to learn how to build such a complex scheme and to establish a meaningful connection to the surrounding environment.

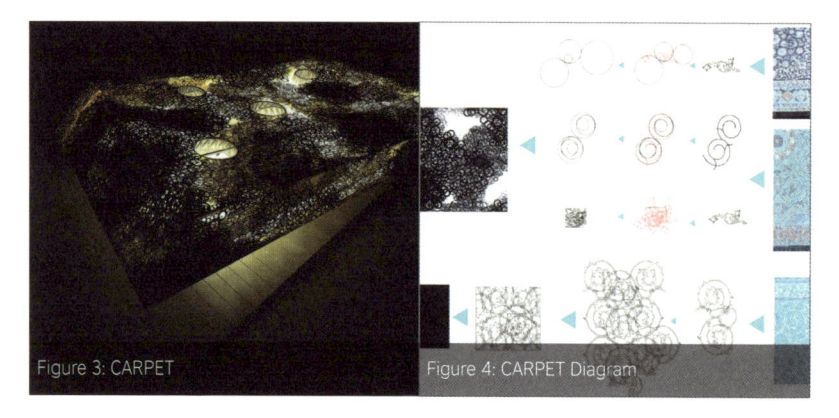

Figure 3: CARPET

Figure 4: CARPET Diagram

I still had to graduate from the Iran University of Science and Technology (IUST). We both decided to take my diploma project as an opportunity to work further in cultivating the knowledge which we were planning to leave the country for. We did not know where to start until the day Amin found an article in the newspaper upon which an American scientist gave us further information on the potentials presented behind the mathematics of Islamic geometries. Peter J Lu, a PhD researcher from Harvard, found that by 1200AD a conceptual breakthrough occurred in which girih patterns were reconceived as tessellations of a special set of equilateral polygons (girih tiles) decorated with lines. These tiles enabled the creation of increasingly complex periodic girih patterns, and by the 15th Century, the tessellation approach was combined with self-similar transformations to construct nearly perfect quasi-crystalline Penrose patterns, five centuries before their discovery in the West. Hence, we had found the subject for exploration. This was a starting point for studying the underlying rules of Islamic geometries and using them to answer some of the questions that were emerging in the modern world, ie: seeking novel structural, spatial and environmental solutions. Penrose tiling, as well as numerous other mathematical geometries that are used in Iranian vernacular architecture, presented us with an interesting opportunity. They had a cultural connection with us including the capacity to fill a surface or space in an unlimited manner. We started this research in Iran and later continued in the UK after learning advanced design and production methods. We are still working on this subject and hope to extend the current boundaries in this field. Benetton Headquarters, a residential proposal in France, the Venice Biennale Wall proposal, deFUSE and Introvert Light are some of our design projects utilising this method.

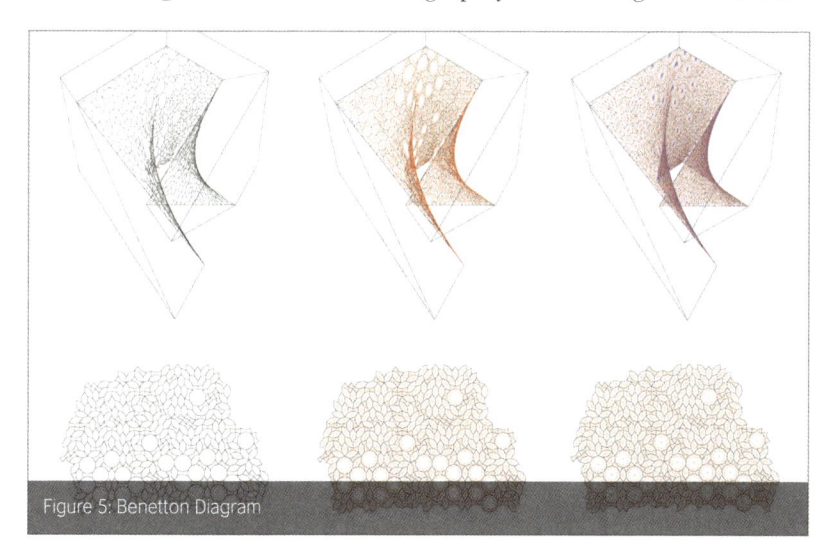

Figure 5: Benetton Diagram

Figure 6: Benetton Design 1. *Photo by Angus Leadley Brown*

    Benetton Headquarters has been one of the most successful design attempts we have made based on this method. The project was a competition entry for the headquarters of Benetton in Tehran. We based the project on creating a tight interior canyon by rotating a U shape around the vertical (z) axis. The canyon would create a central courtyard acting as an urban plaza which was shaded and naturally ventilated. Access to the courtyard and natural ventilation were made possible by opening one of the sides of the courtyard towards the street. Benetton Headquarters was designed when we had already reached the stage in our research where we could apply quasi-Crystalline Penrose geometry onto complex doubly curved surfaces using only a few base modules. This helped to simplify the fabrication logic of the complex's central courtyard which was a response to the climate of Tehran. Here, we managed to synthesise environmental studies with mathematical knowledge to respond to a given brief in a dense urban environment and the local culture.

    deFUSE was another example in which we used the same method in a small scale lighting design. However, the resulting object is significantly different in appearance, showcasing the diverse potentials of such an approach across different scales. It evolved from the base geometries of the Penrose tiling. These base modules are re-arranged, re-scaled and de-formed on a rectangular grid. The grid is then defused into a smooth geometry to leave a gentle light and visual affect in the room while having a strong presence.

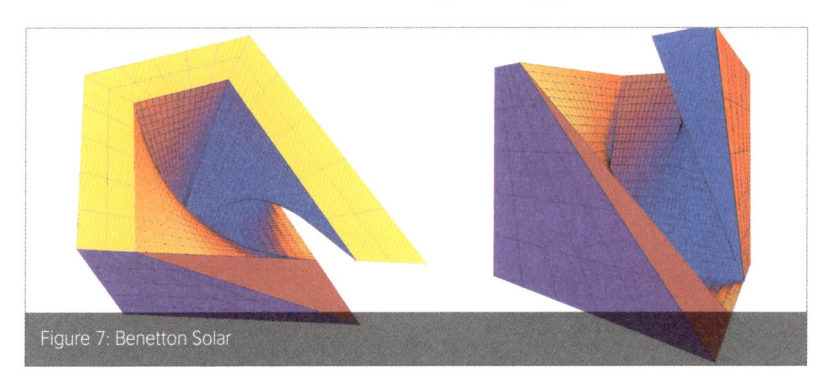

Figure 7: Benetton Solar

One year after the lecture in Tehran, on 27th September 2007, we arrived in London to start studying at the Emergent Technologies and Design programme. The AA was a life changing experiences for us. We studied natural systems and biomimetics to learn how nature makes use of its available materials and resources, in addition to learning smart strategies that respond and adapt to different environments. Michael Weinstock, our professor and our current colleague, taught us about evolution and methodically showed us how incremental and random changes over many generations can improve the overall performance of species, as well as provide enough flexibility to survive under environmental changes. We looked into embryonic development and understood how the species grows from a single cell into complex organisations through a series of simple instructions. Some of the questions that still occupy us were beginning to take shape at that point.

Have central courtyard houses in Iran excelled as a result of evolution? Have their performance been improved gradually and incrementally over many generations? Why are they the dominant building types in the hot and dry climates of Iran? Are there similar typologies in other countries with similar environmental conditions? If so, is it possible to study them in similar ways that we study nature? What about culture? What is culture? Is there an entwined relationship between culture and ecology? Does culture evolve? If so how can we adapt to new environmental social challenges? These questions will remain unanswered throughout our lifetime, we believe. Yet they allowing us to search through historical examples, learn their underlying principals and adjust them to contemporary scenarios, both in architecture and design.

Our first endeavour in researching a historical building through a contemporary lens and tools started in London, when we were working on our Masters' dissertation project entitled Adaptive Pneumatics. Adaptive Pneumatics was about devising a smart building system which used a lightweight inflatable structure with the capacity of adapting to its surrounding environment to provide comfort while minimising the need for electro-mechanical devices. The project seemed quite different at first, but soon it became apparent that in order to reach a reliable result we had

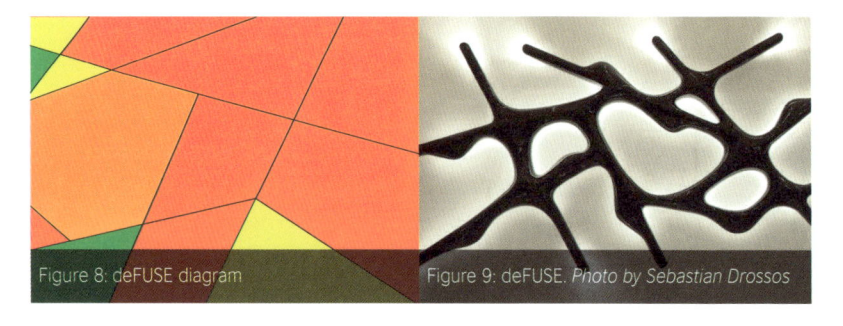

Figure 8: deFUSE diagram

Figure 9: deFUSE. *Photo by Sebastian Drossos*

to study successful precedents. We realised that the principals of environmental design remained the same, but we had to use new tools and materials to improve the outcome and find answers to some of the emerging challenges. We decided to look into some vernacular buildings that could provide a comfortable interior environment in extreme climatic conditions without using any additional and environmentally harmful devices. We selected the Borujerdis House in Kashan as a case study. Inside Borujerdis House it is 12 degrees cooler than outside without compromising the quality and aesthetics of its interior spaces. However, there were not many reliable resources available for us to base our research on. We had to analyse and understand the building ourselves and use its sustainable design strategies in our project which had no apparent connection to the historical precedents.

Figure 10. Borujerdis House   Figure 11: Borujerdis House

After our graduation in early 2009, events developed at a much faster pace. We worked on academic projects, joined a few offices in London to gain work experience on international projects and developed the foundation of our own practice in London.

Adaptive pneumatics won a competition and was awarded a grant by some of the leading UK design and engineering firms such as Arup to be developed further. We received expert advice, talked to fabricators and received funding to develop our ideas further. The prototype of the project became a part of the London Design Festival in 2009 and won the 2010 Sustainable Award across academic projects. This was our first international achievement and also the beginning of a long research project in relation to vernacular Iranian architecture.

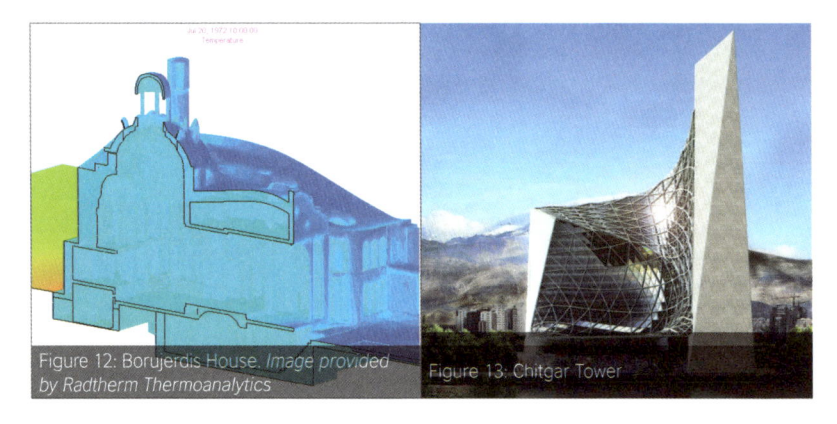

Figure 12: Borujerdis House. *Image provided by Radtherm Thermoanalytics*
Figure 13: Chitgar Tower

In parallel, we teamed up with Michael to guest edit an issue of *Architectural Design* (AD) entitled *Iran: Past, Present and Future*. The proposal and detailed agenda took around a year to be prepared. The first chapter aimed to raise the awareness of the role that vernacular Iranian architecture can play in the contemporary world, as well as creating a reference so that the knowledge which was gained could be used in future to create a better built environment. It included studies on historical Iranian buildings through a contemporary and analytical point of view. We picked seven carefully selected case studies and understood their underlying environmental principals. This research was significant for us, as it established a cross-cultural relationship between our colleagues in the UK and Iran. More than 30 people across borders collaborated with us to realise this project. They ranged from students, researchers and cultural organisations in Iran and the UK, including our colleagues in Foster and Partners, the AA, Isfahan University and cultural organisations.

In the final chapter *AD Iran* showcased the contemporary architectural works both by Iranian architects inside Iran (at home) and outside (the diaspora). It was the first time in 30 years that the architecture of Iran was being shown on such a scale. The magazine displayed the contemporary scene of Iran to the world and reminded Iranians of the importance of their heritage and architecture. Preparation of the magazine took two additional years and it was launched in the summer of 2012.

In 2009 we both started working in practices such as Foster and Partners and Plasma studio. During that period we worked on large-scale projects such as the Kuwait International Airport, the Apple Campus in California, Masdar Zero Carbon City and the

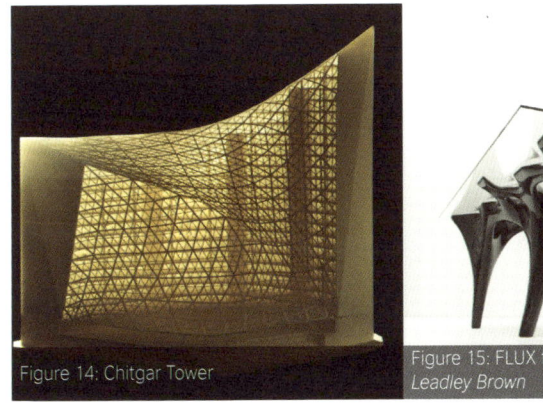

Figure 14: Chitgar Tower

Figure 15: FLUX table. *Photo by Angus Leadley Brown*

Xian Horticultural Centre in China, which is now one of the ten wonders of the world from above. It was at Foster and Partners that we were given the chance to work on some fantastic projects where culture and environment could play an important role shaping the buildings. I played a significant role in developing the concept and scheme proposal of Kuwait's future airport and Amin did the same for the Apple Campus proposal in California. At Foster and Partners we learnt how large and sustainable projects are developed in large teams and in close collaboration with the external and internal consultants. This experience was extremely valuable and later gave us the confidence to start our own practice in the UK.

It was around 2010 when we were approached by Archen, an Iranian architectural firm based in Tehran, to design a large scale commercial and office complex. The benefits of using pneumatics, the material system which we intensively explored in the AA, came to the forefront when we were designing the Chitgar complex. Its lightweight and highly differentiable geometrical capacity make the construction of a complex building, in a seismic zone, feasible. Its environmental potential to control solar gain

Figure 16: FLUX table. *Photo by Angus Leadley Brown*

Figure 17: GeMo. *Photo by Sebastian Drossos*

and insulation facilitated the creation of a climatic skin in Tehran. Our studies of vernacular buildings in Iran allowed us to use the principle of wind towers and stack effect for natural ventilation. All together, the on-going research projects that we learnt at the AA in London enabled us to propose a better-built environment for the inhabitants through innovative spatial conditions and geometries. The project's integrated approach in creating an environmentally friendly, programmatically effective, culturally responsible building helped us obtain a construction permit from the local authorities in Iran and the client, despite its apparent differences to the current dominant construction theme. The project is still under development and will hopefully become an active urban node once it is completed.

In August 2011 we established studio INTEGRATE based in Hackney in London and I became its first employee, later joined by Amin as soon as his residency was settled. Upon leaving Foster and Partners, I was invited to become a tutor at the AA for the same course that we had studied, the Emergent Technology and Design programme. We are now both teaching at the AA, in addition to running our studio. Going back to the AA was an opportunity to keep the research projects alive and bring the knowledge back to the studio.

Ever since, studio INTEGRATE has provided a platform for us from which we can lead architecture and design projects through research. Considering the human sense of beauty and comfort as the most crucial aspect of design, we try to synthesise spatial quality, material performance, and relationship of design with its context, culture and the environment.

The projects at our studio can be characterised as buildings, installations, product design, and academic workshops. These are all interrelated and informed from the overall interdisciplinary experimental agenda of our studio. Through product design and small-scale installations we are provided with the opportunity to test our ideas, realise them and receive feedback before applying them on buildings. In products and furniture, we aim to experiment with digital design and fabrication techniques and test different materials. This assists in the understanding of geometrical principals of historical art and architecture, enabling us to evolve them further.

Figure 18: GeMo. *Photo by Angus Leadley Brown*

The ability to put our own research findings into action through various projects and products is an exciting experience, as every project introduces unanticipated challenges. We often use mathematics to identify elegant and simple solutions for complex queries. As Iranian-born architects and designers, we are particularly interested in exploring the complexity of Middle Eastern art, architecture and culture by thoroughly understanding the underlying mathematical principals behind them. Islamic art and architecture, predominantly that of Iran, is largely characterised by complex geometries in patterns, ornaments and structures. Similar to the process of growth in nature, most of these patterns and geometries can be described as sets of instructions. These instructions can be interpreted as their DNA, whereby each of the steps as their Gene. Consequently, through changing the order of the genes, modifying the magnitude of their impacts or duplicating them to add extra layers of information, novel artefacts are discovered. We anticipate these artefacts to untap novel objects and spaces, which are simultaneously rooted culturally. Therefore to fulfil this task, our design method necessitates a shift within the conventional design paradigm and utilises contemporary modes of design and fabrication.

The FLUX table exemplifies a design piece that obtains its complex pattern and 3D form from a basic Islamic pattern. The strictly geometrical pattern at the surface fuses with the bottom layer through a series of multi-directional arches. The legs of the table emerge at the convergence points of the base pattern and stretch towards the outside to provide its balance. This leads to a novel and complex geometry that maintains its original roots. Starting from this point of departure, the final result leads to an unfamiliar and innovative artefact that can no longer be produced using conventional methods of production. This procedure proliferates the geometrical and cultural possibilities to those that presently exist. This practice is similar to the process of speciation in nature by which several different species emerge from the same ancestor over many generations.

GeMo (Genetically Modified) is the latest and perhaps most successful project that we have designed using a biological and mathematical method to evolve a traditional motif into novel artefacts. It is a mass customised series of vases that are generated using symmetrical multi-sided polygons, deriving from one of the fundamental components of Islamic art. The same geometries of existing typologies are used to create the form of each vase; however they are differentiated by the orders of combination and duplication. This method of formulated geometry retains its cultural roots, yet enables us to achieve novel geometric expressions. GeMo is realised by 3D printing techniques and embodies the potential of what 3D-printed fabrication is truly offering to contemporary design culture. This technique enables the creation of a wide range of over 500 variations to be 3D printed that are virtually impossible to be produced by any other techniques.

Through designing the GeMo series we are further familiarised with the 3D printing industry and have become further established in the world of designers and makers in the UK. After one of our the seminars regarding 3D printing we were invited to move our studio to Somerset House in London, one of the most vibrant art and culture organisations in the UK. Being based in such an environment has expanded our cultural activities and the possibilities of our journey. We have also recently reunited with our colleague and an old friend from our university in Iran, Amir Gholami, who has accomplished similar architectural and cultural activities. This year Amir started studio INTEGRATE in Sydney, hoping that we'll pursue our research and professional goals in Sydney along with the London studio.

The journey will continue and our London studio will remain as the heart of all of our activities. It is not yet clear how it will all unfold, but it has become increasingly evident that our bond with our culture has become much stronger along the way. At the beginning of our journey we asked the question: 'How can we design architecture and objects that are relevant in the world of today while staying rooted in our culture?' Ever since, we have been searching for the answer and we hope that our work will ultimately demonstrate the possibilities in the contemporary world of design by dipping deep into the pages of history.

Notes

Figure 1: Dolat Abad Garden
Located in Yazd-Iran and built around 1750AD, it is one of the tallest wind towers, with a height of 33m, which catches the wind above the trees and directs it into interior spaces.
Figure 2: CARPET image
The design proposal for the International World Carpet Trade Centre competition.
Figure 3: CARPET
Night View: the design proposal for the International World Carpet Trade Centre competition.
Figure 4: CARPET Diagram
The diagram of a derived geometry of facade, through the study of patterns and motifs.
Figure 5: Benetton Diagram
Penrose tiling has the capacity to fill a surface or space in an unlimited manner with three simple shapes.
Figure 6: Benetton Design 1
Design proposal for the headquarters of Benetton in Tehran.
Figure 7: Benetton Solar
The U-shaped central courtyard at the ground floor is open towards the street to create a public platform, rotating at the top floors to create self shading.
Figure 8: deFUSE diagram
The design evolved from creating a polygonal division pattern on a rectangular region. The borders of the divisions provide the skeleton of a porous volume that diffuses the light. While the branches distribute the light on a planar surface, the differentiated sizes of voids add a subtle dynamism to the effect, due to the changing levels of light intensity.
Figure 9: deFUSE
The design objective for the deFUSE light was to create a lighting piece that suffuses large areas with a combination of diffused and directional light. The polyurethane-coated and CNC-milled piece is lit with linear LED's spread across its top face.

Figure 10: Borujerdis House
Borujerdis House: Central court yard with pool to increase the humidity and decrease the temperature through its evaporative cooling effect.
Figure 11: Borujerdis House
A porous dome lets the warm air exhaust through the openings and lets the indirect sunlight penetrate into the space.
Figure 12: Borujerdis House
The solar load analysis shows the difference between the temperature inside and outside.
Figure 13: Chitgar Tower
Chitgar Tower: The environmental skin turns from the facade to shade the public platform at the ground floor.
Figure 14: Chitgar Tower
The architectural model of Chitgar Tower assists in understanding the geometry and structure of the facade.
Figure 15: FLUX table
The FLUX Table is the Golden A'Design Award Winner 2013–14. FLUX is an exploration of traditional Islamic art with contemporary modes of design and digital fabrication.
Figure 16: FLUX table
Flux's pattern is derived from a basic geometry, used in Iranian architecture. The end product is CNC polyurethane and hand finished.
Figure 17: GeMo
GeMo is a mass customised series of 3D-printed vases. The form of each vase in the series is generated using symmetrical multi-sided polygons, deriving from one of the fundamental components of Islamic art.
Figure 18: GeMo
GeMo 3D-printed in Resin.

Irregular Channels

LEYLA DAMAVANDI[*]
Leyla Damavandi is a filmmaker and academic who splits her time between living in Iran and the United States.

Introduction
Television has been popular in Iran since being introduced in 1958, when TVI (Television Iran) was established as a privately owned and commercially operated monopoly given and granted a concession of five years, repeated by a second. A southern branch of Television Iran, based in Abadan, was established in 1960. The National Television Network (NITV) was established in 1966, a separate entity, which catered for a more educated public than the light entertainment and dubbed American shows of TVI. TVI was nationalised in 1969, becoming a government monopoly. Full colour programming began broadcasting in Iran in 1978. After the 1979 Revolution the NIRT was renamed *Seda va Sima-ye Jomhouri-e Eslami-ye Iran* (Voice and Vision of the Islamic Republic of Iran), and known as the Islamic Republic of Iran Broadcasting (IRIB) in English.

Although satellite dishes are banned under a 1994 law, the research centre of the IRIB estimates that they're used by up to 70 per cent of Iranian households, exceeding the number believed to use the Internet. Despite the ban on satellite television, dishes dot many Iranian rooftops and people have access to dozens of Persian-language channels broadcasting a daily dose of politics and entertainment. Despite being repeatedly jammed, the BBC Persian channel had a weekly audience of 7.2 million in 2011.

*pseudonym

In October, the EU called on Tehran 'to lift restrictions on communications, including internet censorship, and put an immediate end to jamming of satellite broadcasting'.

In the following, Leyla Damavandi imagines a scenario in which the IRIB comes to terms with the influence of Manoto TV, the popular satellite channel which broadcasts from London into Iran, in its own particular way.

'We have to change the way we present the news. We're losing audiences,' Amin Ezzati, known only as Mr Ezzati in the office, said emphatically, tapping his index finger on the wooden table in the conference room. Ali, his back plastered with sweat to the plastic-covered chair, sat with eyes cast down, staring intently at the steam that rose up from the cups of tea clustered in the centre of the table. It was July and the heat poured through the windows despite the blasting air conditioning. He silently debated whether he should offer up his suggestion about how to change their news programme in order to regain audiences. A good 15 years younger than the other five people in the room, Ali was hesitant about rocking the boat. Though he felt more secure in his position than before, having now worked for two years at the state broadcasting service, he was constantly aware that there were many others waiting to take his job.

'Our youth watch our programme, Mr Ezzati. We're not losing audiences,' the predictable Mr Shirazi chimed in. The eldest in the room by far, Shirazi, who had worked in broadcasting for 25 years, still sounded absurd in all the meetings. Ali dug his knuckles into his left cheek, and willed his eyes to stare even more intently at the tea. He always had to try so hard not to show a reaction when Mr Shirazi spoke. Though none of them actually respected Shirazi, he was a lifelong bureaucrat who they could not get rid of and they had to cater to.

'Mr Shirazi,' Mr Ezzati calmly responded, 'Of course we still have an audience, but the number of viewers who respond to our surveys during the show with text messages has dwindled. Just last week the boys on set had to invent the audience messages themselves so it would look like we were getting responses.'

The meeting dragged on as usual and it was decided at the end that they would add more colour to the set, put a more 'joyful' introductory song to the show, and try faster editing whenever possible to make the show feel more dynamic. As if that could make up for poor content and boring anchors. Ali went to his desk, deflated. None of that would increases audiences, and they all knew it.

Reza walked up to Ali's desk, leaning in: 'Give them your suggestion, Ali. They'll listen. They will have to eventually.' Ali looked into Reza's encouraging face. He just needed to speak his mind, he knew that. His eyes fell to the picture of Reyhaneh, his two-year-old daughter, framed on his desk in her pink birthday dress. His wife, Amineh, had stopped working when Reyhaneh was born and they lived on his salary alone. His parents were middle class, retired teachers from Bushehr, which meant they had no money to help cushion Ali and his family. And Amineh's parents had two younger daughters to worry about. Plus, her father had helped enough in getting him this job at the broadcasting service. Without his father-in-law to vouch for him, Ali did not have the right connections to get this state job.

So who was he to all of a sudden suggest they start modelling their show after the 'News Room' on Manoto's station, aired via illegal satellite from Britain? Did he really want to be the one to say publicly what he knew they all thought privately: that the satellite opposition news stations from London were stealing their audiences because they had higher production values and fresher insights?

Reza was always the one telling Ali to relax, to not be so afraid at work to ruffle feathers. Reza and the other young guys at the station had a confidence about them that came through their privilege. As the son of the deputy director at the station, Reza's position was secure and he could more easily speak his mind and get away with pushing the envelope. Ali knew just as well as Reza that the directors of the broadcasting network wanted change and knew all the problems with state television. He had sat in on meetings where the station directors aired their frustrations and it sounded exactly like the conversations Ali had with his own friends after work: the shows were dry; the sets were horrendous; the anchors too stiff on camera; the topics too safe. He walked past his directors' desks at work, their attention turned to the opposition websites from outside the country for news from Iran that they themselves could not report.

'They'll like your idea, trust me,' Reza said to him as he walked back to the editing room with his signature slow gait. Ali pulled up the proposal he had been working on the past few months. He had run his ideas by his university classmates who now worked in small production houses throughout Tehran. Ali trusted their opinion and he didn't want to lose their respect. He knew that his former classmates thought of him as a sell-out when he decided to join the news team at the Islamic Republic of Iran Broadcasting. But he had no choice, as far as he saw it. His classmates' families could afford to support them as they worked as independent filmmakers and they all seemed to have connections abroad to get their films into festivals. Ali had no family outside of Iran and besides the work trips he'd taken to Lebanon to shoot a short documentary for the station, he'd never travelled internationally. It was quite literally a foreign world to him and he didn't know how to navigate it. His university classmates, on the other hand, spoke as if getting their work recognised abroad was almost easier for them than navigating the media industry in Iran.

He would visit his friends at least once a month in their studios. They loved his idea, though they were sceptical that Ali would get it approved. But this was exactly the crowd that his television programme wanted to attract: young urbanites. Ali knew that if his station actually took this idea seriously and developed it, they could make a dent and gain more viewers.

Ever since Manoto Television started broadcasting on satellite from London in 2010, the students at the arts universities in Iran were hooked. The production values of the shows were high, the topics interesting, and great serials, like Downton Abbey, were professionally dubbed in Persian. In fact, Downton had won many fans for its particularly British charm. Manoto wasn't overtly political and it actually carried quality programming, unlike the stations broadcast from Los Angeles, that looked worse than those broadcast by the state in Iran, stuck in the 1980s. Above all, to have quality programming that was of international standards broadcast in Persian was a blessing for Ali and his university buddies, who although they understood English, found it easier to watch and pay attention to the editing and storytelling if the programme was in Persian.

The show that caught everyone's attention was the station's 'News Room', a clever 30-minute news programme run by five journalists the same age as Ali and his friends. It was refreshing to see such young faces on camera speaking seriously about news and breaking all the traditional format rules about how to present news. Plus, it didn't hurt that they are all good-looking with good taste in clothes – the accessories that the female anchors wore became all the range in Tehran the following day.

On the programme, the 'anchor' stands in the room and asks

each of the journalists to speak about a pressing issue of news in Iran. The other journalists sit in cubicles with large touch-screen computers in front of them. They address the report to the anchor and air their packages about the issue at hand. They call each other by their first names, a practice unheard of on Iranian news media, where formality is the rule.

Ali's idea was to create a state version of 'News Room', with young journalists in front of the camera and a more informal atmosphere. He knew they still wouldn't be able to create packages about taboo subjects but at least they could provide a quality news show that would retain audiences. All his younger work colleagues loved the idea, but Ali wasn't sure his bosses would approve of this copycat show of a much-maligned satellite station.

It didn't matter. The idea had wormed its way into his brain and devoured all other thoughts. He could not shake it. It wouldn't leave him, this idea that could cost him his job.

After one more week of sitting in pointless meetings, Ali made the decision to propose the idea, come what may. Not wanting to put the presentation together at work, he made an excuse that he had to do research for a new segment, and left for the afternoon. He travelled downtown to the part of the city he felt the most comfortable: Revolution Square, home to the University of Tehran and the plethora of bookstores and computer stores that surrounded it. He felt invisible in that part of town, but invisible with a purpose. It wasn't the feeling of being lost and angry that he felt in other parts of the city. Here, he felt like he had worth, like he could return to the person he used to be, the person who had dreams of making a difference with his art. I guess, he thought, this is what most people feel when they leave university and enter the workforce. Everything changes so drastically. The things you thought you'd do are so different from where you end up. At least that was the way it was for him. And so, when he desired that return to purpose, he came back downtown. In those crazy busy streets with fliers advertising tutoring classes for university entrance exams strewn on the sidewalk, the relentless pollution ceased to bother Ali. The bookstores lined the street, the stores empty, but the windows enticing those who cared to take a look. It was here that he needed to come to get into the mode of making his presentation. He walked into the internet cafe he had used all those years while at the university. The damp smell of the basement room with its old rolling chairs hadn't changed. He gave the owner a familiar handshake. 'I thought you were done being a student!' he said to Ali with a laugh, 'It's good to see you, buddy.'

With his thumb drive in, Ali pulled up his proposal. He read it over four times before deciding to print it. He'd already proofread it and edited at least 20 times, but he just had to make sure the wording was right: not too critical, not too pushy. Just enough flattery.

He had decided if he was going to do this, he'd do it right. He had created a PowerPoint presentation to give to his bosses, outlining exactly how the show would work. He printed out ten copies of his presentation, bound everything, and he was ready to go.

The next morning, Ali arrived early to work and set out his bounded presentations at each seat in the conference room. He asked Hossein, the tea-bearer of the office, to bring sweets and fruit into the room and to set it all up nicely in the centre of the table.

'You've already gotten married, Ali. What other exciting news do you have to tell us that you've gone to all this trouble?' Mr Ezzati asked delightedly as he walked into the room. 'He must have gotten a new car, and wants to treat us all,' Mr Shirazi chimed in, his round belly moving up and down as he laughed to himself. Ali hated the sight of that belly and he cringed at the sound of Shirazi's laugh. But today he laughed back.

With everyone finally in the room, Ali began: 'We all know that although our show remains the most popular news show on television, we're losing younger audiences. I know how hard we all work and how capable everyone in this office is, and that's why, with the help of many friends here, I've been wracking my brain trying to think of a humble solution that could potentially help us.' He opened his PowerPoint and the projection light came on.

'Unfortunately, our youth are being tricked by all of this Western media coming through satellite stations and the internet, and they think what they see on these stations is somehow better than what we have to offer them. We have to show them that we can be cutting edge and joyful, just like those stations. But instead of lying to them, like the satellite stations do, we can offer them good news. But we need to tweak our format a bit.' Ali couldn't believe he was saying these words out loud. He sounded like a real state bureaucrat. Shirazi looked at him with one eyebrow raised, his face contracted and dour. Ali directed his gaze to the screen, took a deep breath, and continued. 'A few colleagues and I have surveyed young people in Tehran, and what they're watching for news are all those programmes beamed into the country. The most popular is Manoto's 'News Room'. I propose that we create our own 'News Room' to appeal to those young viewers.'

'You want us to copy those liars and traitors?' Shirazi leaned into the table, raising his voice.

'Give him a chance,' Ezzati replied, pulling Shirazi back in his chair. He gave Ali an encouraging look, and nodded for him to continue.

Ali outlined what the new show would be like, how they would produce it, what he imagined for the set design, and who the anchors could be. 'I like the idea very much,' Ezzati chimed in, once Ali had finished. Shirazi scowled at him. 'We take what is so popular with our youth, but we infuse it with the truth, with the good news,' Ezzati said directly to Shirazi. 'What could be so wrong with that?'

Ali took a breath. At least one of the elders in the room was for his idea. Much to his surprise, his bosses, save for Shirazi, did not debate the issue for too long. They all acknowledged that Manoto's 'News Room' was popular – 'my kids even watch it', one of the bosses said, 'I hear the programme from the other room,' was his explanation for knowing all the details of how the show ran. Although Ali hadn't expected the discussion to go so well, he knew what his younger co-workers had told him all along, that all of their bosses watched these very same satellite stations that they publicly railed against. And they secretly enjoyed them. They all just had to act as if they didn't. That's just the way it was. Acting 'as if' all the time.

'Let's see a mock up for the show,' Ezzati said to Ali as the meeting ended, 'and we'll go from there.'

Overjoyed, Ali stayed at the office every day until nearly 10pm. For the first time in his life, he was motivated to work. This was his idea and it had been validated. And, what's more, there was the possibility of creating something new on television and pushing the boundaries even a tiny bit more.

Ali worked for three weeks on the mock-up for the show. He convinced three of his young colleagues to stand in as anchors and he focused the show on three news items: Iran's nuclear negotiations with the Western powers; the controversy over mismanagement and cronyism in Iran's National Football Team which was about to head to Brazil for the World Cup; and pollution issues in the capital, which posed alarming levels of danger to citizens. Though he wanted to present more of the social issues that made Manoto popular, he knew he had to take small steps and not alarm the likes of Shirazi. Instead, these three news items allowed him to tangentially touch upon the way the conservatives attacked the pragmatic president, corruption in high places, the unwieldy mismanagement of resources, the effect of Western sanctions on the country, and the unaccountability of officials when it came to poor decision-making.

Like artists who were preparing for their opening night on the large stage, Ali and his colleagues worked through the butterflies in their stomachs. They had never worked with such guts and passion. They paid attention to every detail, from the dress of the anchors, to set design, to the graphics of the show. They wanted to communicate freshness and sophistication. This was no longer about getting through the day to take the paycheque home.

When they finally presented the show at the end of the month to their bosses, even Shirazi was impressed. They could tell because he stayed silent and had no rebuttal, a first in the years that Ali had been at the broadcasting service. It was agreed that the show would air by the new year, and that they would have to do some sort of audience testing by asking viewers to text in their votes on certain questions. That was the only way they could gauge how many viewers the show had.

As the winter drew to a close, the blossoms came out in Tehran, and the New Year was upon them, Ali decided to send his wife and daughter alone to Bushehr to visit his family. He stayed back through the holidays to put the finishing touches to the show. When the show finally aired three weeks later, Iran's vibrant blogosphere and social media sites lit up with criticism that although the show attempted to bring a fresh perspective, without an ability to broach more political issues, it was ultimately just more of the same.

Ali ignored the criticism. He just kept working from week to week to ensure that the show would go on. He knew, just like anything else that attempted to exist officially in Iran, that he had to proceed slowly. He continued to work tirelessly on the show, as the summer months beat down on Iran with their oppressive heat. The show continued through the autumn, the heat relentlessly pulling back and allowing people to finally breathe again. All the while, Ali continued, week by week, to put the show on. This was enough of a victory for now.

Working together through language

Bridge or Wall? English Language in Iran

MARYAM BORJIAN
Dr Maryam Borjian is Assistant Professor and Director of Language Programs in the Department of African, Middle Eastern and South Asian Languages and Literatures at Rutgers, the State University of New Jersey. She is the author of *English in Post-Revolutionary Iran, Indigenisation to Internationalisation*.

> We shall one day learn to supersede politics by education. – Ralph Waldo Emerson

Introduction

Languages can serve as a bridge to build peace between and among nations, against the backdrop of today's world filled with unhealthy tensions. Ngũgĩ wa Thiong'o (2012), the Kenyan-American scholar and a focal supporter of linguistic justice, draws upon the metaphor of 'wall vs. bridge' to argue that languages can serve as a conduit to promote peace. In his view, a wall is a barrier that blocks contacts and exchange, like the wall of elitism that has been built by the many dominant languages, English in particular, all over the world. But language can equally serve as a bridge to cross the gulf. Such bridges facilitate two-way traffic, allowing transitions, crossing, and continuities between and among nations.

Using Ngugi's analogy as a point of departure, I will examine the place of English in post-revolutionary Iran, in which English has served both as a bridge and as a wall, but mostly the latter due to many reasons including an uneven economic and political power relationship between Iran and its English speaking counterparts in the West, US and the UK foreign policy towards Iran, and the enormous desire on the part of Iranian politicians to combat the global domination of Anglo-American language and culture. These factors have contributed to the formation of a wall of isolation around Iran, with actions and attitudes on both sides preventing a two-way exchange and transition of ideas since the 1979 Islamic Revolution.

Following a brief historical account of English in Iran, this chapter looks at the unique position of English in post-revolutionary Iran. Unlike most nations that equate English with economic growth and prosperity, and thus, enthusiastically borrow English-language teaching (ELT) norms, models, and practices from the English-speaking West, Iran has turned its back on the Western world to resist the global domination of Anglo-American cultural and linguistic norms. In spite of thirty years' resistance, English education in today's Iran is marked by two diverging and seemingly incompatible models: the indigenised or culturally – and ideologically – adapted English vs. the international or Anglo-Americanised English. This paper reflects on the who, what, how and why of the two models since 1979, reflecting its strengths and shortcomings, with recommendations and a conclusion.[1]

The past

English first entered Iran in the 19th century, when Christian missionaries of various denominations (often in a stiff competition with one another) invested new-found interest. Iran was nominally a sovereign nation; as such, unlike in the colonies, the power of missionaries was limited as they had to seek permission for their operations from the local authorities. In addition, they had to learn how to peacefully co-exist with other rival religious denominations, as a verdict issued in 1841 by Mohammad Shah Qajar welcomed Christian missionaries from all denominations and nationalities to open schools in Iran as a means to modernise education.[2] As a result, from the 1840s scores of foreign missionary schools were founded, including those of the French Lazarist Catholics, British Angelicas, American Presbyterians, and to a lesser extent, German Protestants.

Among these denominations, American and the British missionaries (close allies, and rivals of the French Lazarists) promoted the English language alongside their religious practices and medical activities. Dividing Iran into two spheres of interest, American missionaries were active in the northern sphere and held the cities of Tabriz, Hamadan, Kermanshah, Qazvin, Rasht, and Mashhad, whereas the British were active in the southern sphere and held the cities of Isfahan, Yazd, Kerman, and Shiraz. Tehran, the capital, occupied a central position between the two missionary allies. American and British missionary schools are credited for introducing more modern educational initiatives, including literacy both in English and local languages – first to Iranian Christians, Armenians, and Assyrians, and later to the country's Muslim population, especially women.[3] However, the missionaries are equally criticised for converting Iranian Armenians and Assyrians to their own version of Christianity and for having less-than-altruistic motives (economic, political, and religious) for offering education to the Muslim population;[4] thus, English was used as both a bridge and as a wall. American and British educational establishments attained a positive reputation among the general Iranian population and government officials, and some children from the royal family attended these schools. However, it was French that enjoyed the position of the primary foreign language in the country's modern schools and among the country's intellectuals. This could be attributed to the global status of French worldwide during that period, as well as the more neutral role of the Imperial France (unlike its British and Russian counterparts) in Iran's internal and external affairs.[5]

Following the foundation of the Pahlavi dynasty in 1925, progressive steps were taken towards establishing a modern nation. Among many initiatives, the government was able to establish a national, tuition-free, and modern education system at primary-school level in urban areas; thus, European missionaries were asked to turn over their schools to the newly established Ministry of Education. By 1940, all missionaries had left the country, being compensated for their financial losses.

It did not take long for the UK and USA to re-establish themselves in Iran through alternative organisations, including the British Council, the Iran-America Society, and many other aid supported initiatives. After World War II, the internal and external circumstances contributed greatly to the rise of English and its sustainability in Iran's education system, with Iran's economic, military, industrial and educational ties with the West during the Cold War helping the process. The educational reform of Iran in the 1950s and 1960s, the ample financial and technical support from the US, and the presence of thousands of American and British experts, laid the foundations for the rise of the English language. From the early 1950s English began to replace French as the first foreign language in the country's education system, and by the early 1970s French had entirely lost its status in comparison to English. English was dominant (the first foreign language), but this domination was perceived as an unequal, one-way flow of ideas from the English speaking West to Iran (thereby as a wall) by the revolutionary leaders, who came to blame the Pahlavis for the country's excessive modernisation and Westernisation. However, what was not taken into account was the fact that Pahlavis equally promoted Persian language and culture in the West (thus, using language as a bridge). The Islamic Revolution of 1979 in Iran eventually put an end not only to the country's monarchy but also to the UK and USA's formal educational operations in Iran following the country's Islamic Revolution of 1979.[6]

The present

Under the Islamic Republic (1979–present), English has continued to enjoy the status of first foreign language within the successive national curricula. However, it is marked by two diverging models: 1, the indigenised English that is used in state-run education programs; and 2, the Anglo-Americanised English that is used by private-run education programs. Although the two models co-exist, the latter model is most popular among Iranian learners. The account provided below reflects on the who, what, how, and why of the two models.

Indigenised English

Indigenised English is a product of the indigenisation movement that began after Iran's 1979 Revolution, which put an end to the country's monarchy and replaced it with an Islamic Republic or the governance of religious jurisprudence (velāyat-e faqih).[7] At the time, the country's ideo-political horizon was dominated by third-worldism, anti-imperialism, and anti-Western sentiments. Driven by the uncontested power of religion and bent upon an Islamic state, the country's new leaders were no longer interested in implementing the Westernised version of modernity and development. The goal was rather to craft a homegrown model of development free from the influence of the West (capitalism) and the East (socialism) – in the words of the grand revolutionary motto of the time, it was to be an 'Islamic Republic,' 'self-sufficient' (*kod-kafā*) from the West and the East (*na sharqi, na gharbi*).

The drive towards 'indigenisation' became a policy as soon as the newly established government undertook its Cultural Revolution (1980–82), in which the two underlying pillars of 'Islamisation' and 'purification' regulated and institutionalised the newly constructed discourse of indigenisation.[8] Within such a climate, the attitude towards foreign languages was profoundly negative. Foreign languages (which effectively meant European languages), were treated as 'suspicious subject matters' and tools used by the imperial powers to practice their cultural imperialism. Among foreign languages, English was most disfavored as it was closely associated with the United States of America (referred to as the 'Great Satan') and its closest ally, the United Kingdom. Instead, emphasis was placed on Esperanto and Arabic, arguably because the former did not belong to any particular European nation, and the latter was the language of Islam. Although positive attitudes towards Esperanto did not last long, Arabic was praised as a medium of communication among Muslims with different linguistic backgrounds.[9]

Although Arabic still enjoys the 2nd foreign language position in Iran's school curriculum, it is English that holds the primary position. The revolutionary leaders were quick to recognise the importance of English as an international language. In one of his speeches, Ayatollah Khomeini emphasised the importance of learning foreign languages as a means to achieve scientific growth and self-sufficiency, as well as to export the message of the revolution to the outside world. As such, English remained in Iran's education system,[10] but it was heavily modified to fit the newly constructed discourse of the nation.[11]

Field Picture 1   Field Picture 2

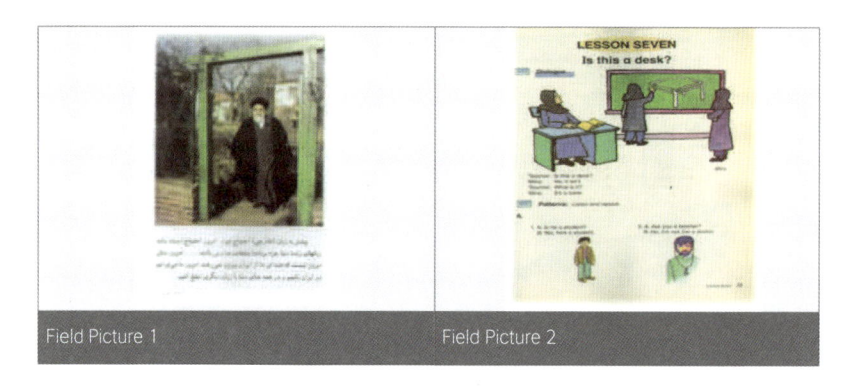

In attempting to expel foreign cultural values and elements from English, Iran followed in the footsteps of earlier post-revolutionary nations (the Soviet Union, Cuba, and China) who tried to eliminate all variables associated with the cultural imperialism of the English speaking West. Thus, in Iran, all foreign language schools were shut down, including those belonging to the British Council and the Iran-America Society, the most active centers of English language teaching in pre-revolutionary Iran.[12] Moreover, all foreign teachers and professors were expelled from the country. In the absence of exogenous forces or official representatives from the core English speaking nations, the government took charge of Iran's English education. Soon, a state publishing house – the Organisation for Researching and Composing University Textbooks in the Humanities, better known by its acronym, SAMT – was established to produce indigenised, homegrown textbooks for local use.[13]

An indigenised curriculum and textbooks were needed as English materials of the pre-revolutionary era were Anglo-American in content, and a site of interaction between English 'native speakers' and 'non-native speakers': between 'Muslim' Iranian speakers of Persian, who were said to have been alienated from their 'true' past, and their Christian American or British counterparts, and native speakers of English, whose names were often 'Jack,' 'Joe,' 'John,' 'Mary,' 'Catherine,' or 'Elisabeth' in pre-revolutionary school textbooks. Such a site of interaction had to be revisited and appropriated, and thus, it was targeted for indigenisation or 'liberalisation' from the 'unwanted' foreign elements. Some aspects of English were selectively accepted (phonology, morphology and syntax), whereas the cultural elements of the language were all removed for fears of being a threat to the nation's 'tradition.' As a result, Jack, Joe, John, Mary, Catherine and Elisabeth all disappeared from school English textbooks and were replaced by new characters whose names were Mohamed, Ali, Fatima, etc., all pious Muslims who dressed modestly, visited mosques regularly, and read the Koran daily. They had one goal in common: to learn English only to empower the nation in its new stage of bottom-up, localised, indigenised development. A new form of English was born; a form that many of my research participants, notably Iranian English professors and teachers, regarded as a 'flat, lifeless, and context-free language,' which has been taught to generations of school children via the state's approved homegrown English textbooks ever since.

Today, despite a dramatic change of attitude towards English on the part of the country's politicians (discussed further below), indigenised English still exists and is being used and taught in all formal school settings.[14]

Field Picture 3

Anglo-Americanised English

This model of English was the product of policies implemented in Iran during the presidencies of Ali Akbar Hashemi Rafsanjani (1989–1997) and Mohammad Khatami (1997–2005). Faced with a war-ravaged country (after the Iran-Iraq War, 1980–88), the administration of Rafsanjani was the first to suggest that Iran had to abandon some of its early revolutionary promises and accept technocratic solutions to domestic problems – in order, it was hoped, to support the rebuilding of the nation, stimulate Iran's ailing economy, and train a qualified labor force to meet the needs of the country's economy. Both Presidents advocated opening up towards the international community and exchanging antagonistic attitudes towards the West with more moderate ones: President Khatami, called for 'moderation and tolerance' at home and a 'dialogue of civilizations' on the international scene.

One of the many outcomes of this re-orientation was the arrival of international organisations that offered their technical and financial assistance to help Iran with its macro-economic planning. In addition to the opening of various United Nations agencies (UNDP, UNICEF, UNFPA, UNODC, and UNESCO), the World Bank resumed its loan lending to Iran between 1991 and 1993, and then from 1997 onward. In return for receiving loans, Iran was compelled to implement the World Bank's 'structural adjustment policy,' a neoliberal economic policy that favors privatisation and decentralisation of state-run agencies, reduces the presence of government and government subsidies, and transfers ownership from the public sector to private sector.[15]

This led to a push towards school privatisation in Iran. It was a controversial policy for a country whose leaders had claimed unconditional support for the deprived and dispossessed (*mostaz'afin*). However, rapid growth in the school-age population throughout the 1980s due to the abandoning of pre-revolutionary family planning laws had created a demand for education that could not be met solely by state-run schools. While the school curriculum and textbooks (at K-16 levels) remained largely indigenised, privatisation led to multiple, decentralised curricula in private language institutes.

In the 1990s private English language institutes were established on an unprecedented nationwide scale, targeting fee-paying students across all ages and proficiency levels. These institutes were allowed to offer their own curriculum and textbooks, while following the government's broader rules and regulations. This has resulted in the private sector participating in the educational decision making process, albeit indirectly and on a limited scale.

To attract students, the private sector looked abroad in order to emulate promising English language teaching models and practices. The result was the importation of English-teaching methodologies (including Communicative Language Teaching, or CLT), and textbooks (e.g. *Headway* and *Interchange* among many others) and audio-visual products from various English-speaking nations, and from the UK in particular. This process was accelerated by Iran's failure to observe international copyright law for works (books and audio-visual products) published abroad. Accordingly, 'Jack,' 'Joe' and 'Mary' and 'Elizabeth' returned to the English textbooks of private language institutes with minimum modification of content.[16]

Another strategy used by the private language institutes to attract fee-paying students is to advertise themselves as a representative of foreign universities, primarily British ones. Such claims could be either real or phony, and it is sometimes difficult to distinguish between the two. All these factors have greatly contributed to the popularity of private English language institutes, particularly those who desire to be part of the international community, and particularly among the 55%

of the population who are below the age of thirty. At the same time, indigenised textbooks and curricula have fallen out of favour, because they are seen to promote little more than reading and grammatical skills.

The size of the English language teaching market in Iran at present is difficult to estimate in the absence of official statistics. However, given that the international examinations market alone in Iran is worth over £4m annually, and that some private language schools have over 150,000 students, it is safe to estimate that the total market size must be well in excess of £25m, if not much more.

Table 1: pirated books published by a local publisher, 2007–2008

Book Themes	# of books	Book Themes	# of books
English, Children's Education	152	English, Grammar	59
English, Adult Education	96	Teaching English and Linguistics	54
English, Listening	16	English, Vocabulary	36
English, Conversation	18	English, Comprehension	20
English, Illustrated Dictionaries	12	English, IELTS	42
English, Dictionaries	32	English, TOEFL	18
English, Slang and idioms	22	French	19
English, Writing skills	29	German	10
English, Testing	6	Turkish & Russian	8
English, Reading	44	English Language Stories	480
Total: 1173			

Source: Catalogue of X Publications 2007–2008.

Pirated textbooks also give us an insight into the English language teaching market, and the data presented above reveals several interesting facts about English teaching and learning in Iran. First, contrary to the isolation strategy of the country's politicians (or perhaps because of it), there is a high demand for learning about the culture (and cultural icons) of English speaking nations. Out of 1173 books pirated by the above publisher in 2007–2008, 480 were English fiction, of which only 59 were from America, with the remainder from the UK. The majority of these narratives were about Western icons like Leonardo DiCaprio, Michael Jordan, Tom Cruise, Julia Roberts, Bill Gates, Princess Diana, and Mr. Bean. British books have become the primary source of emulation for Iranian publishers. Also, although English continues to be absent from primary school curricula, there is a high demand for English at pre-school and primary-school levels (152 titles) which suggests that parents perceive an importance of learning English for their children. Finally, the data also reveals a high demand for academic books, most particularly in the fields of teaching English and applied linguistics (54 titles).

The data could also be seen to reflect indirectly the country's high rate of brain drain, as seen in the 42 titles on IELTS (International English Language Testing System), an exam required for migration to English language speaking countries such as the UK, USA, Canada, New Zealand, and Australia. According to a report by the International Monetary Fund, Iran ranks among the worst affected by loss of talent through migration among developing countries, with an annual estimate of 150,000 migrants (200,000 according to the Islamic Republic's official statistics).[17] Thus again, language can be seen as a bridge to other nations for aspirational Iranians, although a bridge with long term negative consequences for the country.

Field Picture 4

Although the private sector in Iran pioneered the introduction of Anglo-American English to Iran, it would be misleading to assume that the government of Iran was against it. Between 1997 and 2005 under the Presidency of Mohamad Khatami, a moderate-pragmatic clerical figure, English took a new role in Iran, and was perceived as the key language for scientific and economic growth. It entered the country's policy documents when the government pledged to improve the quality of school curricula and textbooks in the areas of mathematics, science, and English language – though such aspiration mostly remained at the policy discourse level as illustrated here:

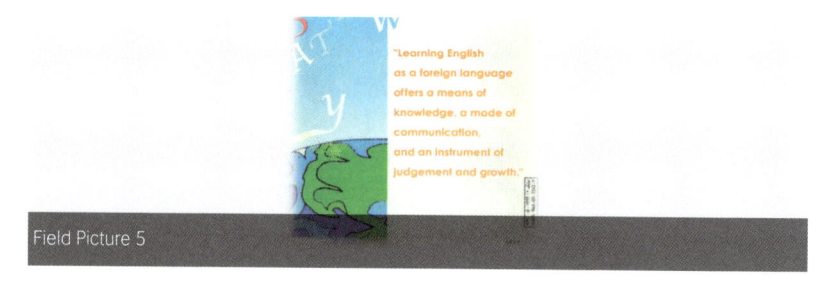

Field Picture 5

In 2001 the government of Iran sent a somewhat surprising invitation to the British Council to resume its operations in the country after a hiatus of two decades or so. Although the Council was prohibited from offering English language courses, between 2001 and 2009 it collaborated with Iranian government agencies and departments in various arenas, including English Language teaching (training language teachers and offering workshops), professional networking, scholarships, arts and higher education.[18]

During the Presidency of Mahmoud Ahmadinejad (2005–2013), the Iranian government became less trustful of the outside world and implemented policies to minimise the influence of exogenous forces. One such a policy was the closure of the British Council. In December 2006, Iran's Ministry of Intelligence accused the British Council of conducting 'unauthorised' social, cultural, and educational activities in the country. The accusation was soon followed by an official order from the Ministry of Intelligence prohibiting all state-run organisations, ministries and universities, from collaboration with the British Council. By July 2007, the website of the Council was blocked, and its IELTS Exam Center was shut down. The Council was prohibited from organising public events such as workshops and conferences, and a kiosk was placed by the Ministry of Intelligence outside the Council's offices to monitor visitors, and to prevent the entrance of more than two persons.[19] On January 31st, 2009, the Council was instructed to suspend all its activities in Iran. Local staff were laid off, and the following note was posted on the website of the British Council Iran:

With regret, we have had to suspend all our operations in Iran, effective 31 January 2009. Our hope is that we will be able to secure the agreement of the Iranian Authorities to allow us to resume as soon as possible education and cultural programmes between Iran and the United Kingdom for the benefit of the peoples of both countries.

Under the Ahmadinejad Presidency the Iranian government was not in favor of collaboration with the West, but it would be too simplistic to assume that politicians were fully opposed to English. It was during this phase that English was allowed to be used as the medium of instruction (rather than a subject matter) in selected universities (a policy that was approved at the policy discourse level but has not been implemented).[20] It was also during this phase that a high score in an international English test, such as TOEFL and IELTS, became a prerequisite for university entrance in various fields (including sciences, medicine, and engineering) at the graduate level.[21] In addition, pressure on professors and doctoral students to publish English articles in international journals has increased given that it is now a condition for graduation and promotion. Since late 2007, clerical figures have been appearing on state-run television to stress the importance of learning English for the nation, equating the mastery of English with an Islamic Jihad.[22] Last but not least, it was during this period that Iran's state-run TV began to broadcast programs aimed at teaching American and British English.[23]

Under the more moderate-pragmatic administration of President Hassan Rouhani (2013–present), English continues in a position of strength in Iran. One illustration of this is the following certificate, issued for an Iranian medical student who presented a paper in an international medical conference held in Tehran in May 2014. Although the paper

Certificate of Presentation
This is to certify that
Mr. XX XXX
Presented the article entitled
XXXXXXXXXXXXXXXXXXXXXXXXX
In the 12th International Congress of Immunology & Allergy (ICIA)
Tehran-Iran
April 29–May 2, 2014

Source. Fieldwork data, Iran, Summer 2014

was presented in Persian and the conference was bilingual (Persian-English), the issued certificate is monolingual (English) – reflecting a increasingly common practice across academic fields.

The Ministry of Education has launched a new English language curriculum and textbook for the current academic year, and while it is too soon to assess the impact of these reforms, the first indications are that the curriculum is much more learner-centred, that the pedagogy is more modern, and that the materials represent an improvement on past models.[24]

Although it is beyond the scope of this paper to detail and analyse, the internet and mobile technology have also had a major impact on English language teaching and learning in Iran. Internet-based learning is growing in popularity, and the potential for mobile learning is great – Iran has almost 100m mobile phone accounts, 25m more than the UK (with similar population sizes), and more than one per head of population. Iran was among the top 5 countries in the world for downloads of English language teaching applications for mobile phones in 2011–12. There are a great many risks and opportunities involved in these developments, with the potential for English and technology to act again as both a bridge and wall in some respects. Research is ongoing, and will be highly instructive.[25]

The result of these complex and frequent ebbs and flows with regards to English education in Iran is that indigenised English and Anglo-Americanised English co-exist in today's Iran. Apart from international organisations and the private sector, which are often credited (or blamed) for the promotion of the latter model in Iran, the Iranian government should equally be credited for playing a key role in promoting Anglo-Americanised English in Iran. This has been done via the implementation of many cross-sectorial policies, such as structural adjustment and education reforms, whose intended and unintended outcomes included the promotion of English in Iran.

Current challenges

Iran's educational indicators demonstrate notable quantitative growth and improvement in English education. Since 1979, locally-produced English textbooks and materials have been produced in mass, counterweighing the smaller quantities of internationally-produced materials. Moreover, Iranian professors and teachers of English have been in charge of teaching English locally, counteracting the importation of foreign experts and specialists from core English speaking nations. But has this quantitative growth been matched with equally important qualitative growth? Despite its improvements, English education in Iran suffers from serious shortcomings; improvements are essential for producing a labor force that meets the needs of the country in the global economy.

Firstly, other than those who study English or its various sub-fields at university, the majority of Iranians lack proficiency in spoken English (both for academic and personal purposes). This is partly due to the absence of listening and speaking exercises in the indigenised textbooks and the official local English examinations. In addition, the courses offered at private language institutes offer proficiency in spoken English for personal purposes but not academic or vocational English. Furthermore, Iran remains somewhat isolated a nation, with only limited ties to the international community; few foreigners visit for tourism or investment in Iran due to many constraints including the difficulty in obtaining a visa and the country's economic instability and high rate of inflation. As such, Iran is a homogenous society, in which Iranians mostly see each other and use Persian in all formal and informal domains. Consequently, there is little need for Iranians to speak English and few opportunities to practice. As a result, those who study English on their own may eventually let go of their English proficiency, find a job locally, or leave the country permanently – most often the latter, judging by Iran's high rate of brain-drain.

Another challenge is the writing of academic articles in the English language. True, qualitative improvement requires Iranian scholars to close the gaps in knowledge between themselves and their transnational counterparts. Regardless of the politics of academic publishing in international journals (which have their own biases towards non-native English speakers) much research conducted in Iran deserves publication in peer-reviewed English journals, especially in the fields of medicine and science. Yet a majority of locally produced papers appear unqualified to meet this aim, partly due to a lack of training on the part of Iranian scholars and students in writing academic articles in English. Since publishing in international journals is, for example, a prerequisite for promotion to university professor, there are now many writing centers that produce academic English papers, books and even dissertations for anyone who can afford to pay a high fee – a practice that is not hidden from the public, but is rather quite legal and commonplace in Iran.

Another challenge concerns Iran's English teacher training programs, in which theory and practice are perceived as two separate entities. Whereas the former is the business of academicians, the latter is that of teachers. As a result, universities do not commit themselves seriously to the production of practical knowledge in training pre-service English teachers. For example, teacher training programs at graduate and undergraduate levels rarely offer a practicum course, in which student-teachers would have the opportunity to go directly into the classroom to teach English under the close supervision of their instructors. In order to have a balanced teacher training program, academic curricula should give more weight to practical courses as opposed to just learning the theories of second language acquisition.[26]

Another difficulty is the lack of student and teacher-exchange programs which might encourage Iranian students and teachers of English to put into use their knowledge of English by collaborating with their transnational counterparts. And last but not least, there is a pressing need to fundamentally revise the country's locally produced materials to go beyond grammar and reading skills to include all language skills especially listening, speaking, and writing to increase the country's competiveness in the global market economy. Other recommendations on this subject are proposed by Iranian professors of English in a three-volume work in English (Kiany & Khayyamdar, 2005–2006), which covers the first English for Specific and Academic Purposes Conference in Iran.

Conclusion

'Gone are the days when a wall could be built around the country. Today there are no more walls'.

This was the presidential campaign slogan of President Hassan Rouhani, through which he was elected by winning especially the vote of women and youth in 2013. This illustrates the clear desire on the part of Iranians to be part of the international community, as well as the aspiration on the part of the current administration to take the country out of its international isolation.

The re-thinking of the UK-Iran cultural relationship on the part of the British Council is a welcome attempt to rebuild a trust between the two nations that has repeatedly been shattered in modern times. Perceiving languages as a bridge could perhaps be a good start for both sides in rethinking their cultural relations, if both sides keenly aspire to build this linguistic bridge as a means to enable a two-way, mutual exchange of culture, ideas, and understanding.

Field Pictures

Field Picture (1). This quote by Ayatollah Khomeini decorates the first page of all Iranian locally-produced indigenised English textbooks. It reads: In the past, there was no need for learning a foreign language. Today, however, learning foreign languages should be included in school curricula... Today is not like yesterday, when our voice could not reach beyond the national boundary. Today, we can stay in Iran but advertise [our religion and export our revolution] to other parts of the world in different languages. (Author's translation).

Field Picture (2). A page from a homegrown English textbook for sixth grade, in which all the cultural aspects of English language have been removed. In addition to having Iranian names, the characters dress modestly, following the State-approved dress-code.

Field Picture (3). The picture illustrates a page from a modified version of a pirated British textbook (Headway by John & Liz Soars, 1996) that was used in Iran throughout the 1990s. The picture of the woman in the book was modified by the Ministry of Culture and Islamic Guidance to fit the Islamic dress code. This type of modification is no longer practiced in Iran and the illegally reproduced Anglo-American textbooks are used in their original versions.

Field Picture (4). Instances of signs used by Iranian private language institutes to illustrate their collaboration with foreign educational establishments.

Field Picture (5). The cover of an indigenised English Textbook for Sixth Grade, produced by the Iranian Ministry of Education, 2003, illustrating English's role since 1997. The language is no longer the language of the enemies, but rather a means of 'knowledge, communication, and an instrument of judgment and growth'. Examining the content of this textbook and comparing it with those of previous years, it would appear that except for the change in the cover page and few other minor changes, the content of this locally produced textbook was identical with those of previous years. This is a good instance of conflict between what politicians say, policy discourse, and what is actually being practiced on the ground. Many policies set in post-1997 Iran thus stayed merely at the policy level and have never been translated into practice, due to constant sectarian tensions within the ruling elites.

Notes

1 Methodologically speaking, this paper is part of a larger original research (Borjian, 2013) – a chronological, vertical, and horizontal case study, for which I applied multiple means of data collection, including an in-depth fieldwork (2007–2008 academic year, followed by several short country visits between 2009 to 2014) across various research sites, whose operations were perceived in having a direct or indirect impact upon the country's education and its subfield of English education at the national, sub-national and supra-national levels. Other means of data collection included: document analysis, school and university visits, visits to various publishing houses, the headquarters of the international organisations operating in Iran (including the British Council, the World Bank and various UN developmental agencies), as well as conducting structured, unstructured and semi-structured interviews with various stakeholders, including ministry officials, representatives of international organisations, English professors, teachers and students. My research drew primarily from qualitative data, enhanced by quantitative data collected via electronic surveys from 88 professors and 102 students of English.
2 Using a multi-level and multi-layered research design suggests that the lens we are applying here in understanding the place of English in post-revolutionary Iran is an academic lens (as opposed to a journalist one), in which subjectivity and bias are minimised by the multiplicity of research instruments. Since this paper is written for a broad audience and is meant to be concise, it highlights the findings of my previous research with limited references to my original fieldwork notes and data sources.
3 See (Ashraf, 1997). Also, to a lesser extent, English was also promoted by the local modern educational establishments, though their student populations were rather small (e.g. the Sate Translation House, Moshiriyeh School and Dar-al-Funun).
4 See Borumand, 2002.
5 For more on missionaries in Iran, see Francis-Dehqani, 2008; Mansoori, 1986; Ringer, 2001.
6 For more on education under the Pahlavi dynasty, see Ashraf, 1997; Menashri, 1992; Slocum, 1970; on English language under Qajar and Pahlavi, see Borjian, 2013.
7 Persian: ولایت فقیه, velāyat-e faqīh.
8 For more on Iran's cultural revolution, see Habibi, 1989; Shorish, 1988; Sobhe, 1982.
9 'We accept that Arabic is the language of Islam, and... the world's holiest language... We believe that in the future Arabic, not Persian, will be the international language of Islam. We believe that, on the day the united Islamic government is established, certainly its language cannot be anything but Arabic' Ali-Akbar Hashemi Rafsanjani's 1981 speech. At the time he was the IRI's parliamentary spokesperson, and was to be president of IRI,1988–1997.
10 English is taught via localised school textbooks and curriculum from the first year of the middle school (Year 6) to the end of high school (Year 12) for two to three hours per week. At the tertiary level it is taught via local English for Specific Purpose (ESP) textbooks.; two such ESP courses are required for undergraduate students to meet their graduation requirements.
11 On favorable attitudes towards Esperanto, see Harlow, 1998; on indigenised English see the insights of Tahere Saffarzadeh, better known as the poet of the revolution, Saffarzadeh, 1990.
12 German and French schools and cultural institutions were also closed temporarily, but were soon invited back to resume their operations.
13 For SAMT's track record, see the official website, SAMT, 2014.

14 For more on indigenised English in Iran, see Borjian, 2013.
15 Various reports on Iran produced by the listed international organisations are available on their websites; on Khatami and education, see Mehran, 2003.
16 For more on private English language institutes, see Borjian, 2013.
17 It is beyond the scope of this paper to go into more depth on the associated problems of brain drain, but see Harrison, 2007.
18 For more on the British Council's operations in pre – and post – revolutionary Iran, see *EIr*, 1989 and Borjian, 2011 respectively.
19 Personal interview with the Staff # 1 of the British Council Iran, Tehran, Qolhak, April 2008.
20 Regulation No. 619, issued November 6th 2007 by the Supreme Council of Cultural Revolution, in charge of supervising the operations of all cultural and educational activities in Iran.
21 The given TOEFL exam is locally produced with a focus on reading and grammar, and is administrated by the Ministry of Higher Education.
22 *Iranian National TV*, Fieldnotes, December 2007–May 2008.
23 For more on my English in early 21st Century Iran, see Borjian, 2013.
24 A fuller analysis of the new curriculum and materials will be in the forthcoming British Council publication on English Language Teaching in Iran, to be published in Spring 2015.
25 Again, see the forthcoming British Council publication on English Language Teaching in Iran, to be published in Spring 2015.
26 For more on this, see Beh-Afarin, 2005; Namaghi, 2006.

Works referred to

Ashraf, A. (1997). Education: viii. General survey of modern education. *Encyclopedia Iranica*, vol. VIII, Fascicle 2: 189–96.
Beh-Afarin, R. (2005). ELT teacher development: The case of Iran. ILI Language Teaching Journal, 1 (1), 75–89.
Borjian, M. (2013). *English in post-revolutionary Iran: From Indigenisation to internationalisation*. Bristol, Buffalo, Toronto: Multilingual Matters.
Borjian, M. (2011). The rise and fall of a partnership: The British Council and Iran (2001–2009). *International Journal of Iranian Studies*, 44/4: 541–62.
Borumand, S. (2002). The Operation of British church missionary society (CMS) in Iran under Qajar dynasty. Tehran: *Moassese-ye Motaleat-e Tarikh-e Moaser-e Iran*.
EIr. (1989). British Council. *Encyclopedia Iranica*, vol. IV, Fascicle 5: 455–56.
Francis-Dehqani, G. E., (2008). Great Britain: xv. British schools in Persia. *Encyclopedia Iranica Online*, Retrieved 7 April 2008, from www.iranica.com.
Habibi, N. (1989). Allocation of educational and occupational opportunities in the Islamic Republic of Iran: A case study in the political screening of human capital in the Islamic Republic of Iran. *Iranian Studies*, 22/4: 19–46.
Harlow, D. J. (1998). Esperanto: An overview. Retrieved 28 December 2008 from *Wikipedia* Free Encyclopedia: http://en.wikipedia.org/wiki/Esperanto.
Harrison, F. (8 January 2007). Huge cost of Iranian brain drain. Retrieved 6 May 2008 from *BBC News* at: http://news.bbc.co.uk/2/hi/middle_east/6240287.stm.
Kiany, R. & Khayyamdar, M. (eds.) (2005–2006). *Proceedings of the first national ESP/EAP conference*

(three volumes). Tehran: SAM.
Mansoori, A. (1986). American missionaries in Iran, 1834–1934. Doctoral dissertation. Ball State University, Muncie Ind.
Mehran, G. (2003). Khatami, political reform and education in Iran. *Comparative Education*, 39/3: 311–29.
Menashri, D. (1992). Education and the Making of Modern Iran. Ithaca: Cornell University Press.
Namaghi, A. (2006). Forces steering Iranian language teachers' work: A grounded theory. *Reading Matrix*, 6/2: 90–105.
Ringer, M. (2001). *Education, religion, and the discourse of cultural reform in Qajar Iran*. Costa Mesa, California: Mazda Publisher, Inc.
Saffarzadeh, T. (1990). Preface. In R. Deedari, M. Ziahosseiny & M. Varzegar (eds.), *English for students of medicine*. Tehran: SAMT.
SAMT. (2014). The official website of the Organisation for Researching and Composing University Textbooks in the Humanities: http://www.samt.ac.ir/.
Shorish, M. M. (1988). The Islamic revolution and education in Iran. *Comparative Education Review*, 32/1: 58–75.
Slocum, J. B. (1970). Iran: A study of the educational system and guide to the admission and academic placement of Iranian students in colleges and universities in the United States. Washington D.C.: American Association of Collegiate Registrars and Admissions Officers.
Sobhe, K. (1982). Education in revolution: Is Iran duplicating the Chinese Cultural Revolution? *Comparative Education*, 18/3: 271–280.
Thiong'o, N. (2012). The challenge – ndaraca ya thiomi: Languages as bridges. In V. Papatahana & P. Bunce (eds.), *English language as hydra: Its impacts on non-English language cultures* (pp. 11–17). Bristol, Buffalo, Toronto: Multilingual Matters.

Persian Language Teaching in the UK: challenges, potential and initiatives

M WIMBLE[*]
Dr M Wimble is a writer and developer of text books and materials for language learning in English and Farsi.

Learning the language of Persia and modern Iran is vital for the cultural identity of those in the UK and for the future relationship between the two countries. Teaching is enthusiastic but its uneven quality and outreach may be holding back new learners.

Persian, including its different dialects, is the official language in Iran, Afghanistan and Tajikistan and has more than 100 million speakers around the world. The language is called Farsi, Dari and Tajiki in these native countries respectively. Although there are some minor differences between these Persian dialects, regarding pronunciation, vocabulary and grammar, they have many more similarities and share more or less the same cultural values and heritage.

Outside the homeland of the Persian language, it is spoken widely by millions of migrants from these countries particularly Iran and Afghanistan.

This great population of Persian speakers want their children and grand-children, who are the second and third generations of Iranians, to learn the language of their forefathers (Persian as a Heritage language) and communicate with them and their other relatives in this tongue. They also want them not to forget their roots, culture and values. Therefore they believe knowing Persian and being able to read and write in this language is key in reconnecting these children to their culture.

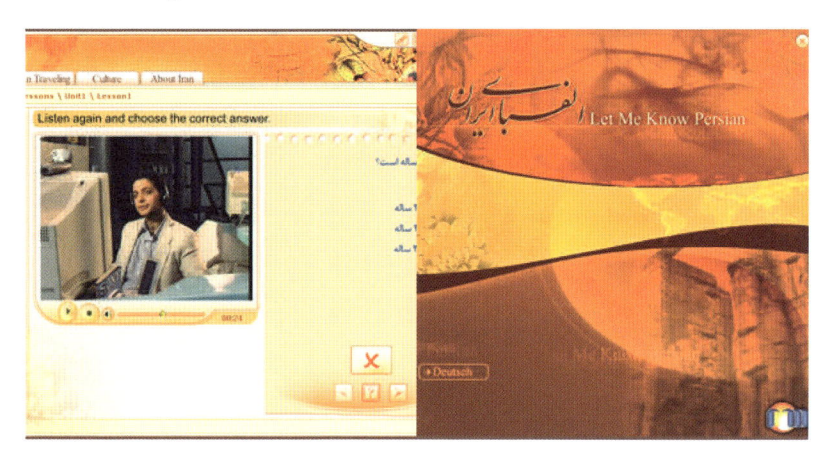

On the other hand, Persian is the language of people who have a very rich literature, history and culture. Therefore many people, researchers, scholars, and students in the world have given great attention to it and have studied it in order to be able to read and study Persian literary works in the source language and further to translate them into other languages for the public to enjoy. For the very same reason, many universities and institutions established programmes in Persian studies and Iranian studies and offer Persian language courses.

In general, in the last century, the importance of language has been emphasised as it is not only the main communication tool, but also knowing other people's languages would help with understanding those nations better and improving cultural exchange. In the case of the Persian language, this has been of more importance since the Islamic revolution in Iran in 1979 and particularly in the last two decades because of the increasing tension between Iran and western countries that seems to be largely due to misunderstanding.

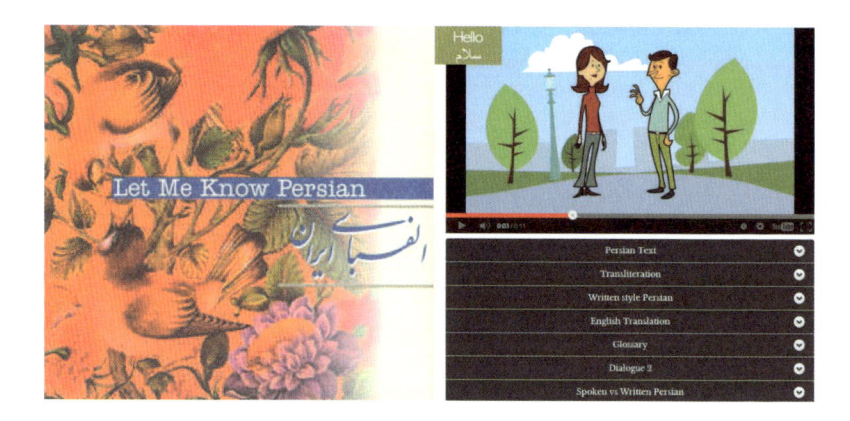

Based on what has been mentioned so far, we can divide the learners of Persian language into two main groups in the UK. The first group is the children of native Persian speakers. The second group of Persian learners are non-Iranian adults who study the language at university. However, apart from the two main groups of potential learners of Persian language, there are some Persian learners in other centres. Some of these centres belong to Persian or Iranian foundations which have courses in the UK throughout the year. There are also some private language companies and institutions which offer Persian as one of the languages on offer. In addition, The Foreign and Commonwealth Office and Ministry of Defence have their own Persian programmes.

In this article, I will focus only on the main two groups. The first group, which are children of Iranian origin, are usually encouraged or, in some cases, pushed by their parents to learn the language; here there is a lack of internal motivation amongst the learners. There are different factors involved in how Persian is used at home. Usually if both parents are Persian speakers, they usually communicate to each other in Persian, so the children are at least exposed to the language and learn the language unconsciously, particularly the vocabulary. In the families where these parents speak in Persian with their children, these children have a better knowledge of Persian particularly in spoken skills. But usually their language doesn't go much beyond the routine everyday language for communication. If only one of the parents is a Persian speaker, the only way the children are exposed to Persian is when that parent talks in Persian with them. Although this would be ideal, in reality it does not happen and both parents speak in English with their children. The other factor is the age of the children when they moved to the UK. Usually if they are born and lived in the UK, then their knowledge of Persian would be much less in comparison to those who came to the UK when older. Other factors can be the extent to which the family are in contact with other Iranians, how often they have Iranian visitors, or how often they visit Iran and their older Iranian relatives. The other factor is how important the parents feel the Persian language is for their children and how much they focus on Persian as a heritage language. The way the parents look at it can be the main external force or motivation for the children to learn the language. Often when they explain to their children how knowing a second language, and particularly Persian, can give them an advantage over their monolingual friends in future and how it can help them and opens lots of doors to them when they are older, the children are more willing to learn and are motivated to develop their knowledge by attending Persian classes. The other motivation is when a trip to Iran is arranged for school holidays or when one of their close relatives is going to visit and stay with them for a long time.

 Often, teaching this group takes place in less academic situations. The children are home-tutored by parents or private teachers, or go to the so-called Iranian schools which hold their classes mainly once a week.

There is another important factor in why we should pay attention to this group of learners. The students who learn Persian in the Iranian schools can use it to communicate with their relatives, read Persian books and maintain their link with their roots, country, and cultural heritage. In addition they can sit for Persian language exams for their GCSE and A-Level. As Persian is among the 22 languages for OCR-accredited (Oxford, Cambridge, RSA) examinations, the Iranian students have the opportunity to get high marks in Persian exams and raise their profile and chances of getting into higher education. Although the Persian in OCR examinations is very well developed and it seems there are professional examiners and markers in developing that test, there are no specific course books written for this purpose, except some textbooks developed by Rostam school for these exams as well as past papers and sample tests published by OCR.

The second group of Persian learners, usually non-Iranians, are more mature in comparison to the other group and have different internal and external motivations which trigger the learning. Sometimes they fall in love with the beauty of Persian poetry and literature or its fascinating history and culture or they want to learn the language for its usefulness and to enhance their employability. This type of learning usually happens in more academic environments such as universities. In these cases, the learners attend one of the Persian programmes around the world and pursue their studies in higher education where they can get a degree.

Readers may know that in the UK alone there are about 10 higher education institutions including the prestigious Universities of Cambridge and Oxford as well as SOAS, Manchester, Exeter, St Andrews, Edinburgh, Westminster offering Persian programmes at Undergraduate and/or graduate levels. Furthermore, there are more or less 30 Iranian schools in the country, some of them large like

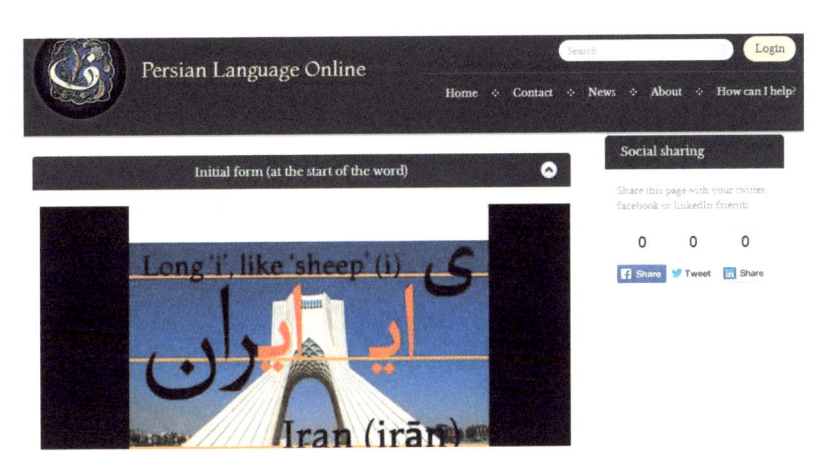

Rostam School in London with hundreds of students a year and some very small. These Iranian schools (Farsi medium Saturday schools) play an important role in helping the Iranian families to teach Persian to their children and connect them to their roots.

However the journey towards learning Persian is not easy for either group. There are different types of obstacles to the promotion of Persian language all over the world including the UK.

In the UK, there are more than one hundred thousand Iranians. For this heritage language group, there are insufficient Iranian schools to accommodate all the potential second and third generation learners. The available schools are mainly in London and other big cities which have their classes on Saturdays. Therefore, there are many smaller cities with enthusiastic parents who cannot find such schools in their towns.

In addition, not all the teachers in these schools are professionally trained to teach Persian as a second or heritage language. Some of them are ex-teachers who were used to teach in primary schools back in Iran to native speakers, and the same is true with many private teachers. Parents, who home tutor their own children or work in such schools, are not of exception either.

Unfortunately there is no professional development training for Persian teachers and lecturers in the UK. Some Iranian schools have their own teacher-training workshops where more experienced teachers will share their findings and skills with younger colleagues or schools invite well-known speakers from universities or Iranian societies. These workshops are available in many schools and sometimes the trainers themselves do not have professional qualifications in second language or teacher training.

We should admit that the teachers are gaining great experience through the years teaching in the Iranian schools, which in turn is very valuable and we have to accept that it is true that at the end the children who receive tuition in these classes do learn Persian to some extent. However, the question remains: could we do better? It is not easy to measure financially the extra time and energy spent in teaching Persian to children to remedy deficiencies in the knowledge of second-language teaching methodology.

The second issue is that to run such courses needs time and financial commitment. Unfortunately after a while, smaller schools are closed because they cannot afford the expenses and costs.

The other obstacle is that there are not that many resources available to meet all the needs, to be used as self-study or in class to support the process of teaching and learning Persian.

In general, the course books published for teaching Persian to non-Persian speakers are written by authors who have written books based on their experience teaching foreign students over time. These books do not follow a particular methodology and are not based on the principles and basis of writing language books for second-language learning. The Sa'adi Foundation in Iran which is responsible of teaching Persian to non-Persian speakers in Iran or liaising regarding Persian courses outside Iran, particularly

Iranian schools and those centres in connection with the cultural sections of Iranian embassies, have regulated only one single text book among many other competitors to be used. Some of these competitors are much better in terms of methodology, design, quality, and supplementary materials. Moreover, for different needs and audience, a particular textbook is needed. The teacher should not use a book designed for adults to teach young learners.

Some of these Iranian schools have made their own resources. These resources are mainly written by their own teachers based on their experience of teaching in these schools. However, it seems that they lack the methodology which is needed to underpin any course book for language teaching. Some schools use the books which are already available in the market and we also mentioned earlier what is wrong with majority of them. There are a few schools including the London Iranian School (affiliated to the Iranian government and runnning on all day from Monday to Friday) which use the same books taught in Iran in the primary schools to native speakers. Unfortunately this is a great mistake, because these books are designed for children who already know the Persian language: their listening and speaking skills are developed, they are living in a Persian speaking context and country, and the books are designed to teach literacy, reading and writing skills. So it is misguided and potentially harmful to use them to teach the children who barely have any knowledge of Persian at all.

The situation for the second group of learners who learn Persian language at universities is completely different. For a majority of potential university students, their employability is the main factor motivating them to apply for a particular course. Therefore when they decide to learn a non-European language, they choose the one from the nations and countries with which their own countries have a strong political and commercial relationship.

As far as Persian is concerned, in the recent years the number of students deciding to learn the language in the UK has decreased mainly because there is no direct political relationship between Tehran and London after the closure of their embassies. One of the other main factors for major UK universities in attracting the students to study one of the middle-eastern languages is the year abroad opportunity. In this year of their programme the students have the chance to go to one of the native countries in the region and explore for themselves and in their own way the language, society and culture of the Middle East. Again in case of the Persian language, due to the decrease of political relations between the UK and Iran and because of the restrictions imposed by the western powers on Iran for its nuclear programme, the students found that it is very difficult for them to travel to Iran. Therefore they decide not to take Persian courses at all, or at least not as their main subject.

In addition, when there is not that much demand from the students for particular courses, the university is less likely to support running them. Thus such language courses need to get their financial support from external entities, mainly the governments of the native countries. Unfortunately, among the three Persian speaking countries, Tajikistan and Afghanistan do not have sufficiently strong economies to support Persian programmes and the Iranian government does not financially support universities in the UK offering Persian language courses. It seems that they are more willing to promote Persian in Asian or a few Eastern-European countries. Currently the support of some Iranian organisations such as Soudavar Memorial Foundation, Fereydoun Djam Charitable Trust, Iran Heritage Foundation, the British Institute of Persian Studies, etc. and support from some Iranian businesses such as the donation of Bita Daryabari to the Shahnama Centre in Pembroke College at the University of Cambridge have maintained the existence of Persian studies and Persian programmes in the UK.

As readers may know well, because of the same reasons, i.e. employability, the political and commercial relationship between the two countries and financial support from the native-speaking countries, languages like Arabic, Chinese and Japanese have chairs in all major universities in the UK and are among the top Asian and Middle-Eastern languages that UK students prefer to learn.

There are only a few Persian language lecturers in the UK universities who have professional training and qualification in teaching Persian to non-Persian speakers or as a second/foreign language. This is one of the main challenges in this sector. The majority of lecturers are graduates of Persian literature, comparative literature, linguistics, media or cinema studies and have not had any language teaching courses during their entire academic life. They merely teach this language based on their knowledge of Persian, their experience after some years teaching or as the result of any training in teaching English as a second language. As it has been proved regarding other languages, being a native speaker of a particular language or having a degree in the literature or linguistics of a particular language is not enough to be a good language teacher. On the contrary, training in language teaching is necessary and required if one wants to teach a language, however this by itself does not guarantee becoming a good teacher.

For these lecturers, there is even less opportunity for teacher training and teacher development. It is only the lecturer themselves who may attend some international conferences or workshops in order to hear talks on current issues and trends about second language teaching.

In universities, again the problems with the resources used persist. Some lecturers use the books currently available in the market as discussed before. Some lecturers have written and published their own course books based on their experience and their students' profiles. Although these books may be found suitable for their students, they have not been written based on the principles of language learning and may not suit the students in another university. But there are some instructors who are more flexible and use different resources available including books, extracts from newspapers and magazines, audio/video clips from different radio and television channels, online resources, films, etc. based on what their students need.

As is well-known, the resources for teaching a particular language are not limited to books and other published materials. And the challenges are bigger for other kinds of resources which need more money to develop. In the area of online resources, there are more and better opportunities available but one of their main weaknesses is that, usually they have not made the most of the features of online language learning. Usually features like integrating audio and video, interactive activities, instant marking and scoring, reporting and giving feedback, monitoring, etc have been overlooked. Some of them are so basic that it seems that instead having the content on the paper, it is delivered on the screen without any online functionality. In other words, one can only print and read through them.

When it comes to mobile learning and mobile apps, the situation is even worse. There is no app for teaching Persian in the market which is fit for purpose in my view. The number of mobile users is increasing and the users' age is decreasing. Many primary school students in the UK take a smart phone to school in their pockets, and spend a large amount of their time playing with one of these mobile gadgets. Therefore paying attention to mobile learning and game-based learning is crucial as it can change the habit of young learners in the very near future.

To address how to solve these problems we need to take some big steps and make decisions in different areas. It is important to improve the political, commercial and cultural relationships between Iran and the UK. This should enable a better understanding between the two governments and nations and having a clearer vision about their future career and employability, the students would be persuaded to learn Persian.

Financial support from the Iranian government, large Iranian cultural institutions and successful businesses is a key factor in maintaining such programmes in UK universities which in turn will lead to more research in the field of Iranian and Persian studies, attracting more students and researchers to travel to Iran, promoting Persian language and Iranian culture, and resulting in stronger cultural relationships and understanding.

Training our current teachers and arranging on-going language and pedagogical workshops and seminars for them will result in better outcomes for Persian courses in Iranian schools.

Developing functional and professional resources is a key element in helping the teachers and learners to achieve their targets more quickly and efficiently. As it is really difficult to detach people from their gadgets (laptops, tablets, smart phones, etc) these days, it is essential to think about more technology-based resources since they can potentially reach learners in remote areas where they do not have access to school or face-to-face teaching. These resources should be online, interactive and motivating and designed in a way to be used for self-study or extracurricular tools. Furthermore, if the resources can be developed as apps and made mobile compatible, they can be more easily accessed and more widespread. The key feature of mobile learning and online learning tools is that they can be used worldwide and are not country-specific.

It is important to look at and learn from other countries that have gone this way in promoting their languages for a long time and have much more experience. As we all know, English Language Teaching (ELT) has a long tradition and it is the language most widely learnt and studied. Plenty of research has been done on teaching English as a second language. As this is an international language with a strong economy, politics, culture and power behind it, there has been a great demand for learning it all over the world. Therefore, there are plenty of resources, teacher training programmes and course providers worldwide and English language teaching has been seen as a great business.

Regarding Persian, the case is completely different. It cannot be looked as a business which generates significant revenue. On the contrary, it should be looked as a project which needs funding for non-financial outcomes and cultural reasons. Thus, to promote Persian, we can learn from the achievements and outcomes of ELT, particularly its experience and history in teacher training and resource development.

At the moment, there are a few course books available on teaching Persian, some of them with audio and video supplementary materials. As I have mentioned before, there are also some online programmes. These online projects and teaching tools are very helpful, but there are few available and the existing ones cannot completely fulfil all the needs.

The most recent online teaching tool, an innovation in the field, is Persian Language Online which is a free interactive website for learning Persian at three levels developed by the Persian Language Foundation in London. This is more advanced than any other Persian language teaching website and capitalises on the capability of online teaching. Before designing this website, a survey study was made on language learning and what had already been developed in the field. The academic committee responsible for developing the content are experts in the field of second language teaching, Persian language teaching, Persian as heritage language, Persian literature, and Online teaching from the major universities in the UK such as SOAS, University of St Andrews, University of Cambridge and Rostam Iranian School. The animations on the website are developed by a professional animation company. The design of the website with all its functionality is done by an expert web design company. The high audio quality confirms the importance of recording in specialised studios and by expert voices.

    A careful look at the website confirms that there has been an excellent teamwork behind a project of such quality. However it has to be admitted that although it is richly featured, still more could be added to it to improve its functionality and help it achieve its goals. But the fact is that adding the extra features to this website needs a huge budget and much greater investment. However, of all areas in the teaching and learning of Persian it is one of the most important for the future.

Abalish: how English changed the language in Abadan

Pardis Azi Abbassian*

Pardis Azi Abbassian, was an Abadani teenager during the first half of the 1960s. He joined the oil company in the late 1960s and continued his success until he became the head of his department. He lives in Abadan.

The British presence in Iran's southern province of Khuzestan, and in Abadan, the hub of the Anglo-Iranian Oil Company, led to a mixing of lifestyle and language that created its own unique culture and patois.

In 1901 when William D'Arcy obtained the concession for oil exploration and exploitation for 60 years in Iran's Khuzestan, no one, including him, could have imagined how completely his journey would affect Iranian life and culture, even down to the style and construction of housing. Mr D'Arcy could never have imagined how the speculation for his next adventure – he had made his fortune with gold mines in Australia – would come to affect me and my family, and a whole generation of southern Iranian people whose youth, education and employment was formed by the presence of the oil company and the British in Iran.

After more than seven years of failure, on 28 May 1908 D'Arcy hit oil in Masjid-i-Suleiman and with that first rainfall of back gold began a new and different chapter for Iranian people in the state of Khuzestan, and the path of history changed. Near the site of the first oil well, there was a triangle of land lurking in the delta of the Tigris and Euphrates rivers, some 30 miles from the pearl-stitched water of the Persian Gulf, known as Abadan. Abadan sits on its own island along the eastern bank of Shatt-Al-Arab (*Arvand-Rood*) bounded on its west by the Shatt, and the east by an outlet of Karun river, Bahmanshir. The river kept depositing silt and eventually the delta of the Shatt extended and, like a forlorn and disappointed lover, the coast of the Persian Gulf gradually drew further and further back from Abadan so by the time that intrepid Arab traveller and geographer Ibn Battutah visited in the 14th century, he described it as little more than a large village in a flat, salty plain.

Unpromising though its location, Khuzestan has a charm that gets under the skin. The Shatt fishermen navigating the languorous waters in dhows as old as time, date growers trading their syrupy fruit in the covered bazaar, the ethnic Arabs squatting on their haunches as they sort their catch on the river banks, the women mixing the herbs, spices and garlic which they stuff into the belly of the cleaned fish before putting them over some hot coals in the yard to cook. There is cool air from the water as evening draws in and the chorus of cicadas and frogs joins the chatter of the population.

When it became clear that the refinery necessary to process the crude oil now fizzing out of the ground would have to be located in Abadan – the ever-reliable Shatt could provide anchorage for tankers and allow them a way to the Gulf – the Westerners found a village whose way of life had been unchanged for 3,000 years and they had no idea, with their ambitious plans for industrialisation and a modern technology, that they too would become enamoured of the heat and the dust.

Abadan's transformation had begun.

The Anglo-Persian-Oil-Company was established in 1908 (APOC) and changed name to the Anglo-Iranian-Oil-Company (AIOC) in 1935 and everything was transferred from APOC to AIOC, including the ownership of the Abadan Refinery lands.

Abadan's refinery was the largest overseas asset of Britain, which owned 51% of the oil company. In 1933 there was a new agreement between the oil company (APOC) and the king of Iran, Reza Shah, which included, as well as Iranian loyalty pay by the oil company, an agreement that APOC should pay Iranian labour fairly, and also to start building schools, hospitals, roads and a telephone system. The Abadan General Hospital was built in the late 1930s, Abadan Fire station was built in 1927 and the Bawarda swimming pool was built in 1933, and this is how Abadan was reborn.

My name is Pardis and I am a former teenager from Abadan, and this is the story of my home town of Abadan, the city with its own culture and its own language, a mix of Persian and English, a patois that I don't call Abadani, but prefer to call Abalish, and still whenever I speak Farsi, I speak Abalish instead.

The city held the world's biggest oil refinery (with the capacity of 635,000 barrels per day) which took four years to build, being finished in 1912. During these four years, lots of houses were built in different styles for different positions of employees, but they all had something in common; the style in which they were built, which was completely different to the traditional Iranian style. They were English-style houses with fireplaces, gates and a garden on the outside, rather than walled-in traditional houses which had their gardens contained inside the houses, tucked away.

One of the most important changes in the style of housing was the use of baked bricks instead of adobe bricks (the Farsi version is *khesht*) which up to that time the people of Abadan used for building their houses, and it was a big revolution in housing construction for that time. Another big revolution in city design was the sewerage system and piped water lines for company housing, Abadan became the first city in Iran which had a sewerage system, which was very sanitary and prevented of lots of disease which are carried by insects called *botol* (the Abalish version of 'beatles').

I am proud to be Abadani. Abadan was the only city in Iran besides Tehran the capital that had an international airport, and the city that had one of the most beautiful cinemas in the country, built in the late 1940s and named Cinema Taj. Cinema Taj showed British and American movies and until the late 1960s was the larger, the most modern and fashionable cinema which was for the *staff* (Abalish for 'managers') of the oil company. They also they built an outdoor cinema, which had same shows as Cinema Taj, for labourers called Cinema Bahmanshir. The Abadan Symphony Orchestra, which was established in 1946, had another big effect on the lifestyle of Abadan. Abadan was Iran's first really modern city with a new culture, the city which bloomed a better future and education for the next generations. And I am so proud to say that I am Abadani and what follows are snatches of my life story in Abadan.

I remember one day as a boy, I went with some friends to the riverside to kill some time and have some fun. I forgot the time and when I went back home it was after sunset and already dark. My mother asked me: 'Where have you been?' I replied: 'I went with my friends to the riverside, near *jetty #3* (the Farsi version is *eskeleh shomare seh*), next to gate *hijdah* (the English version is 'gate 18' and Farsi version is *dawazeh hijdah*), she got upset and asked me: 'Is that the one close to *lever hoffice* (the Abalish version of 'labour office', the Farsi version is *kargozini*). 'Don't do it again, it's a dangerous place,' she continued, 'I want you to change that burnt *lamp*, let me get a *globe* for you (the Farsi version is *cheragh*).' My mother, the generation before me, already spoke Abalish, it wasn't something that my generation invented, it went deeper than that and spoke of the long relationship that already existed then between the Abadanis and the British.

My father worked in the *workshop* (the Farsi version *kargah*) of the *company* (the Farsi version is *kargar-e sherkat*). He was a kind, nice and respectful person, but he was not at all organised, and I remember how every morning he would lose his temper and accuse my mother of losing his *lamber* (the Abalish for 'number', which was his ID pass). He was always in a rush and a hurry in the mornings, with my mother looking on patiently. Every afternoon when he came home, he brought with him one *looft* (the English version is loaf) of bread and six *bakhsam* (the Farsi version is *noon sefid*) from the *company store* (the Farsi version is *forooshgah*) which were my favourites. But she used to scold him when he brought home stuff from the *salvige* (the Farsi version is *ghorazeh khoneh*, the English version is 'salvage') which were given to him by his boss.

Before the company gave my father a *bangeleh*, (the English version is 'bungalow') we used to live in Seyd Moosa lane (pure Abalish. The Farsi version is *koocheh*). On his day off he helped my mother with the shopping, buying *tamateh* (the Farsi version for 'tomatoes' is *gojeh farangi*) and cooked for us. He had a very close friend who was like an uncle to us and we used to call him Uncle Mo. He and his family were the best friends of my parents. Uncle Mo was *espactor* (the Abalish version of 'inspector', the Farsi is *gashti*) in the oil company and always had a good story for us about how he caught people who tried to steal equipment from the company. I use to be good friends with his son, Karo, we had been in the same class since elementary school, and he was a very good football player. At the age of 17 he was a member of the city football team, and whenever he had a game, I used to go to *gran-e shapouri* (the Abalish version of *ground*, the Farsi version is *zamin*. These days, it is called *stadium*) and watch his game. He was so dangerous whenever he managed to *head* (the Farsi version is *zarbeh ba sar*) the ball.

I had two sisters and one brother, one of my sisters attended the *nursing school* (Farsi version *madreseh parastari*) and the second one hired by *company* (Abalish) as a *secreter* (the Abalish version of 'secretary', the Farsi version is *monshi*). My brother attended the Abadan *technical school* (the Farsi version is *amoozeshgahe fani*), also named the Abadan Institute Of Technology (AIT), after he finished his high school, the Technical School built by the British in 1939 under the name of Abadan Technical School, in the clause of Anglo-Iranian Oil Company (AIOC). It was a school of engineering, which was dedicated to educating and training engineers and managers for the Oil Company. It was extremely selective in its admissions and it was so hard to get in that, in fact, only one per cent of applicants were successful and then only 50 per cent of student would make it to graduation. Several factors counted in the admissions process. Its founder and first president was Iranian Dr Reza Fallah, and the curriculum and management of the school was more or less British in nature. Later on, the school decided to expand and update the education offered in several branches of engineering and the capacity of student admission and Dr Walter A Groves from Lafayette College of Easton in Pennsylvania became president (1956–1961) but still the British were among the teachers. Therefore, 1966 was the last year of general engineering graduates and the school thus opened another door of opportunity for young Iranian students which was a great and positive change in young Iranian students' lives and high school graduates from all over the country applied for the entrance exams.

Education by the British was not just restricted to the academic level. My mother told me about different programmes to develop the talents of Abadani women, training them in their own houses and praising them for improvements, for having the best garden, for sewing and cross stitching. They wanted to help the employee's housewives in finding their own abilities.

Back to my brother, he was so happy because his future was guaranteed, but his greatest happiness was the *saykel* (the Abalish version of 'bicycle', the Farsi version is *docharkheh*) that my father bought for him as his transportation. He was happy that once a while, he could go to a garden party (there is no Farsi version), which was held in the company's club. He had many dreams for the future, he was constantly telling my parents who he was going to be and what he was going to do, repeating it every day, and so I knew that when he graduated from technical school, he would be hired by the oil company as *staff* (the Farsi version is *karmand*) and they would hire him as a *grade 8* (the Farsi version is *rotbeh hasht*) and he would be given a big *bangeleh* in the best part of town. He was very successful and had a very comfortable life and got married and took his wife there with him. My parents were so happy for him and his family, and I was too.

Let's talk about my sisters. The one who worked as a secretary at the Oil Company married a very nice gentleman who was Oil Company Staff and held the head of the engineering department position, Abalish version *head-e mohandessi* (Farsi version *raeise edare mohandessi*).

Now let's talk about my life and the good memories which started from childhood and continued till I became a young man, from the time I was wearing Mothercare clothes till I was wearing *boots* (the Farsi version is *pootin*) and Ray-Ban sunglasses, lots of memories from school, especially from when I was riding the *bass* (the Abalish version of 'bus') with all my friends.

I was a very small and skinny child, and I remember that my mother used *brasses* (pure Abalish for 'braces') to hold up my trousers, but according to my grades in school and my teachers, I was a smart boy. Growing up in Abadan, everything we had there was normal for me and I assumed this was the way of life everywhere in Iran, until I travelled to my grandparents' hometown to visit them and various other relatives I didn't know very well. That's when I realised the difference between me and others of my age, my peers, the difference between us in the level of knowledge and thinking, culture, style of clothing, and even language. I realised that everything about me, from how I looked to how I was planning for my future, was a product of growing up in Abadan, that I felt that the world was open for me, that I could be anything that I wanted to be, I was the one who could make decisions for my own future, not just let others map my future and if I didn't meet their expectations, blame it on destiny. I learned that I am the one who makes my own destiny, and all this just because I lived and was raised in Abadan.

By adapting the mixture of English and Iranian culture, I learnt how to be independent and make good decisions, and how I could have a positive role in my country's economy. Living in a city which was the backbone of my country's economy gave me the opportunity to have many chances for my future, and gave me the chance to go to different technical schools at different levels, such as *Artisan School* (the Farsi version is *kar amoozan*), after finishing elementary school, Technical High School (the Farsi version is *honarestan-e san-ati*), after middle school, and the Abadan Institute Of Technology (Farsi version *daneshkadeh naft*), after high school.

That's why I believe D'Arcy couldn't imagine how his journey would affect mine and millions of other people's lives in such a positive way, which continues to this day. When I look back, I realise how I learned to hope, to challenge myself for success and set a goal for my life, how to be creative and a role model for the next generation. I felt that if D'Arcy didn't give up, I shouldn't, and so I learned not to be a quitter and how to follow my goals. I am, as an Iranian Abadani, thankful to him and those who issued the oil exploration license to him. I, as an Abadani, was a witness to how the life of the people and their methods of living in Abadan changed. I learned how we can live together and exchange knowledge and cultural aspects, and adopt the best one for a better life. During the time of the British presence in Abadan, from the days of exploration to the time of exporting the oil, everything progressed positively towards better living, and we lived together with respect for each others' culture, never forcing any one onto the other. We respected each other's beliefs, dignity and culture; for example, from 12noon to 1pm was the lunchtime for oil industry employees, but it could be used as praying time too. In the 1950s and 1960s, this sort of tolerance was not the norm in corporations.

When I look back to those times, I understand how lucky I was. I learned responsibility and respect. We lived together with trust, believing in each other as people, co-workers, neighbours and human beings, and that's how we also learned the best from each other.

Owersettin the Rubaya'iat of Omar Khayyam

RAB WILSON
Rab Wilson is a Scottish poet and dramatist who writes mainly in the Scots language. His works include the collections *Accent o the Mind*, *Life Sentence*, and *A Map for the Blind* and a play called *Beggars*, a re-imagining of Robert Burns' 'The Jolly Beggars'.

Here he writes about how and why he undertook a Scots translation, or *owersettin*, of the 11th Century Persian poem, the Rubaya'iat of Omar Khayyam and how, for him the work resonates in contemporary Scottish culture. His introduction is followed by the first 20 verses: first in his translation, then in that of Penguin Classics by Peter Avery and John Heath-Stubbs from which he worked. References to all the books can be found at the end of the chapter.

Omar Khayyam in Scots – an introduction by Rab Wilson
'Myself when young did eagerly frequent
Doctor and saint and heard great argument
About it and about: but evermore
Came out by the same Door as in I went'.

I was about twenty-two years of age when I first heard of Omar Khayyam. Six years previously I left school and commenced an engineering apprenticeship with, the then, National Coal Board. After failing almost every theoretical and practical exam they could devise for me I was eventually consigned to a dead-end menial job on the pithead. One day, in the workshop where I was now based an older, wiser colleague repeated the above stanza to me. I have always loved poetry and literature and I was entranced by the profundity of this intriguing quatrain. I asked where it came from and who had written it but being a good teacher he left me to find out the answer. Thus began my life-long love affair with the *Rubaya'iat of Omar Khayyam*.

Years passed and my interest in the *Rubaya'iat* grew and deepened. Life moved on, I married, moved house, had a family and changed careers but during this time I never forgot Omar.

That a Scots version of the *Rubaya'iat* was possible had occurred to me. Yet I felt, due to a strange allegiance to FitzGerald's verse, that it would be wrong to re-work his version of the *Rubaya'iat*. Working as a nurse I was serendipitously introduced to a literal translation of the *Rubaya'iat* by Peter Avery and John Heath-Stubbs. The discovery of a literal translation immediately fired my imagination. Here was the opportunity that I had been waiting for. My aim was to convert these immortal quatrains into Lowland Scots. I firmly believed that profound ideas expressing some of the great metaphysical problems of life and death could be expressed in the everyday language of the street.

In an age where established beliefs are increasingly eroded the *Rubaya'iat* represents a set of guidelines adaptable to modern life. It encourages us to make the most of our lives by accepting the bad times and enjoying the good. In his appreciation of this ideal FitzGerald, like Omar, was far ahead of his time.

My vision was to use a simple language that ordinary folk would understand without losing any of the magic, mysticism, wonder and profundity of the original. The following three versions of the same quatrain (no.60 in FitzGerald's 2nd edition, no.48 in the Penguin Literal Translation and the version in Scots) shows how the work has evolved. The new work in Scots restores some of that 'simplicity' of the original. It shows that the fundamental problems of everyday existence have not really changed for any of us over the last thousand years.

Penguin Literal Translation;
I saw an old man in the wine shop,
I said, 'Have you any news of those who have gone?'
He replied, 'Take some wine, because, like us, many have gone, none has come back'.

FitzGerald's 2nd edition;
And lately by the Tavern door agape,
Stealing through the Door an Angel Shape
Bearing a vessel on his Shoulder, and
He bid me taste it, and 'twas the Grape!

New version in Scots;
Ah met an auld boy ootside Victoria Wine,
Ah asked him if he'd heard ony news.
He said, 'here, hae a slug o this –
The news is aa the same.'

But what is the *Rubaya'iat*, who was Omar Khayyam, and who was Edward FitzGerald? Firstly, the *Rubaya'iat* is a collection of ruba'i. A ruba'i is simply a four lined quatrain verse form. It is a succinct, self-contained poem that usually makes a profound philosophical point or observation. Much the same effect is achieved with a classical Japanese haiku, the humorous observation of a limerick, or a guid auld Scots proverb – 'As the auld cock craws, the young cock learns!'

The *Rubaya'iat*'s pithy, witty verses became popular among the ordinary people of medieval Persia. Viewed as subversive and dangerous the country's authorities tried to ban them. Composed anonymously and circulated in secret, they became firm favourites in the satirical armoury of the Persian intellectual and philosophical elite.

Western readers regard Oriental poetry as being steeped in mysticism and abstraction. Yet the ruba'i is often a truly pragmatic and common sense assessment of the realities faced daily by all of us. Full of a strong sense of fatalism, the ruba'i veer between pessimism and optimism and back again. Exhorting people to live for the moment and seize the day!

Omar Khayyam is probably better remembered today as a mathematician and astronomer instead of the greatest composer of the Persian ruba'i. His theories and work on algebra and geometry were centuries ahead of their time, perhaps the equivalent of Isaac Newton or Einstein. Born in the important trade-route city of Naishapur, situated on the 'Silk Road', (the Golden Road to Samarkand), in 1048, he died at the age of 83 in 1131. He lived through times of great social and domestic upheaval. Northern Persia was constantly under threat and invaded regularly by foreign powers. However during Omar's lifetime there was a period of peace and stability and Naishapur became a renowned centre of intellectual learning. The leading academics of the time willingly embraced the Greek philosophies of Aristotle and Plato. Yet there was a hard-core group of fundamentalist detractors opposed the new 'free thinkers'.

Scientists throughout history have often been viewed with scepticism and suspicion. Similarly towards the end of his life Omar suffered persecution and victimisation from fundamentalists. One of Omar's students remembered him prophesising that his grave would be in a spot 'Where the trees will shed their blossoms on me twice a year!' This prediction seemed impossible to his pupil. Years later, when he visited his old master's grave he found it next to a garden wall supporting pear and peach trees. So much blossom covered the grave that it was almost completely hidden from sight. Recalling his master's prophecy Omar's pupil broke down and wept by the graveside.

The Rubaya'iat of Omar Khayyam is said to be one of the ten best known poems in the world, and probably the most popular piece of Oriental literature in the Western World. This work could very well have been lost to us, and it is almost a miracle and perhaps an act of fate that the writings of Omar Khayyam should have survived, but survive they did.

A set of almost supernatural circumstances occurred that brought this collection of quatrains to its standing today. Firstly, an unknown middle-eastern scribe saved the writings of Omar Khayyam in the 1460s, by copying 158 of the original quatrains in purple ink on yellow paper and powdered in gold, more than 300 years after Omar's death. This manuscript was then serendipitously re-discovered by Professor Edward Cowell in 1856, after it had mysteriously made its way to the Bodleian Library, Oxford. Cowell brought the newly discovered Persian manuscript to the attention of Edward FitzGerald, who had been studying the Persian language since 1852.

Struggling with the break-up of a disastrous marriage, FitzGerald – with his deep and abiding interest in the Victorian fashion for 'Orientalism' – was so taken with these 'Epicurean tetrastichs by a

Persian of the eleventh century' that during this period of personal crisis he translated them and created his great literary masterpiece: the first edition of the *Rubaya'iat*. Fitzgerald states in a letter to Cowell on completion of his first draft, that 'My translation will interest you from its form, and also in many respects its detail, very unilateral though it is. Many quatrains are mashed together, *and something lost, I doubt, of Omar's simplicity, which is such a virtue in him*. But there it is, such as it is' [my italics].

FitzGerald attempted to get his *Rubaya'iat* published and had he not persevered, after being rejected by *Fraser's Magazine* and paid to have his first translated version of 75 quatrains published, it probably would have been no more than a scholarly exercise. The first edition was a commercial and critical failure and the publication itself would have died on Piccadilly Street had Whitley Stokes, a well-known Celtic scholar, not plucked a copy from the London bookseller, Bernard Quaritch. Stokes then gave a copy of FitzGerald's *Rubaya'iat* to his friend Dante Rossetti in July 1861, and the translation was introduced to the influential literati of the day. FitzGerald's translation passed from Rossetti to Charles Swinburne to George Meredith to William Morris to Edward Burne-Jones to John Ruskin to the Brownings and on and on, even to America, and the romantic verses kept gaining in popularity, necessitating more and more editions to be printed.

Over the decades *The Rubaya'iat of Omar Khayyam* has achieved a global cult status of gigantic proportions (just type 'Omar Khayyam' into your search-engine and you'll see what I mean). Edward FitzGerald died peacefully in his sleep on 14 June 1883. On his grave grows a rose tree cultivated from cuttings from the rose bushes growing on Omar Khayyam's grave in Nishapur.

***

But, tae oor tale. One of the key features of the *Rubaya'iat* for me is its beautiful quality of timelessness. Almost a thousand years have elapsed since the *Rubaya'iat* was written, yet the struggle of daily life remains, for the most part unchanged for the majority of ordinary people. The unique language of this new version captures the epic struggles of our mundane existence, portraying the universal problems of the human condition, asking the great unanswered questions that still remain unanswered. I have always believed there exists in Scots poetry the ability to distil great ideas and concepts into a handful of words. This unique ability can only enhance a re-working of the *Rubaya'iat*. The simple language enables us to grasp clearly concepts that could easily be lost or obliterated by the use of a more elaborate language. Robert Burns had this wonderful gift. You only have to consider some of his incomparable work to recognise this:

The best laid schemes o mice and men
Gang aft agley,
An lea'e us nought but grief an pain,
For promis'd joy!

Or:

O wad some Power the giftie gie us
Tae see oursels as ithers see us!

Scots poetry still exhibits this native ability of expressing fantastic concepts with crystalline clarity, impressive imagery and stunningly beautiful simplicity.

Therefore I decided to try to subtly update the *Rubaya'iat* by using modern imagery, names, phrases and language, to try to re-capture some of that 'simplicity' that FitzGerald felt he had lost. The *Rubaya'iat* has always appeared to me to be firmly placed in an urban setting. Omar would have been a city dweller. No doubt many of his musings and observations were influenced by his metropolitan lifestyle. Therefore it felt natural to talk of city landscapes, parks and pubs, football stadiums, off-licences, newspaper vendors and down-and-outs. The *Rubaya'iat* in Scots is a conscious Burnsian/Rabelasian celebration of an underclass who are often ignored and therefore remain largely unseen though they are all around us every day. Their primal fears are exactly the same as their Persian forebears, a thousand years ago. Eftir aa, we're aa Jock Tamsons bairns.

Today no one really knows how many hundreds of editions have been printed from FitzGerald's translations alone, not to mention other English and foreign translations. Now you can sample for yourself the latest version of this remarkable work, set out entirely in Scots.

I wonder what Omar would have to make of it all. Hopefully he'll be sitting, glass in hand, in some celestial tavern. Perhaps Edward FitzGerald is sitting with him as he casts his observant and sardonic eye over all this, enjoying the joke, and chuckling merrily to himself.

The Rubaya'iat of Omar Khayyam in Scots.

1 Aye, ah'm a braw fellah, an handsome tae!
   Ruddy cheeked an stracht as a Scots pine.
   But the answer tae yer question? Ah'm no quite shair
   Whit an why the reasons are that ah wis planted here.

2 Ah wis born wi certain inbuilt restrictions;
   Limitations that hiv knockt me tapsalteerie.
   Ah dasht frae the block at the stairtin gun
   An nou, as ah reach the feenish line, whit wis it made me run?

3 The Wheel o Fortune's spinnin, but it's no duin ocht fir me,
   But then, tae be truthfu, ah nivver expectit it tae.
   Ach, it'll aye be the same, a gemme fur mugs an losers,
   But the shout frae the tables aye the same –
   'There's naebody made ye play'.

4 Ye can search yer soul for answers that've bate better men than you,
   An even if ye figured it oot, could ye pruive that it wis true?
   We micht as weel enjoy a hauf
   While we examine aa the clues.

5 If, in yer heart, ye truly professt tae ken it aa
   Jist think hou easy Daith wid be at the last kick o the ba,
   But, the day, jist think aboot it, whit dae ye really ken?
   An the morn, when ye're awa, will it maitter onywey?

6 Ye'd be as weel tryin tae lay a course o bricks oan the sea,
   As listen tae aa they idiots toutin their daft beliefs.
   An onywey, Rab, wha says that there's a Hell?
   Or a Heaven? Whaur's the pruif? Hae you been there yersel?

7 Weel, ah don't ken, an ne'er dae you, the meanin o it aa;
   An if we hud eternity, we'd baith still fidge and claw.
   Mortality's a puir viewpynt tae try an see things frae
   Beyond it? Well, we'll ne'er ken – we'll no be here tae see.

8 This Earth's jist teemin wi life; whaur did it aa come frae?
   We can aa hae a guess at whit's beyond reality.
   An ah should ken, ah think ah must 've listent tae them aa,
   But ah cannae say ah've heard ocht tae enlighten me at aa.

9 The enigma o life beyont the stars
   His gi'en wise men their doubts;
   But tak care no tae lose yer grup oan things
   Fir theories they cannae refute.

10 We're aa oan the Infinity Bus-route,
   Jumpin oan an aff;
   A Grand Mystery Tour wi nae hint o explanation,
   Blinly contemplatin oor eventual destination.

11 Thon Cosmic Inventor, beaverin awa wi aa his toys
   Suin tires o them, suin loses interest.
   His worst work? Weel, ye could weel unnerstaun,
   But e'en his very best? – *He flings it oot.*

12 Aa thon geniuses oan tea-towels an stamps,
   Ladent doon wi aa the Glitterin Prizes,
   Deep doon, they must've wunnert, 'Whit's it aa aboot?'
   Gie'd us their bedtime stories, then pit oot the licht.

13 Aye, they aa come an go, kiddin theirsels oan.
   Ach! gie's anither drink,
   An ah'll whisper ye a secret:
   It wis aa juist a load ay blethers!

14 We listen't tae aa thae Con men
   Wi their variety-pack opinions o the truth,
   Kiddin oan that they kent it aa.
   Weel, whit did they ken? Whaur ur they nou?

15 Aa thon astrology: 'Ah'm a Taurus, ectually.'
   Bull markets, bullish behaviour – bully fir you!
   Open yer een. Ur ye blin'?
   It's aa a load o bull!

16 Thon young yins, hingin roun the bus stop
   Wi their comfortin bottles o Buckie,
   Blamelessly swillin each bitter moothfu,
   Contemplatin their bitter lives.

17 They niver askt tae be here;
   If they had a choice, they'd raither go
   Awa frae this run-doon dump, whaur, in reality,
   They've nae choice.

18 Whit's tae be gaint frae their comin or gaun?
   Whit's the pynt o their lives?
   They're aa dancin tae the same score: the music o the spheres
   Fadin in – burnin oot.

19 The shame o it. Aa they auld yins jist fadin awa,
   Cut doon in the great celestial harvest.
   The pity, the sorrow – in the blink o an ee,
   Wishes unfulfillt, intae oblivion.

20 Okay. Ye micht've slept wi a whoor or twae,
   An leeved in the fast lane aa yer life,
   When ye come tae the slip road, ye can kiss it aa goodbye,
   An yer life micht as weel hae been juist a dream.

Stanzas and introduction reprinted with kind permission of Luath Press

The Rubaya'iat of Omar Khayyam
Translated by Peter Avery and John Heath-Stubbs

1 Although I have a handsome face and colour,
   Cheek like the tulips, form like the cypress,
   It is not clear why the Eternal Painter
   Thus tricked me out for the dusty show-booth of earth.

2 He began my creation with constraint,
   By giving me life he added only confusion;
   We depart reluctantly still not knowing
   The aim of birth, existence, departure.

3 Heaven's wheel gained nothing from my coming,
   Nor did my going augment its dignity;
   Nor did my ears hear from anyone
   Why I had to come and why I went.

4 Oh heart you will not arrive at the solving of the riddle,
   You will not reach the goal the wise in their subtlety seek;
   Make do here with wine and the cup of bliss,
   For you may not arrive at bliss hereafter.

5 If the heart could grasp the meaning of life,
   In death it would know the mystery of God;
   Today when you are in possession of yourself, you know nothing.
   Tomorrow when you leave yourself behind, what will you know?

6 How long shall I lay bricks on the face of the seas?
   I am sick of idolaters and the temple.
   Khayyam, who said that there will be a hell?
   Who's been to hell, who's been to heaven?

7 Neither you nor I know the mysteries of eternity,
   Neither you nor I read this enigma;
   You and I only talk this side of the veil;
   When the veil falls, neither you nor I will be here.

8 This ocean of being has come from the Obscure,
   No one has pierced this jewel of reality;
   Each has spoken according to his humour,
   No one can define the face of things.

9 The bodies that occupy the celestial vault,
   These give rise to wise men's uncertainties;
   Take care not to lose your grip on the thread of wisdom,
   Since the Powers That Be themselves are in a spin.

10 The cycle which includes our coming and going
    Has no discernible beginning nor end;
    Nobody has got this matter straight –
    Where we come from and where we go to.

11 Since the Upholder embellishes the material of things,
    For what reason does He cast it into diminution and decay?
    If it turned out good, why break it?
    If the form turned out bad, whose fault was it?

12 Those who dominated the circle of learning and culture –
    In the company of the perfect became lamps among their peers,
    By daytlight they could not escape from the darkness,
    So they told a fable, and went to sleep.

13 Those, boy, who went before
   Have been laid in the dust of self-delusion;
   Go, drink wine and hear the truth from me,
   It was all hot air that they spoke.

14 The uninformed who pierced the pearl of meaning,
   Spoke concerning the wheel with a variety of opinions;
   Not encompassing the secrets of the world,
   They first bragged and then lay silent.

15 A bull is next to the Pleiades in the sky,
   Another bull is hidden below the earth;
   If you're not blind, open your eyes to the truth,
   Below and above the two bulls is a drove of donkeys!

16 Today is the time of my youth,
   I drink wine because it is my solace;
   Do not blame me, although bitter it is pleasant,
   It is bitter because it is my life.

17 If my coming here were my will, I would not have come.
   Also, if my departure were my will, how should I go?
   Nothing could be better in this ruined lodging,
   Thank not to have come, not to be, not to go.

18 What is the gain of our coming and going?
   Where is the weft of our life's warp?
   In the circle of the spheres the lives of so many good men
   Burn and become dust, but where is the smoke?

Reprinted with kind permission of Penguin Books Ltd

Further reading

Avery, P and Heath-Stubbs, J, translators, *The Rubaya'iat of Omar Khayyam* Penguin Classics, 2004.
Hedayat, S, *The Rubaya'iat of Omar Khayyam: Taraneh-Haye Khayyam. A Persian edition of the Rubaya'iat* H&S Media, 2011. The original Farsi text ordered and edited by a giant of 20th Century Iranian literature, Sadeq Hedayat.
Wilson, R, *The Rubaya'iat of Omar Khayyam in Scots*, Rab Wilson, Luath Press 2004.

Working together in education and science

Higher Education in Iran, and UK-Iran cooperation

REZA KERMANI*
Reza Kermani has worked for over twenty years in the Iranian education and higher education system at senior levels. He lives in Tehran.

This chapter details the historic ties between Iran and Great Britain with regards to higher education, looking at the modern history of Iran's higher education sector, its establishment, development and the changes it has undergone since the formation of the Islamic Republic in 1979. The essay examines current collaborations between the two countries in this sector and highlights hopes and plans for developing this further in the future for the mutual benefit of both countries.

Historical Context
Iranians have been distinguished throughout history by the effort they have made to seek knowledge, enrich it with wisdom, and bestow that back onto the world. The importance that Iranians have historically given to education can be traced back as far as the

time of the Sasanid King, Shapur I, when the first known academy of science was built. According to historians, it was located at Gondeshapur, the intellectual centre of the Sassanid Empire located in the south of Iran, the home of teaching of medicine, health and a centre of higher learning. The first modern institution of learning was established by Amir Kabir (1807–1852), the chief minister of Naser al-Din Shah, during the Qajar era.

Amir Kabir invited experts, teachers and professors from a variety of disciplines from Europe to teach there, and established branches of science in the school of Darolfonoon in Tehran. His establishment expanded as the time passed and decades later many parts of Darolfonoon were turned into the university of Tehran. The investment in education at a higher level was expanded during the Pahlavi era (1925–1979) when universities, colleges and polytechnics were established. These entities were mainly Western oriented with an emphasis on medical and science-based subjects. They gained their methodologies in teaching and education from the West, especially from Western Europe.

With the establishment of the Ministry of Higher Education in 1967, higher education underwent profound change. New policies were introduced and scholars were sent abroad, mostly to Europe, to provide the academics and staff needed for newly established colleges and universities in Iran. Efforts were made to improve the infrastructure and maintain the academic system in Iran and on their return scholars occupied seats in the newly established academic entities, expanding the network of higher education institutions in modern Iran.

At the same time international cultural and academic centres opened branches in Iran. The British Council from the UK, the Goethe Institute from Germany and the cultural section of the French embassy represented efforts to establish international cultural and educational dialogue and partnership between Iran and European countries. Before the Islamic revolution, the British Council's operation in Iran was their largest in the world, with branches in six major cities around the country.

After the victory of the Islamic revolution in 1979, fundamental and mostly obligatory changes in the different systems of Iranian bureaucracy were applied and the higher education system was not exempt from these changes. The Council of Revolution ratified the establishment of the High Council for Culture and Higher Education, which was responsible for the 'Cultural Revolution' in Iranian universities. As a result, some of the well-known academics and professors who had been educated in the West were marginalised or dismissed. Under the banner of the Islamisation of Iranian universities, the Cultural Revolution began to change higher education entities and universities according to Islamic norms and principles. These radical changes in higher education provoked some protests from the academic sector and resulted in the closure of all academic institutions for one year (1980–81).

With the establishment of the Supreme Cultural Revolution Council (SCRC) in 1984, new laws and regulations were ratified and implemented in academic institutions. Guidelines were also provided for the selection and recruitment of academics in accordance with revolutionary policies. Major changes in the curricula and textbooks, especially in social sciences, were implemented immediately.

These changes, along with the Iraq-Iran war (1980–1988), arguably restricted the growth of Iranian higher education, causing the system to become politicised at the expense of academic development.

In 1985, the Ministry of Higher Education was changed to the Ministry of Science, Research and Technology (MSRT) and in

2000 the Ministry of Health and Medical Sciences, (MHMS) was established by hiving off the medical and public health education section of MSRT.

Around 1985 a new bursary scheme was introduced by the new generation of revolutionaries. The stated objective of the scheme was supposedly to train and educate new generations of academics and researchers who could contribute to the growth of science and research and undertake the future governance of state-related services in Iran. Carefully selected students from different subject areas received state scholarships and were sent overseas (mostly to the UK, Canada, and Australia) for multiple purposes, including studying postgraduate courses. However, some students who were sent abroad did not have adequate academic qualifications. The selection procedure was mostly non-academic and subject to purposes outside of academic interests.

Some of these state scholars never returned to Iran, but many of those who came back started working in leading key positions, including cultural, political, educational, and economic positions. It is interesting to note that some of these graduates, whose children and families still live in the West, are opposed to closer bilateral relationships with the countries in which they formerly studied, including the UK.

The scheme was evaluated carefully in 2005; the evaluation concluded that less than 40 per cent of the academic objectives had been met. The lack of efficient academic monitoring, questionable selection procedures, the small numbers of returning scholars, and economic hardships were named as the main reasons for failure. The potential benefit for better relations between Iran and other countries including the UK during these exchanges was far from maximised.

By the end of Iraq-Iran war and the reconstruction years led by President Rafsanjani (1989–1997), a new phase of Iran-West research and academic collaboration started. Rafsanjani was a powerful president and is now the head of the Expediency Discernment Council[1] in Iran. Mr Rafsanjani supported the privatisation of the economy and initiated a new phase of relationship between Iranian universities, research centres and academic institutes and their counterparts in the West, especially in the US and the UK. He also reinforced the expansion of the first and only private university in Iran, the Islamic Azad University.

In 2000–2008, the political relationship between Iran and the UK entered a new phase. President Khatami supported cultural and educational relations between Iran and the West. The British Council returned to Iran in 2001. However, in 2009, after almost a decade of operation in Iran, the British Council was accused of unacceptable activities by members of the ruling elite and was forced to close its office under direct political and security pressures.

The relationship between Iran and the UK in the field of higher education has always been a contentious political issue. Reformists in Iran have traditionally worked better with the West in many areas especially in higher education, compared to more conservative stakeholders, but even amongst those who are more westward inclined, the relationship has often been characterised by historical mistrust.

Current higher education cooperation

Today Iran, with a population of nearly 77 million and more than 2,500 universities, colleges, and institutes working in higher education, is considered a well-established country in terms of higher education in the region. Around 318 of the universities in Iran are managed by MSRT with the same number affiliated with MHMS. The Islamic Azad University has about 400 branches in different cities around the county. The Open University, known as Payam Noor, has approximately 570 branches active nationwide.

It is easier to compare the higher education system in Iran with other countries in the region than with the West and the UK. Large numbers of an impressive, young and talented population (over 50 per cent of the population are below the age of 30) who wished to enter university forced the authorities to expand the sector, and to hastily agree to register more students without adequate infrastructure and facilities for such expansion. This has resulted in an increasing number of Iranian graduates for whom there are not enough jobs, and high levels of graduate unemployment. In the most recent report by Statistical Centre of Iran, affiliated with the Vice Presidency for Strategic Planning and Supervision of the Presidency of the Islamic Republic of Iran, 22.2 per cent of the population between 15–29 years old are unemployed. According to the Minister of Economy, unemployment rates in Iran, especially among university graduates, have reached a critical stage.

Despite the rapid growth in the number of institutions to accommodate the local demands for higher education, the quality of education and research has come under scrutiny by independent monitors. The Tehran University of Medical Science is ranked 348 among 2,400 internationally recognised medical universities while Sharif University of Technology and Tehran University are ranked around 800 in the list of top international universities. The place of Iranian universities in the world rankings reflects the socio-cultural and political challenges faced by the educational system in the country.

According to a report by the Deputy of Research and Technology, Iran's share of academic output increased from 0.1 per cent of the world's total academic publications in 1980 to 1.62 percent in 2013. However, low rates of graduate employment, and an incompatibility of the skills taught at universities with the demands of the market have been raised as evidence of the poor quality of research and academic education in Iran (as opposed to the scale or size of the output). It has therefore not been surprising to see an increase in the number of Iranians studying abroad. In 2010–11 up to 3,500 Iranian students studied in the UK while 5,626 registered at international universities in the US, showing a 19 per cent increase from previous years.

According to the report by the International Monetary Fund, in 2009 Iran ranked first in the rate of 'brain drain' amongst 91 developing or under-developed countries. In 2012 a report was published in the Iranian Parliament stating that about 60,000 educated Iranians left Iran in only one year for better, living and studying or research opportunities. Indeed, many of those responsible for the higher education system in Iran ensure that their children study in Western countries, including the UK and the US.

In the absence of an independent body to appraise, monitor, and advise stakeholders in higher education in Iran, the efforts of individuals who have tried to change the system have faced bitter resistance from the older generation of policymakers.

While the scale and structure of higher education provisions are changing around the world, certain parts of the education sector in Iran suffer from policies rooted in an outdated understanding of educational methodology. The independent thinking that is essential to academic progress has been challenged in social sciences, although the natural sciences have managed to achieve successful development. The achievements however are mostly the result of individual factors such as talented students and dedicated academics rather than the outcome of the system as a whole.

Some parts of the higher education sector suffer from over-controlled policies ratified and imposed by bodies which are affiliated with the status quo and who do not necessarily have expertise in educational practices. This prevents changes to the structure and the quality of teaching and research. For example, instead of putting students in control of their learning or designing programmes that are in compliance with the social changes and the demands of the modern world, educational programmes and curricula are tightly controlled, supporting the interests of a few bodies outside of the education system.

Unlike higher education systems in the UK and other developed countries that value critical and analytical thinking, education in Iran is authoritative, non-participative and passive: it has been widely criticised within Iran as being 'mono-vocal'. Higher education institutions in Iran are not independent of the government and therefore are subject to major intervention from non-educationalists.

Cooperation with the UK in higher education

Iran's interest in science and demands for international cooperation go back as far as the mid-20th Century, when scholars and politicians who were educated mainly in Europe and the US tried to connect Iran's higher education institutions with their international counterparts. Many branches of science, as well as fine arts, law, engineering and medicine flourished because of the endeavours of those who studied both in Iran and overseas.

The public in Iran generally has a positive view towards scientific collaboration and contacts with Western countries, especially the UK. This view partly originates in the recognition of the UK as an advanced country in terms of education and science.

The tradition of sending Iranians to be educated abroad has continued in recent years: overseas scholarship schemes were launched by officials as an investment to support talented students in order to benefit Iran on their return. At the same time, Iran made considerable advances through education and training in the sciences; the Iranian scientific community remained productive even when the purchase of research equipment was restricted and publishing academic papers in international journals was difficult. With the support of some more outward looking members of Iran's ruling establishment, international connections in areas of science and technology were expanded. In the meantime the presence of the British Council (most of 1942 to 1975, and again 2002 to 2009) provided a secure platform for academic exchange giving the UK a unique opportunity to expand scientific ties with Iran's higher education entities. Conducting academic joint ventures and scientific projects broadened the prospect of advanced collaboration between the two countries in different areas of science and technology. The high quality of Iranian scientists and researchers facilitated by these collaborations has resulted in a noticeable improvement in the academic relationship between Iran and the UK.

Although the political relationship between Iran and the UK has been turbulent, individual initiatives and university joint ventures have maintained the higher education ties. The contribution of Iranian scientists in advancing different branches of science and technology in the UK should also not be ignored. Without a doubt, a mutual interest exists in the areas of science and higher education which can facilitate ties between the two countries and defuse political tensions which have caused pressure at both ends.

Although interest exists within the scientific community in collaboration with the West, accusations made by certain authorities in Iran have spread concern among those who want to engage in legitimate interactions with their international counterparts in the West, especially in the UK. These accusations, and sometimes threats, are rooted in the politicised system of education in Iran combined with security concerns and a lack of trust for the outside world.

At the same time, the lack of intellectual freedom and independence of universities to some degree have also prevented the advancement of science in Iran. This is obviously counterproductive to state-endorsed efforts to promote Iran's scientific achievements internationally. However with advancing technology and the process of globalisation, avoiding international academic and scientific collaboration seems impossible. This explains why the academic society in Iran has been struggling to break unwanted and mostly politicised curbs and make progress towards establishing joint ventures and projects with overseas institutions, especially with those in the UK.

With the closure of the British Council in 2009, the Iran High Council of National Security, the highest coordinator of national security rules and regulations in Iran, prohibited any connection between Iran and the UK in the fields of cultural, social, and especially educational and scientific collaboration. The Council warned those who ignored the order that they would be considered as violators of the law and face unpleasant consequences. However, it advised that economic ties be kept to a minimum but not stopped.

This agenda was obligatory for all Iranian universities and research centres: individuals and offices were authorised to monitor the implementation of this act of the Council. In some cases academics who tried to bypass the order and make connections with their counterparts in the UK were summoned and faced limitations in their academic positions. The political pressure on academics was blamed for the increase in the number of well-educated Iranians leaving the country for a better environment for study and research. The reality of talents leaving Iran has been covered in the media; the former minister of MSRT, Dr Faraji Dana, went further than the 2012 report quoted above, and claimed that every year about 150,000 of the Iranian elite emigrate from Iran, costing the economy more than US$150 billion.

However through the persistence of a few academics and the support provided by some individuals in key positions who had a personal interest in expansion of the relationship with the UK, collaboration – although inhibited – was not stopped.

Since the new president, a PhD holder from Glasgow Caledonian University in the UK, came to power in 2013, efforts to expand academic ties with the West, especially the UK, have increased and demands for lifting the prohibition of academic collaboration have been growing. Although the path is difficult, some progress has been made in mutual academic relationships and negotiations have been started with Western academic establishments.

For Iranian academics, men and women of knowledge and science, it is vital to initiate and maintain connections with their counterparts in the West, especially in the UK. But some parts of the Iranian State exert direct pressure on the President regarding the prospect of opening doors for mutual relations with the West at different levels, using their influence inside and outside of the government.

Let us divide opponents of collaboration into categories
Traditionally there is some ideologically and religiously rooted opposition towards old colonial powers, believing that any connection with the West will endanger the independent existence of Iran.

Some political hard liners are against ties with the UK as this would be a measure of the success of Rouhani's government in delivering the developments promised at the time of the election themselves, without external – especially UK – support or assistance. Another area of resistance comes from those whose political survival depends on the idea of a conspiracy theory that places Iran as a target of the rest of the international community. At the same time the role of those who financially benefit from hostility with the West, which means more trade with powers in the East such as Russia and China, should not be ignored.

Recently the President's office conducted a comprehensive review to examine different areas of relations with the UK. Experts from different backgrounds were invited to take part in a series of meetings discussing related subjects; academics, historians, university professors, researchers and even students were invited to exchange ideas on Iran's international relations in a wide range of areas.

The result was interesting. Participants in these meetings, while acknowledging the gloomy shadow of history over any such relationship, were nevertheless in favour of allowing a relationship between the two countries. The view expressed by most participants, even those previously opposed to links with UK, favoured the initiation of relations by allowing bilateral exchange of expertise and knowledge in different areas.

Collaboration can potentially benefit Iranian and British universities both academically and financially, but the existence of a heavy shadow of some authorities is a serious challenge to any Iranian effort to develop contacts with UK.

It is often argued that restarting a relationship between two countries with a history of conflict should be initiated in less politically sensitive areas such as culture, education, science, economy and sport. Only later can the relationship be expanded to a political level but security issues may remain a dilemma. However, starting a relationship between Iran and the UK in non-political areas has proved to be difficult. This may be partly due to the authoritarian nature of Iran's political and religious structure and partly due to the tendency of British policymakers to follow US and EU policies, which are perceived as hostile in Iran. This encourages deep-rooted conspiracy theories and results in accusations of 'soft war' against Iran.

Hence there is a long held belief, supported by historical facts, among religious policy-makers and hardliners that culture and science are the two areas by which Western powers impose their policies on countries like Iran. Considering the authoritarian political structure in Iran, it is recommended that cultural and academic collaborations should initially be proposed and discussed officially. The presence in such negotiations of officials from the UK would require the corresponding presence of Iranian officials from Iran; authorisation of collaboration at such a level would facilitate relationships at an institutional and individual level. Although this view many not be shared by independent organisations such as the British Council but this should be considered as an initial step toward build trust between the two countries.

Starting new ventures at any level requires deep understanding of the history of relations between the two countries. The realities should be acknowledged while encouraging both sides to take risks and create opportunities based on mutual respect and reciprocal interests.

The work of the British Council has a vital role; it can facilitate collaboration at an individual level by initiating official and ministerial contacts. The British Council has the capacity and experience in assisting cultural and academic institutions to work side by side.

Since any contacts with international partners are under vigorous scrutiny in Iran the procedures for joint ventures should be drafted with consideration of political and social sensitivities; the protocols should be clear and transparent to avoid any misunderstanding from Iranian officials.

One of the strategies that has been proven to be effective is generating regional projects under British Council offices in the region. This could be a short-term solution until diplomatic relation between the UK and Iran is re-established.

In recent years political conflicts have caused considerable deterioration of diplomatic relations between Iran and the West. In the absence of powerful competitors, some Eastern countries entered the economic and industrial market in Iran and expanded their network to include the academic level. Although these relationships are endorsed by officials, the Iranian public has remained sceptical towards the nature and efficiency of collaboration with Eastern countries and is looking at Western alternatives. On the other hand the reputation of the UK in areas of science and technology with its longstanding history in successful academic structure is recognised and appreciated by the people of Iran. Another asset, which puts UK in a higher position than other competitors in the field, is the wide and strong network of UK alumni that over the years are working in different levels of administrative, industrial and academic institutions; this network manages to maintain and renew itself continuously.

Many untouched areas offer opportunities of collaboration between the two countries; for example, with increasing concerns over environmental issues in Iran, investing in renewable energies is a unique opportunity to start the academic exchange. The Iranian Oil industry is another intact area ready for research investment. Medical research and health education are also important but less sensitive and could be a platform for sustainable collaboration.

There is no doubt that the reestablishment of an academic relationship with the UK may not receive united approval from powerful institutions in Iran. The resistance has mainly come from different commissions in parliament and the executives of military and political bodies in Iran. Pressure has been exerted on members of the cabinet to resist any formal relationship with the West especially with the UK.

Some basic steps could be taken to facilitate collaboration between the two countries. Reports produced by British media illustrate a questionable image of Iran. In particular, most of the reports from BBC Persian reflect a one-sided and negative image of Iran. Iranians are proud of their history and their achievements. The fact that Iranian tradition is intertwined with religion should be respected and recognised. Highlighting controversial issues may satisfy a limited number of individuals outside but will not facilitate the establishment of a long-lasting relationship.

It is important to use the power of social networks and mass media to connect individuals from inside of Iran with those in UK. Websites for introducing Iranian culture and history and natural beauty to the public in UK can certainly help in building mutual trust for future collaboration.

Bilateral and multi-lateral dialogue between the two countries and even with the EU can keep doors open for possible relationships in different areas. The importance of public diplomacy and the role of elites in academic relations cannot be ignored. Means of establishing connections between both sides are eagerly sought. The capacity of the private sector inside Iran is considerable and often undiscovered; following the improvement in internal policies many NGOs in Iran have started exploring opportunities to work with their counterparts outside the country.

Investing in small-scale academic exchanges can certainly facilitate long-term and sustained projects in the future.

Providing online training such as English language teaching that is affordable and efficient can help the general public to be exposed to the level of education in UK. On many occasions researchers and historians have expressed their wish to have access to British archives regarding Persian and Iranian studies. This access would certainly help historians to clarify ambiguous points in the history shared between the two countries

Sports, arts and culture are areas that can engage people at different levels and empower those who want to see Iran and the UK closer together. Iranian and British heritage – scientific, cultural, social and even economic – are areas of potential exchange which is often unfortunately ignored. Tourism should be supported in order to decrease irrelevant sensitivities especially within the Iranian authorities.

Despite a challenging history, the political, cultural and most of all the educational relationship between Iran and the UK maintains potential and interest for both nations. Iran is a powerful country in the region with impressive natural resources and a young educated population.

Countless opportunities exist to initiate inter-university and scientific partnership and to promote mutual understanding and relationships between Iran and the UK. Reducing political involvement in the university system and striving to bring back those who were falsely accused and deprived from studying or teaching at Iranian universities were the promises that helped Dr Rouhani to win the presidential election in 2013.

In his latest remarks in the ceremony for starting the new academic year (2014–2015) at the University of Tehran, President Rouhani also defended his administration's efforts during the past year to encourage international relations and academic collaboration with other countries. He also said: 'Our effort has been the establishment of a stable environment in universities, with all groups having their political views, and for all to know that this is a university, not a political club. It is a centre of partisanship activities, where anyone can be present in socio-political matters.'

Notes

1 In 1988 and after revision to the constitution of the Islamic Republic of Iran, the Expediency Discernment Council was established to resolve differences or conflicts between the Executive Power (the government) and legislature (parliament). The members of the council are appointed by the Supreme Leader with the primary role of advisory body to the Supreme Leader.

Iran and UK on the World Stage in Particle Physics

Farhad Ardalan, Hessamaddin Arfaei, John Ellis
Farhad Ardalan is a High Energy physicist. He is a professor at Sharif University and the Institute for Studies in Theoretical Physics and Mathematics at the Institute for Research in Fundamental Sciences (IPM) in Tehran. Hessamaddin Arfaei is a Founding Fellow, and now Head of the School of Particles and Accelerators, at IPM. John Ellis is Clerk Maxwell Professor of Theoretical Physics, King's College and Guest Professor, CERN, Geneva. All three work at CERN, the European Organization for Nuclear Research.

Three eminent scientists, two Iranian, one British, who worked in the team that discovered the Higgs Boson particle, share their views on working together at CERN and look at the future of scientific research and exchange.

The aim of particle physics is to understand the fundamental structure of matter, and thereby address basic questions about the Universe such as the origin of matter and the nature of dark matter. These subjects are of interest to physicists, cosmologists and people in the streets around the world. As in any science, experiments are the final arbiters between different theoretical speculations. In recent decades, most experimental advances in particle physics have been made in laboratories using high-energy particle accelerators. Nations hosting front-rank accelerators specialising in such experiments include China, Japan, Russia, the United States and Switzerland.

The latter is the location of CERN, the European Laboratory for Particle Physics. This is an international research organisation whose infrastructure has been built up by its 21 member states. CERN is currently operating the Large Hadron Collider (LHC), which is the highest-energy accelerator in the world, colliding protons and heavy nuclei. Its first experimental run led in 2012 to the discovery of the Higgs Boson, a particle hypothesised in 1964 that is a manifestation of the mechanism whereby elementary particles acquire their masses. Its discovery led in 2013 to the award of the Physics Nobel Prize to François Englert and Peter Higgs, two pioneers of this theory. This discovery was possible thanks to the efforts of thousands of physicists and engineers from dozens of countries around the world, as shown on the map. Although centered at CERN, this discovery was truly a global effort.

Iran's rich intellectual tradition includes mathematics and theoretical physics, and the Iranian mathematical physics

Distribution of All CERN Users by Nationality on 14 January 2014

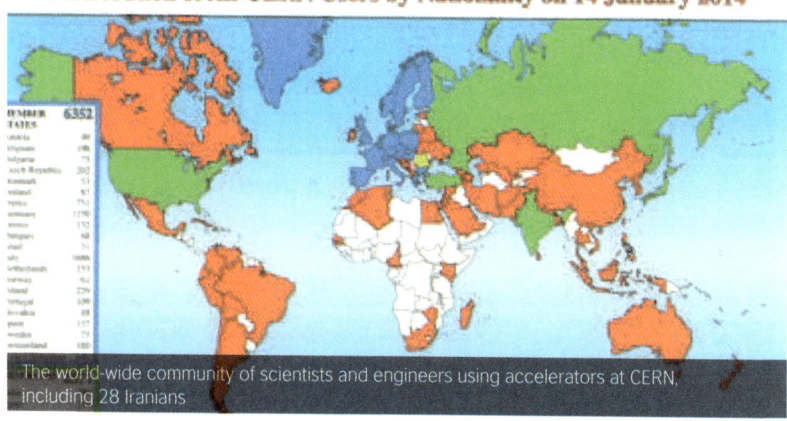

The world-wide community of scientists and engineers using accelerators at CERN, including 28 Iranians

community is well known and respected worldwide. It has maintained and developed its profile in the years following the Islamic Revolution, in particular via the Institute for Research in Fundamental Sciences in Tehran, formerly known as the Institute for Theoretical Physics and Mathematics and generally known by the acronym IPM.

In this article we describe how Iran has become a member of the global community of particle physicists and came to participate in this discovery. We also discuss other international research activities in which Iran is open to collaboration, including astronomy as well as other applications of accelerators. We also present some considerations about obstacles to enhancing Iran's international scientific collaborations and measures that could help overcome them. We emphasize in particular measures that the United Kingdom could take, both on its own account and as a member state of CERN.

We are theoretical physicists who have known each other for over 25 years. Two of us (FA and HA) are senior physicists at IPM, and one of us (JE) worked at CERN for many years. He was advisor to successive CERN Directors-General on relations with non-European countries, after heading the CERN theoretical physics division between 1988 and 1994. It was during this period that he first visited Iran, giving lectures in Tehran and Shiraz at the invitation of FA. The motivation was to share progress in constructing models of particle physics and their experimental tests with the Iranian theoretical physics community, which was very strong in mathematics and abstract theory, and sought closer contact with experiment. At the time, Iranian participation in actual experiments at CERN seemed a distant dream.

The breakthrough came thanks to the support of the UNESCO office in Tehran and the personal efforts of its head, Galileo

Violini, in particular. At the suggestion of JE, FA and Violini arranged to invite the then CERN Director-General, Luciano Maiani, to Tehran to promote collaboration between Iran and CERN. As Maiani's advisor on relations with non-member states, JE accompanied him on this visit, whose highlight was a meeting with the then Science Minister of Iran, M. Moin. This led to the preparation of a Memorandum of Understanding between the Iranian Government and CERN, which was approved without controversy by representatives of the CERN member states in its Council, and subsequently signed by Director-General Maiani and Minister Moin in 2001. This Memorandum was officially approved by the Iranian parliament, together with Iranian membership in SESAME, a project to construct an electron accelerator for applied science using synchrotron radiation, a project located in Jordan whose member states also include Pakistan, Turkey and Israel.

The Iran-CERN Memorandum paved the way for official Iranian participation in activities at CERN, the first of which was the CMS experiment at the Large Hadron Collider. Iran contributed equipment for the CMS detector that was fabricated by an industrial engineering company REPCO in Arak, which won an award from the CMS collaboration for the quality of its work. Since there were no experienced experimental particle physicists working in Iran at the time, Iran started its participation in the CMS experiment by sending to CERN, at its own expense, a series of PhD students to learn experimental physics by working on the CMS detector and analysing data. Many of the students have now obtained their PhDs and are working either as academics in Iran or as postdoctoral researchers. The Iranian team in CMS participated in the discovery of the Higgs boson in 2012, and CMS scientific papers currently include 12 authors, including current students as well as researchers with PhDs.

A large part of the CMS detector being lowered into place during assembly. It is supported by a component fabricated in Iran

In addition to participating in experimental particle physics with the CMS detector, Iran is also participating in a research and development project at CERN for a possible future accelerator to collide electrons and their antiparticles at high energies. Apart from the intrinsic interest of this project, this collaboration could help further Iran's ambition to construct a national electron accelerator for synchrotron radiation studies.

All the Iranian participation in these and other projects involving collaboration with CERN is channeled through IPM, which acts as a national centre coordinating advanced research in physics and other fields. This arrangement ensures that only bona fide academic researchers have access to CERN, and that there is no involvement by scientists working on military applications. One of us (HA), a theoretical physicist whose own research interests lie in string theory and related fundamental topics, is charged by IPM with coordinating the collaboration with CERN.

This collaboration now extends to other aspects of capacity development besides PhD training. For several years now, some

Iranian and international participants in a workshop held in Isfahan in 2009 to discuss the prospects for physics at CERN's Large Hadron Collider (LHC)

students from Iran have been participating in CERN's summer internship programme for undergraduates alongside over 200 other students from the CERN member states and other countries. Then, in both 2013 and 2014, Iranian high-school teachers have participated in a three-week programme at CERN (following a national selection competition) alongside some 50 other teachers from around the world, including the United States and Israel. In both years, these participations have been followed by presentations from CERN physicists by videoconference to the annual Iranian national congress of high-school teachers. These initiatives reflect the shared interest in Iran and at CERN in promoting peaceful relations and mutual understanding via science. CERN's slogan for its 60th anniversary in 2014 is 'Science for Peace'.

As could be imagined, the development of the Iran-CERN collaboration has not been without problems. These have usually not arisen from the Iranian side. Indeed, the Director of IPM is one of the Larijani brothers who have been prominent in Iranian politics for many years, including a previous nuclear negotiator and current speaker of the Iranian parliament. However, there have been some difficulties on the European side. For example, although CERN member states were generally supportive of the collaboration with Iran, there was reticence among some CERN member states towards allowing Iranians to access the advanced distributed GRID computing system developed to handle and analyse the enormous amounts of data from the LHC. More problems were caused by the strengthening of financial sanctions on Iran, which made it almost impossible for Iran to transfer money to support students and researchers at CERN, and to pay the Iranian contributions to joint projects at CERN. The collaboration was able to surmount these challenges in part by understanding and support from the CMS collaboration and the CERN management. At the time of writing, these problems seem to be easing, reflecting the fragile thaw in Iran-Europe relations.

Iranians have not had any problems obtaining visas for entry into Switzerland to work at CERN. This is because Switzerland, as host nation under the CERN convention, accepted the obligation to give a visa to anyone invited officially by CERN. On the other hand, the member states of CERN, such as the UK, are under no obligation to give visas to any Iranians who might wish to visit for the purposes of scientific collaboration on CERN-related projects. For example, the UK team in the CMS collaboration could not be sure that the UK would issue a visa to an Iranian for a working visit or a scientific conference: they would have to plan on meeting at CERN.

Conversely, Iran has never hesitated to issues visas to European physicists wishing to travel to Iran to visit IPM or participate in a scientific conference elsewhere in Iran. However, in recent years the Foreign Office has officially advised JE and other UK physicists against travel to Iran, following the break in diplomatic relations and the series of assassinations of Iranian physicists. Other CERN member states have not given similar negative advice.

These assassinations have not affected directly the Iran-CERN collaboration: none of the victims had participated in this collaboration. However, the first physicist to be assassinated was a theoretical physicist and former student and collaborator of FA and HA, who was an Iranian delegate on the SESAME council. In view of the complicated past and present of Iran-UK relations, the Foreign Office was concerned by claims from elements in Iran that the UK was somehow involved in these assassinations, and that the UK would not be able to assist any Briton arrested in Iran as a 'nuclear spy'.

Iran-CERN collaboration is currently in good shape, and the hope is that it will be able to develop more freely now that Iran-Europe relations show signs of improving. However, this tentative hope is contingent on a satisfactory resolution of the nuclear issue. At the time of writing, this is not a 'done deal'. Moreover, there are always unpredictable aspects in the relations between Iran and western countries, and there is always the possibility of some unforeseen incident. Nevertheless, we believe that one should plan for success, and believe that the Iran-CERN collaboration may play a valuable role in confidence-building.

Relations between Iran and the UK are always hostage to the complicated history of relations between the two countries. However, there are several building blocks for constructing a closer scientific relationship in the future. Within the field of particle physics, the UK plays an important role in the CMS collaboration through the experimental groups at Imperial College, Bristol University and the Rutherford-Appleton Laboratory. Several UK physicists have supervised or worked with Iranian students on the CMS experiment, and would be happy to develop this relationship. In addition, the UK has the John Adams Institute in Oxford and the Cockcroft Institute in Daresbury working on accelerator research and development, both with interests in electron accelerators. And, of course, the UK has many university groups with excellent reputations in theoretical physics that would be very happy to collaborate with their Iranian colleagues and their excellent students.

We are not in a position to comment on the possibilities for UK-Iran collaboration in many areas, but would like to mention a couple. The IPM is heading a project to build a national telescope, and the UK is one of the leading countries in astronomy, with a research and development centre in Edinburgh. Another interesting area for developing collaboration may be palaeontology. This is quite developed in the UK, and Iran is planning to establish a national Institute for Earth Sciences with emphasis on palaeontology. Iran has some interesting geological features, since it is located on a tectonic plate that was isolated during a long period and has, in particular, interesting deposits at the boundary between the Permian and Triassic eras.

What could the UK do to facilitate the development of scientific collaboration with Iran? The most urgent need of the Iranian scientific community is to end its isolation, which has been distorting its natural development, preventing it from participating effectively in forefront research in many areas where international collaboration is crucial. Collaboration in particle physics via CERN has been the exception rather than the rule, and was made possible by a combination of special circumstances: the international treaty status of CERN and the impetus provided by a handful of physicists with vision. The aim should be to establish conditions where international collaboration is the rule rather than the exception.

One obvious step that the UK could take would be to liberate funding for academic exchange visits from Iran to the UK and vice versa. These would enable the respective scientific communities to renew acquaintance after a long hiatus, and help to identify areas of prospective collaboration. We have mentioned some above, namely particle physics, accelerator science, astronomy and palaeontology, but there are surely many more. Even short visits would be useful, but 'sabbatical' opportunities for Iranian scientists to make longer working visits to UK universities and research laboratories could be even more helpful. There are potential roles here for the Royal Society and the British Council, as well as more specialized academic organisations such as the Institute of Physics. One of the most fruitful ways to build up future relationships may be via student exchanges. Visits of less than 6 months could already be beneficial, and would not attract the punitive fees that UK universities levy for longer student visits. We are also advocates of programmes for high-school teachers of the type organised by CERN, since even one teacher can influence the orientations and career choices of many pupils.

The recently-announced Newton Fund would appear to be an ideal vehicle for funding academic exchanges with Iran, since it is intended to promote scientific collaboration with emerging economies. However, Iran was not included in the initial list of countries eligible for the Newton Fund, reflecting the continuing existence of sanctions and the generally poor state of relations between the UK and Iran. However, we hope that, if there is indeed an improvement in the diplomatic climate following an agreement on the nuclear issue, Iran will soon be admitted to the Newton fold.

Another step that the UK could take would be to relax the tight visa regime for Iranian scientists and other academics. We think that visiting scholars sponsored by host universities and research laboratories should have their visas approved as a matter of course, no matter where they come from. To do otherwise is to harm UK academic institutions unnecessarily. We hope that the recent re-opening of diplomatic relations between the UK and Iran and a general reduction in tension between our two countries will soon render obsolete restrictions on travel between them.

When and if relations between Iran and Europe are fully normalised, could a closer relationship between Iran and CERN become possible? Membership of CERN is now open to non-European countries, Pakistan has already applied for associate membership, and applications for associate membership are also being considered in countries such as Brazil and India. In the fullness of time, maybe also Iran?

Acknowledgments

Chapter One was first published as 'THE MYTH OF 'PERFIDIOUS ALBION': ANGLO-IRANIAN RELATIONS IN HISTORICAL PERSPECTIVE', in Asian Affairs, vol. 44 issue 3, pp 378–391, November 2013. It is reprinted by permission of the publisher, Taylor & Francis Ltd, http://www.tandf.co.uk/journals.

Chapter Thirteen includes the following, reproduced by permission of Penguin Books Limited: pp. 47–51 from THE RUBAYA'IAT OF OMAR KHAYYAM by Omar Khayyam, transl. John Heath-Stubbs and Peter Avery (Allen Lane1979). Copyright © Peter Avery and John Heath-Stubbs 1979. Also in Chapter 13, 'Owersettin the Rubaya'iat of Omar Khayyam (p248), the stanzas and introduction by Rab Wilson are reprinted with kind permission of Luath Press.

Page 50: 'Gassed' image, © IWM (Art.IWM ART 1460).

The editors would also like to thank all the other people who have contributed to this publication but whom we have not been able to recognise individually.